The BEST

of

Chuck Klein

How Guns, Hot Rods, Police Ethics and Sacred Rights Shape America

[handwritten inscription]

Science & Humanities Press
Chesterfield Missouri USA

Copyright 2013 by Chuck Klein

Inquiries should be addressed: Chuck Klein, 6500 Hillman Ridge Road, Georgetown, OH 45121. http://chuckklein.com

NOTICE: Nothing is this book is intended to suggest or support the violation of any state, federal or local law. The opinions expressed herein are merely such and the author assumes no liability either expressed or implied.

Chuck Klein is a former Firearms Editor for P.I. Magazine, Licensed Private Investigator, NRA Certified Police Firearms Instructor and Police Officer. He is currently an active member of The International Association of Law Enforcement Firearms Instructors (IALEFI) and NRA Certified Firearms and Reloading Instructor. On the subject of firearms alone, his columns, articles and commentary have appeared in P.I. Magazine, Gun Week, Guns & Ammo, Combat Handguns, Guns & Weapons for Law Enforcement, Law & Order, Law Officer, American Police Beat, American Israelite, and other publications. He is also listed, for the 13th continuous year, in Who's Who in America.

ISBN 9781596300866

Library of Congress Control Number: 2013948846

Science & Humanities Press
Chesterfield Missouri U.S.A.
sciencehumanitiespress.com

Also By Chuck Klein

Non Fiction:

THE BADGE, Stories and Tales
From Both Sides of the Law

INSTINCT COMBAT SHOOTING,
Defensive Hand-gunning for Police

GUNS IN THE WORKPLACE,
A Manual for Private Sector Employers and Employees

KLEIN'S UNIFORM FIREARMS POLICIES,
A Manual for Private Sector Detectives and Security Agents

KLEIN'S C.C.W. HANDBOOK,
The Requisite for those who Carry Concealed Weapons

LAWS and IDEAS,
Truths and Observations by Chuck Klein

LINES OF DEFENSE,
Police Ideology and the Constitution

Fiction:

CIRCA 1957
Historically and Technically Correct, Coming-of-Age, Novel
Set During the Early Hot-Rodding and Rock-and-Roll Era

THE POWER OF GOD
A Powerful Novel Exposing a de facto Hole
In America's Civil Defense

THE WAY IT WAS,
Nostalgic Tales of Hot Rods and Romance

For My Daughters:

Amy

Karina

Kelly

Michelle

Foreword

The Best of Chuck Klein...

... Is very good indeed.

His nostalgic tales of hot-rodding and high-schooling in the '50s are like riding in a cherry 1957 Corvette. Imagine cruising through your favorite old haunts—and nothing has changed. There's the patch of rubber you laid last weekend with your new Goodyears. The radio is playing all your favorite songs by the Everly Brothers and the Four Tops. That's it—a four-barrel, fuel injected time machine. You can almost smell the high-octane fuel, burning rubber and Brylcreem. That's Chuck Klein's writing. He has the gift to take you back to the bleachers of your teen years.

But then there is the Chuck Klein that has flashing gumballs on the roof, a wailing siren and a police-pursuit big block V-8. The same guy who evaded the cops while street racing, eventually became one and saw the same picture from the other side of the frame. What's it like for a cop to roll in the dirt, trying to arrest a bigger, stronger man, lose his gun, get shot and shoot back? Klein tells us in gripping, gritty detail.

There's another Chuck Klein in an unmarked car—a private detective. And there's the Chuck Klein today, who looks a lot like the old hot-rodder and drives a very nice old El Camino because anything new off the assembly line would be missing an important part—soul.

But Chuck Klein is not a Corvette or a cop car. He's a man. By the old-school definition. A guy who can do things. Build a car. Race it. Fix it when it breaks. Take a wild and reckless risk and laugh about it later. Wear a gun. Handle it properly and use it if he has to.

He has strong opinions about the way the world should work, based on experience and hard-earned knowledge, not flimsy feelings.

All this makes him stand out in a traffic jam of men who are as about as exciting as the cars they drive that look like shiny new appliances with random numbers and letters on the side where it used to say Bel Air, Thunderbird or Fury.

There are still plenty of men like that around. But their kind is endangered, like the old pre-muscle cars they used to drive and still love. And very few among that few can tell the story. Chuck Klein can write. He can make a story sing like tires on a wet highway. He can take you around a corner on two wheels, or just cruise slowly through a Big Boy parking lot, circa 1957.

Take a ride with him. You won't be sorry.

Peter Bronson, former Cincinnati Enquirer columnist,

now contributing editor for Cincy Magazine.

March, 2013

Preface

From the decades of my writings, I've chosen what I consider to be my best stuff. The subject matter runs from fiction to true accountings, to my columns on guns, police ethics, private investigation, and editorials. Also thrown in are essays, unique concepts and patriotic salutes. None of the pieces have ever won any awards, possibly because I have not entered any contests. The reason is, contests want unpublished material and they insist on retaining the copyright. About 95% of everything I've written was sold to a publisher who had first rights and I do not surrender my copyright. Many of these pieces have seen publication multiple times.

Though the subtitle implies a claim of how America was shaped, I'm not claiming to be a shaper anymore than anyone else who has lived and recorded portions of the American experience. America is founded on and has prospered by ethical and pioneering inspirations from guns to cars to cops to innovative concepts, all of which certainly had an impact on shaping the U.S. of A..

Some of the stories/articles were difficult to classify inasmuch as they overlapped, to wit: *Last Knight* is fiction, but there is a Knights of the 20th Century hot rod club, we did hold a reunion and we do have a tontine (read The Copyright for the rest of the story—but read Last Knight first). Last Knight was my first short story sale. I sent it to a car magazine that had just published a great—full page—review of Circa 1957. When I didn't hear back, I called (long before e-mail) the editor. He said he didn't plan to read it as the magazine didn't run fiction. I told him since he enjoyed Circa 1957, he would surely like this story. He promised to read it. About a month later, and after not hearing—again, I called. Same excuse. This time I said, "Look, it's mid afternoon, get a cup of coffee, take a break and read the story. I promise you, you will enjoy it." We hung up, I got out a fresh sheet of paper and began a letter to another magazine. The phone rang; it was the editor. He loved the story saying, "It made me laugh, cry and remember; it runs in the next issue. Can you send more?"

Another piece, *Sometimes Ya Get Lucky*, is fiction because the names and some of the non-essential portions were changed. The true parts are: I found a guy the Sheriff's Office couldn't find; he did have an alias; a farm in his girl's name; he was a "biker" and the action about finding him, including the lady tending her vegetable garden, and his reaction is verbatim.

Deciding which story or article to be included was daunting—I mean every writer believes all their scribblings are the best ever written, but, to pick a favorite of the favorites? I can't do it—not even the best of each part. You decide—then let me know.

Chuck Klein

2013

Contents

I FICTION STORIES

The Hero

He hadn't been back to his old home town in over twenty years and then it was only for a funeral. The rolling hills of the asphalt interstate looked like the flat side of a giant blower belt cut and thrown casually across the beautiful south central Ohio farm land. He laughed to himself at his unintentional play on words; a blower belt draped around the "farm belt" of the nation. Crossing the county line, his county line, brought a flood of memories. Memories of fun, simpler times and the race, the race for life. Where was it—the spot where the old road had been sliced by this modern highway?

Daydreaming was brought to a rapid halt by the sound of a siren attached to blue and red flashing lights. A quick glance at the speedometer confirmed his suspicions that it was he, for whom the sirens tolled. Swell. Welcome home hero. That's what you get for getting all melancholy while piloting a high powered sports car.

Down shifting his fully restored seventy-four, 454 Corvette he pulled to the side of the road adjacent to what appeared to be the remnants of an old two lane highway. The narrow strip of weed-sprouting black-top was now nothing more than a very long driveway for what looked like the south field to the Mulhouser farm. He wondered if any of the same family farmed it now.

"I've stopped you for exceeding the posted speed limit, sir. May I please see your operator's license," the Deputy Sheriff monotoned.

"I'm sorry officer. I guess I wasn't paying attention," he stated truthfully while searching his wallet—hoping that the license hadn't expired. "Is that the Mulhouser farm over there?" Nodding toward the fields of soybean, the Vette driver asked.

"Used to be. Fellah by the name of Krantz, from up around Columbus, owns it along with about three other farms around here. Absentee owner. Has a family by the name of, of…it'll come to me in a minute, tenant farming it now."

Handing the license to the officer he noted a slight pot belly contained by a sharply creased and neat shirt. This smart looking uniform was embellished with the standard polished brass accompaniments plus gold sergeant stripes. The deputy looked to be in his thirties though his graying hair could place him closer to forty. The neatly lettered name tag, Sgt. Vogt, jarred him. Might be, but Vogt was a common name in this area.

"You from these parts, Mr. Sampson?"

"I was born and raised not far from the old Mulhouser place. Lived here till I went away to college. First time I've been back in twenty years," the Corvette man said. Remembrances of a young, dying mother bounced around in the combustion chambers of his mind like a broken connecting rod in a V8 engine—jagged edges tearing away pieces of the past.

He had been called a hero by some and a crazy fool by others. The county newspaper covered the incident with only a one quarter column saying they were afraid that publicity of that kind would only encourage others to ignore proper procedures.

After graduating from high school he had worked that summer, the summer of fifty-seven, on the Keaton farm. He, and the rest of the farm hands, had just taken a lunch break when the young and very pregnant kitchen helper, white as a sheet and holding a towel under her tummy, stumbled into the mud room

Returning the driver's license the deputy asked, "Sampson. Seems I should know that name. You have any kin here?"

Blinking his eyes to snap back to the present he responded slowly, "Not any more. I was an only child, my mother died in seventy-two. My father lives with me."

"I'm not going to cite you, but I am going to run your VIN number through our computer," the officer said in his official tone as he copied the VIN on his note pad. It'll only take a second or two if the system's up.

As the deputy turned toward his cruiser, Kent Sampson turned to the old stretch of blacktop and back four decades. "Help, please! I fell. I think I'm hemorrhaging!" The mother-to-be gasped as she surged into the kitchen. It only took Mr. Keaton a few seconds to sum up the situation. Knowing that the volunteer ambulance was at least 20 minutes away and the ride to the nearest hospital was over half an hour farther he looked to his young summer helper, "Son, will that hot rod of yours make it to the County Hospital over to Skeetersville any faster than ma old wagon?" The calmness of his employer strengthened him as he shook his head up and down stammering, "Yes sir, Yes sir."

"Well, bring it up here to the back door while the missus and I carry her out. The "missus", blood up to her elbows, was stuffing another towel between the neighbor's wife's legs all the while cooing a soothing message of all's well.

He remembered running to his rod with the only thought in his mind, did he have enough gas for a mercy run to the county seat in the next county over. He'd spent the past year building his pride and joy—a 1935 Ford, three-window coupe. He had, with the help of various hot rod magazine articles, chopped the top, channeled the body, dropped the front axle, installed a LaSalle transmission and hopped up a swapped engine.

He'd done his work well. The full race flat-head fired on the first crank of the starter. Twin pipes, grumbling through Glass-pacs, boosted his confidence as he slipped the tires gently across the gravel barn yard.

There was barely enough room for two, much less a pregnant woman in the altered coupe's tiny interior. As the missus packed towels, Mr. Keaton gripped his arm and in a low steady voice intoned, "Son, she may not pull through, but there's a chance you can save the baby. But you've got to step on it. I'll call over to the hospital and tell 'em you're ah comin'."

He spun gravel all the way to the blacktop, turned east and got on it hard barely getting into third gear before having to shut down for the first set of 'S' bends. Today, he realized, would be the test of his handiwork as he set the little coupe into the first sweeping turn. At the apex, inside front tire on the dirt berm, he poured the coal to the mighty Mercury flathead. The rear tires howled in protest as the power curve of the Clay-Smith cam let in all the fuel the over-sized pistons could suck through the polished ports.

There was no traffic and he used all the roadway he dared. For the next few minutes his concentration was so intense that he hadn't had time to check his gauges much less the condition of his passenger. Just ahead loomed the narrow chicane, the right followed by a hard left at the Mulhouser farm that led to the only section of completed interstate in Spartan County. There he would have a chance to check everything.

Tires baying in dissent, young Kent brought his primer-red rod down to just under thirty-five from well above seventy for the first bend. He powered out of the final curve, tires squealing and engine screaming, to catch a glimpse of old mister Mulhouser out of the corner of his eye. The third generation farmer displayed his disgust at the speeding hot rod by shaking his fist at Kent from atop his John Deere.

Within minutes he was slamming the gear shift into high for the longest straight stretch of the run. Pleased at the sound of the three Stromberg ninety-sevens whooshing air through wide open butterflies he took the time to check the gauges. Oil: eighty pounds; temp: almost 200; fuel: cresting the empty mark; tach: 4200 and climbing slowly; speedometer mounting steadily at 105. He looked to the little lady. Clutching her blood soaked towels, she forced a cringing smile that mocked her vacant stare.

One hundred and fifteen — one-twenty — one-twenty-two. The steering felt light and there was a pronounced vibration. He backed down to just under 120 and the vibration slackened. Water temp hovering at 210, he passed the new green sign: Skeetersville Exit — 5 miles. He was over half way there but, even at 120 miles per hour it felt extremely slow — time wise. Every time he tried to go above 122 the vibration increased alarmingly. It must be those old wire wheels. He'd hand tightened each spoke and wire brushed them down to bare metal but still, true run-out was difficult to attain on those old wheels. He wished he'd had the money to buy new chrome-plated Dayton Wires or polished mags.

Drivers of the few cars he passed, at over twice their speed, stared wide-eyed and slack jawed at him. None dared to race him.

Slowing for the end of the divided highway gave him a final chance to study the interior. All okay except the temperature gauge. Maybe he had blown a head gasket which could, at these speeds, seize his perfectly rebuilt engine in short order. No question though, he would have to keep it floored.

After the zig-zag he ran a short straight tight in second gear and then had to double clutch down into first for the hairpin leading to the final set of 'S' bends. A quick glance at his passenger brought terror to his already over excited mind. Her head was listing at an unnatural angle, tongue visible and eyes half closed. He dared to take his hand from the wheel to shake her. "Lady. Lady," he screamed over the din of the high revving engine as he shook her near wrist. The entire arm flopped like an old heater hose. They were now down to minutes. He pushed the little copper wheeled coupe to its limit at each turn heading into the final straight. Here he'd have to open her up all the way, damn the temperature! Damn the vibration!

The newspaper reported that from the time the call was logged at the hospital to the minute the fender-less hot rod, smoke pouring from its hoodless engine, screeched to a halt at the back door of the emergency room only seventeen minutes had lapsed. The reporter believed it to be a mistake but, young tow-headed Kent Sampson, knew better. The account further noted that Mrs. Vogt died in surgery but the premature baby boy was saved. The Vogt family called him a hero and named the boy James Kent in his honor. The doctor unequivocally stated that had they arrived only a few minutes later the child would not have survived. Contrarily, the police chief admonished his deed threatening to take him to jail if he ever did it again.

~~~~~~~~~~~~~

Sergeant Vogt jarred him into the present with the news that his Vette wasn't on the NCIC hot list. He had broken into a damp sweat, not for fear of the car being stolen, but from reliving the old memories.

Clearing his throat, "Say…ah, Sergeant, is your name, by any chance, James Kent Vogt?"

"Why no, but my little brother was James Kent. How could you know him?"

"Well, ah, I sort of met him once. Knew his mother too, but it was a long time ago. Whatever became of him?"

The officer stroked his chin while eyeing this stranger who was inquiring about his brother and a mother he never knew. "James Kent was a volunteer firefighter. He died a little over two years ago, saving a child from a burning building. Now how could you possibly know my mothe…OH MAN! The name didn't register until just now. Why, why, you're the kid…the hero, who drove a hot rod Ford from the old Keaton place to Skeetersville in seventeen minutes to save his life. Let me shake your hand Mr. KENT Sampson and say thanks, thanks very much."

Uncomfortable as it was, Kent twisted in his seat extending his hand for the obligatory grasp. "I'm sorry to learn of your brother's death…." After the brief awkward silence that imprisoned the grown men in their own revelations, Kent continued, "Whatever happened to the Keaton's, and that police chief and do you know what became of my coupe?"

"The last I saw of your car…say, it's almost my quitting time. Why don't you come on over to the house and we can catch you up on all these things. I'm sure my brother's family would like to meet you."

The Detective

The piercing light was visible long before he heard the two longs followed by two shorts as the Chicago bound James Whitcome Riley approached the Carter Street crossing. Within minutes the E-9, the most powerful of diesel engines, was thundering into Winton Place station. Though the little two piece windshield, just aft of the giant single head lamp, towered over his head he couldn't suppress the smile and memory of last week's Christmas. Then it was he who towered over an E-9, a Lionel with "Santa Fe" splashed in orange and silver across the side of his gift to a wide-eyed nephew.

From his vantage point, near the Western Union window, Kurt Kidwell could see the platform to the right and the parking lot to his left. The target was nowhere to be found. Maybe Miss Dolly had set him up — they were traveling by car and it was a bum steer. He watched, ticket in hand, as the porters loaded and unloaded boxes, grips, trunks and all sizes of suitcases. He watched the passengers embark and disembark, especially the smart looking tan-suited knockout with the matching hat perched atop her stacked honey blond hair. Kidwell never took his eye off the lot. Maybe he was already on-board having caught the train at the Oakley Station.

The man who earned a living watching, watched, with a sinking feeling, as the Brakeman, lantern in hand, got into position at the rear of the train. It had begun to rain. Kidwell stepped toward the Pullman car, Starlight, as the sound of tires straining for adhesion on gravel commanded his attention. Caught in the head lamps of the a dirty black '49 Cadillac convertible, the trademark of Mr. Pogue, Kidwell pulled the brim of his fedora a little lower and the collar of his trench coat up as he stepped onto the Starlight's platform.

The Brakeman began to move his lantern up and down, the signal for the engineer to get underway. Mr. Pogue and his driver, laden with two suitcases and a string tied cardboard box, had to be helped by the Brakeman onto the now moving train.

8

He'd give Pogue an hour or so then he'd look him up. He wasn't going anywhere for at least a few hours—the Riley's first stop. Right now Kidwell needed the men's room and some warm food. Entering the day-coach, El Capitan, he searched the overhead racks for a place to stash his hat and coat. Amid leather suitcases, paperboard composite grips and round lady's' hat boxes with the name of swank department stores emblazoned on the richly colored Krome-Kote wrapping, he found an unobtrusive spot. The car's seats were filled more with small trunks, a few leather trimmed canvas covered grips and gift boxes than the holiday travelers themselves. Tossed on and between were an array of coats and outer wear, a leather flyer's jacket, a smartly creased gentleman's felt hat with a tweed sport jacket and a hangered sailor's dress blues. The lavatory was clean, properly stocked and a great relief.

The dining car was about half full so Kidwell had no trouble settling into a starched linen covered table, complimented with a small bouquet of fresh flowers snugged up to the window. Within a minute the hospital-white clad waiter filled Kidwell's order for a Jack Daniels on the rocks. Complacency settled over the Private Investigator as he casually observed soothed couples' happy faces reflected by the individual table lamps against their personal half-shaded windows. Entrées enjoyed were a choice of Prime Rib, Boursin Chicken or Stuffed Lemon Sole as America's backyards roll by. The dressed to the nines, tan-suited knockout smiled at him over the top of a tall cold exotic something. Kurt Kidwell discretely adjusted his shoulder holster before approaching tan-suit.

"I'm Karl Kinder, may I join you?" he asked, athletically jostling his muscular body into the opposite seat as the train rocked over a set of switches. The pseudo name was one he used when dealing with strangers while on the job. In this business, you never know who's also on the job on the opposite side.

"Seems that you already have, and I'm happy to meet you, I think. My name is Victoria and that, that drunken soldier who just came in has been bothering me. Uh, oh, here he comes again."

"Well … there you are little lady. I thought I lost ya. Is thesh man bothering you," the three-stripe non-com slurred.

"I think it's the other way around, Sergeant. The lady is with me so please refrain from interfering with us again," Kurt said, in a kind manner, rising from his seat while boring his eyes into a set of slightly dilated pupils.

It was really all one move, the words, the stare and the arm lock that crumpled the uniform to his knees. Reducing the pressure enough to allow the intruder to be half dragged, Kidwell deposited the rude soldier in the forward sleeper admonishing him to sleep it off.

Returning to his upholstered dinner table chair beneath the car length, hand-painted murals covering the frieze on both sides of the older 1937 era dining car, the lady named Victoria smiled again, "Thank you ever so much, Mr. Kinder." The soft pastel colors highlighted by the hanging globe lights lent an aura of mystic and intrigue to this calm and sophisticated lady.

During the interlude that preceded the main course the widowed heir to an old manufacturing company and the gentleman with the clandestine demeanor, discretely exchanged pleasantries.

They dined on filet mignon with sautéed mushrooms and fresh spinach au gratin. When the plates had been cleared they sipped Three Star Hennessey as winking roadside crossings lights occasionally flashed across the darkened window. He told her his business was corporate acquisitions and he, also, was on his way home to Chicago.

The train, now at cruising speeds of seventy plus, set up a gentle rocking motion which, between cars as he was seeing her to her bedroom compartment, caused her to fall into him. He steadied her, feeling firm upper arms and catching a scent of Channel Number Five. They stood close to let another passenger pass. The vibes oozed. "I've got some business to take care of," he said, locking into her light green eyes. "If I stop back in an hour or so can we have a night cap?"

She returned his gaze before twisting, brushing against his arm, as she unlocked the door, "I'd like that. I need to freshen up a little, anyway."

Since Pogue hadn't visited the dining car he had to be between there and the club car. Kidwell set out to scout the train. The top half of the outside door to the car just ahead of the lounge car was open, a fact noted by the PI in case anything had to be tossed out. Stepping into the club car, the classic model with a half length mahogany bar down one side, Kidwell smiled to the lone bartender as his eyes scanned the room. Seated in the fore section was a businessman studying a newspaper next to his young, comic book reading son and a fidgeting, beer drinking sailor. Halfway back, Mr. Pogue, holding the twine tied box, and his chauffeur were complacently sipping drinks. Kidwell walked the length of the room and sat at the rear most table — after surreptitiously verifying the door to the observation platform was unlocked. The bartender looked up, but the private dick shook his head while picking up a Life magazine.

He didn't like the situation. He didn't like all the witnesses. He didn't like the driver, if that's what he really was. If he was a driver, then why did he leave the Caddy at the train station and why did he keep looking around — like a body guard.

The diesel horn sounded, two longs followed by two shorts for the approach of a public crossing. The now tense six foot P.I. had been counting since the first. The engineer had been very punctual. Almost exactly eleven seconds after the first blast of the horn the sound of the crossing bells reached the train's passenger cars. The bells, combined with the flashing red lights bouncing through the train's windows, were quite distracting.

The sailor got up to leave, the P.I. started another magazine. It didn't look like Pogue was in any hurry by the number of olive pits in the ash tray. Body guard was sipping something dark with ice through a straw — probably a Coke if he was on the job. Kidwell had hoped to have concluded the business by now, but there had been too many people and he hadn't counted on a body guard.

The mission had seemed simple enough when the phone call came, followed by the packet of cash and directives. All he had to do was trade the package Mr. Pogue was to be transporting for the cash Kurt was carrying in his inside jacket pocket. He was instructed to secure the package at all costs, something about a threat to national security. It seemed his clientele only called when the task was too tough or sticky for lesser agents.

When the executive and his son rose to leave, Kurt signaled the bartender. He asked the practiced elderly Negro if he would be so kind as to check with the kitchen for an order of cheese and crackers. Now there were only three.

"Mr. Pogue, I'd like a word …."

"Mr. Pogue don't talk to nobody, so take a powder, pal," the burly body guard belched forcing his way between them.

Time was short before the barkeep or another passenger would walk in. Kidwell lowered his eyes and turned slightly to send body language messages of capitulation while he searched for words to stall for time and a piece of luck. Softly he began, "I'm sorry sir, I didn't mean to intrude it's only that … the words were lost to the wail of the E-9's horn … won't bother … eight — nine — ten — the bells clanged, the lights flashed, the bruiser's concentration broke as he glanced out the windows. Just like the sergeant, and so many others before him, it was all one move. The P.I.'s foot found the male tender spot just below the belly button an instant before the right hand connected with the jaw of the stunned and buckling galoot.

Mr. Pogue, impaired by the martinis, could only stare, slack jawed, as Kurt dragged the unconscious body through the rear doors and onto the observation platform. The thought of tossing the dead weight over was tempting, but he had confidence that his body guarding days were over for the night.

"Now then Mr. Pogue, before we were so rudely interrupted, we have business to transact. I have here," Kidwell began extracting the envelope filled with cash from his jacket pocket, "A large sum of money that I intend to trade you for the box on your lap."

"What have you done with Bruno. It's not for sale, now please leave me or I shall summon the authorities. Bartender, bartender …."

"I sent him away. It's just you and me. Time is short and you only have two choices."

"What do you mean? Who are you? I'm not selling. All you and your kind want to do is keep it off the market. My invention will …."

As the inventor rambled on, Kidwell took the man's half drained highball from the table top and casually tossed it into his face. The slightly intoxicated keeper of the box reacted before he realized he had relaxed his grip on the box. That was all the practiced P.I. needed. He flipped the envelope on the table and strode out, catching out of the corner of his eye, the opening platform door and the guard struggling in, revolver in hand!

"Is it a present for me?" the golden haired lady impishly chided as she opened the door at his knock. "Or is it a reward from rescuing other maidens?"

His face relaxed and a smile spread to his dimples as he surveyed the room and the silk robe clad lady. But his mind was racing. "Sorry to put you to any trouble, but I'm in a bit of a jam and I might need your help."

He put the box down on the day couch, turned to look her in the eye to see if she was with him. She held her head high and stared back at him. He took her squared shoulders in his powerful hands pulling her toward him. It was a closed mouth kiss, he afraid of relaxing, and she, just to let him know the quid pro quo was sealed.

He told her the box contained medical experiments that a Russian agent, an armed Russian agent on board the train, was trying to steal from him. "Look, I think the train is going to stop soon and when it does I'll need you to get off with me. They won't be looking for a couple, especially one with glasses," he said producing a pair of eye glasses with clear lenses.

It didn't take long before the sound of the thug could be heard in the passage way, banging on every door. There wasn't time to discuss anything.

Bang, bang, bang, "Open the door."

Slowly she opened the door a crack. The bully, gun in hand, pushed, slamming it against the closet. "What's the meaning of this …."

"Shut up. Where is he?"

"How dare you. There's no one in here. Who …." He pushed passed her, looking first toward the beds then at the water closet door.

Kidwell, crouched back to the wall in the tiny, crowded, pitch-black toilet room—eased his HSc Mauser out of its shoulder holster and leveled it at the door. Even over the click-clack of the train's wheels he could hear the distinct click of the door handle as the Mauser's safety clicked off.

Having killed before and in control of the situation, fear was absent, though he was, maybe a mite apprehensive. The little 7.65 pocket pistol, taken from a Nazi officer he had garroted during his days in the service of his country, was a favorite of his arsenal of concealable weapons. Its reliability had been established in past operations.

BlaaaaaaaaaaaaCrack,Crack,Crackaaaaaaaat. The timing of the diesel locomotion's announcement that it was approaching a station couldn't have been more opportune.

The aggressor, dumbfounded at the three thirty-two caliber crimson holes in his shirt front, paradoxically glimpsed the lavatory mirror for his final vision — the face of a dead man.

"Victoria, Victoria give me a hand, he's fallen on me."

The previously formal and composed lady Victoria, ashen and wide eyed, nonetheless dutifully straddled the body and extended a hand.

"Get dressed and put on some lipstick, we're getting off here." She stood there, gaping at the corpse as the impact of the situation began to sink in. Struggling with her suit case, he slapped her hard on the rump. "Get moving, NOW!"

With the smaller of her two suitcases he dumped their contents on the bed, placed the string tied box inside, and packed what he could of the dumped contents around the box.

"What we can't get into your other suitcase, I'll replace," he stated, throwing undergarments and personal items into the larger grip as the train slowed for the station stop.

Victoria, displaying genuine aristocratic style, smiled as she accompanied the P.I. through the El Capitan where he retrieved his hat and coat. As a cold wind whipped at their ankles they snuck across the platform to a waiting cab.

The hotel in this out-of-the-way little burg was, if nothing else, a safe haven. Here, as the lady bathed, he inspected the contents of the box he had killed for.

After his shower, and standing in his under shorts, he moved to take her into his arms, "I just want to hold you."

"You mean gratuitously? For helping you conduct whatever dirty business you're in? Perhaps you better tell who you really are, Mr. Karl Kinder, if that's your real name." She had regained her full stature as a business executive. "You have presented yourself as a gentleman, at least in your dealings with me. Please continue to do so. I have no intention of allowing this room to become a tryst."

"I understand and respect your wishes. All I said was I wanted to hold you. I need a little tenderness now and I thought you might also."

"Who are you? What …."

"It's best that you don't know my real name. I'm a private investigator and sometimes my assignments get a little ah … hairy. I'm sorry to have involved you in this, but making use of you as cover seemed like a good idea at the time. After this matter is concluded I'd like to try to start all over — on a social level, especially since we're both from Chicago. Right now, I think we each could use a little, make that a lot, of TLC."

She came to him. They hugged. The tension dissipated. In a short while they fell asleep.

Hours later he slipped out, paid the hotel bill and, box in hand, wolfed down a pancake breakfast at a greasy spoon two blocks down the street. Finding himself in the seedier part of town he quickly located a pawn shop where he purchased a used canvas suitcase in which to carry the box.

He caught a cab to the station, bought a ticket on the next train to Chicago and found a public telephone. Three rings and he heard his client, "Consolidated Gas and Oil, Incorporated, may I help you?" the sweet voice of a young operator answered.

"Extension 447, Please"

"Yes."

"This is Kidwell."

"Have you got it?"

"Yes sir."

"Where are you? Tell me what's in the box."

"I'm a couple of hours out of the LaSalle Street Station. The box contains a lot of diagrams, blue prints and legal papers plus what looks like a carburetor—a special kind of carburetor."

"Excellent. Come directly to the Drake. We will meet you in the lobby."

He had a half hour to kill before departure. Maybe he could find a little something for Miss Dolly. She had really come through for him, but the thought of a special lady is what was really twisting around in his mind. He took a walk around the block, past a Negro bar where he stopped to listen to a solo coronet crying some blues number that drifted by like a spirit on the winds of time.

Author's note: Rumors have circulated for over half a century that a man named Pogue (or Fish or ???) invented a carburetor that produced unprecedented fuel economy. The rumor includes the scenarios that the petroleum producers, foreign interests and/or the automobile manufacturers, to keep the product off the market, stole the design and to keep Mr. Pogue/Fish/??? quiet, paid him off or....

Christmas Miracle

"OUR FATHER WHO ART IN HEAVEN...." The radio station sign-off paid tribute to the eve of the birth of Christ by invoking the ageless prayer in lieu of the traditional National Anthem. At its conclusion the cab of the single-stack-Mack-with-a-sleeper-on-the-back fell silent, save for the drone of the engine and rush of the wind.

Memories of his father, killed in a foxhole on a like snowy and bitter cold Christmas eve, saturated his mind. Duane Starkholder had always taken the prayer personally, wishing, hoping, believing his father was in Heaven. He was only a small boy in 1944 and had been angry that such sad news had taken the joy from his first electric train, a Lionel with pellet-induced smoking steam engine. Christmases of love brought about by time, marriage, children and now grandchildren had helped suppress remembrances of that paradoxical day and the strong feelings of another traumatic holiday.

The soon to be retired professional trucker reached for the dial in search of entertainment. Refocusing his attention on the task at hand he was surprised that over a dozen miles had been added to the mile markers during what, he thought, was a short trip down memory lane. Right now, the snow was getting heavier and he had better call home to let them know he might be a little late. He was not particularly religious, even though he believed he had witnessed a miracle — some say he was the miracle. Still he would like to be home in time for Midnight prayer service with the family.

Someday he'd show his grandsons the newspaper clippings of the Christmas of '55. He was recently married and just completing his first year with Akers Trucking, driving a 1951 International 5-speed with an electric 2-speed axle. He was young, full of energy and in a hurry to spend his first Christmas with his wife. At the truck stop a few miles back he had called Barbara, his bride of ten months, only to learn that the storm had knocked out all power to their section of town and she was running low on firewood. She had said that she and the baby were sharing a sleeping bag but was scared and cold. So when the State Trooper told him they were closing the road due to the blizzard he dared the officer to try to catch him as he barreled through the road block. With chains on the tandem drive wheels and a 10,000 pound payload in the nose of the trailer he was sure nothing could stop him.

An hour and only 25 miles later he was not so sure. Some of the drifts were up to his running boards and he was tiring from the constant shifting. It seemed like every time he'd get into high 4th the tractor would slam into a drift and he'd have to double clutch the crash box down a gear usually splitting the axle at the same time. Even locating the roadway was taxing his concentration. He was fearful that the rig might jackknife, slide off the shoulder, or worse, run over the top of a stranded motorist though he hadn't seen another vehicle of any kind since the roadblock.

Spending Christmas in the cab of his truck waiting for a rescue team would be humiliating not to mention the possibility of frost bite or even death—his wife and child's! Another hour and a pitifully few miles later he was coming to believe it was going to take a miracle to get him through. Each blast of blowing snow conjured thoughts of Barbara and little David calling his name, as the kindling dwindled and the drafty old house took on the characteristics of a tomb.

Carefully, forcefully, the powerful semi rounded a bend, straining to pick up speed for the long hill into Wesson Springs. A few more turns of the wheel and he'd be warming his family even if he had to load them into this truck and find a motel.

Half way across the flat the beams from the ice encrusted head lamps bounced off a large drift in the center of the road. Failing to see a safe way around the protrusion without risking a jackknife, Duane prepared to plow through the mound. It was only at the last instant that he saw the red glow of tail lights coming from inside the mound! Cursing, double clutching and yanking the huge wheel he fought for control, clamping on the trailer brakes in a last attempt to avoid striking the car.

With a muffled thud or two the thirty-six foot trailer slipped off the shoulder dragging the cab and all hopes for a merry Christmas with it.

18

Dazed, but very aware of the situation, Duane scrambled into the blizzard. He took his bearings, illuminated only by the slowly diminishing flush of the truck's head lamps.

In the forested counties of Northern Minnesota night snowfall renders the surroundings virtually pitch black. There is no reflected light from distant towns and star light cannot penetrate heavy blankets of pure white pieces of dark. Realizing at once the conditions familiar to all locals, he knew he was in trouble. Before the truck lights gave out he secured a flashlight and his hooded coat and gloves from the partially overturned truck and set out to check the stalled car.

Barely audible in the blowing gale force storm, Duane could hear the cries of a man half-calling, half-praying for help. Brushing the snow from the door handle he was aware that the engine was running. In addition to the man's cries a woman's voice, or rather her moans, were filtering from the now recognizable '52 DeSoto.

Cracking open the car's door Duane inquired if everything was alright as his flashlight revealed a terrified man holding the hand of a woman, obviously about to deliver.

"Hurry up and come in, you're letting in all the cold. It must be 20 below out there and Mary Beth's about to deliver. You don't happen to be a doctor or something, do ya?" The man pleaded in run-together words.

Stuffing his large frame into the front seat of the sedan, Duane kept the light modestly trained on the ceiling, though his eyes danced between the woman's strained face and the exposed place from where another being was trying to force his or her presence. About to address the man's question the woman let out a sharp grunt gasping, "It's coming, Jake — help me, quick."

"Hold that light over here mister, please."

With the intensity of a blizzard and the softness of a snow flake a new life was brought forth on this eve of the birth of the Savior. The woman seemed to know what to do, instructing Duane where to shine the light and her husband how to tie off the cord. The moment of euphoric joy only lasted until the reality of the situation was emphatically brought to mind by the exterior conditions. But, what a moment. Amid shouts of joy, all three of them, a man, his wife, and a stranger, trapped together in a snow bound car experienced for one brief jubilant instant the hope and future of the world.

"Thanks for your light. I don't know what we would have done without it. We hadn't exactly planned it this way," the man explained. "We didn't expect little, ah…Stormy, here so soon. But, Mary Beth went into labor just about the time the storm hit. Without a phone to call for help, we figured that we might be able to beat the heavy part of the snow. Our farm's only about four or five miles from here."

"Where did you come from? Do you have a car or…? Can you take us to the hospital?"

Duane explained his predicament, chagrined at his inability to keep his rig from sliding off the road.

"You're welcome to stay with us until help arrives and we're sorry about your truck and…."

"How much gas have you got?" Duane interrupted taking stock of the situation. "It might be a long time before help arrives. They closed the road. I was the last vehicle through and I had to run a road block at that."

"I guess we might have two hour's worth of fuel…closed the road? What are we going to do? A baby can't…we've been here a couple of hours already and Mary Beth's…" he spoke rhetorically in broken sentences, while the dim light of the instrument panel cast coal black shadows of Duane's figure on the roof of their snow cave.

"Well, I thank ya for the kind offer to wait out the storm here. Ordinarily I'd take you up on it, but I got a wife and child at home without any electricity and I aim to spend my Christmas keeping them warm," Duane announced.

"Besides, we can't just let "Stormy" freeze in this old car can we?"
~~~~~~~~~~~~~~

"How 'bout that eastbound single-stack-Mack-with-the-sleeper-on-the-back, come-on," the CB jarred him back to the present as he automatically keyed the mic., "You got the single-stack-Mack, Kick it back, come-on."

20

"How's it look over your donkey? The snow's lighter the further east you go, come-on."

"You be headin' for the heart of it. That there snow be gettin' heavy in your face, come-on."

"Thanks for the update and hope you and all the other truckers listenin' to this ol' ratchet jaw has a merry one," the west bound fellow trucker exclaimed as the two cargo ships of the macadam passed in the night.

~~~~~~~~~~~~

Maybe it was a miracle that he had been able to stumble through drifts, darkness and numbing cold, newborn bundled to his bare chest. With less than a hundred yards of open corn field, Wesson Springs General in view, his clod-hoppered right foot had found a gopher hole. Fighting to keep from falling on the baby he twisted his body enough to break his ankle. He lay there in icy pain, thoughts of his father dying in like circumstance flashing before his mind's eye. Knowing that he couldn't—wouldn't—leave his son the same way, knowing that if he didn't move it would be Spring before they found them, he forced his body to crawl. He had prayed to *his* father in heaven that night and maybe it was those prayers that got them through.

Any fool can walk, or even crawl, through a blizzard. The real miracle was the birth of Stormy. He turned out just fine, with no after effects from the ordeal. The last he'd seen this now grown man was a year ago during a visit to Los Angeles where Stormy was a Police Captain. Duane was even Godfather to Stormy's first born, Paul Duane Peterson.

The blizzard conditions that night hadn't hurt Barbara and David. They were taken in by neighbors with coal stoves. Duane would walk with a cane the rest of his life and Stormy's father lost a leg to frost bite. Mary Beth, Stormy's mother, was taken in by Our Father long before the rescuers came.

This night Duane didn't need any prayers, the snow slacked off and he finished his run on schedule.

Sitting next to her husband in the old downtown church pew, Barbara squeezed his hand at the sight of the lone tear that rolled down Duane's face during the closing prayer: ...Thy kingdom come, Thy will be done.

Boomers And 'Bos

He wasn't sure he heard the first torpedo, but the second got his full attention and that of the locomotive engineer who pulled the throttle full back and yanked the whistle chain. Bartlett, fighting the deceleration, coupled with the coupled cars slamming into each other as the slack between them collapsed, strained to reach the window of the cab.

Number 4, a Santa Fe mixed-freight special east bound out of Needles, California, was highballing in high desert country when the emergency stop signals had gone off. These detonation caps are placed on the track to explode when crushed by the engine's wheels — a warning to immediately halt.

Just before the massive 2-10-2 mountain whaler, hissing a fog bank of steam, ground to a stop aside a red lantern, Bartlett caught a glimpse of horses and riders. Highlighted by the massive headlamp he counted at least five with more movement fading into the deep black woods. As a Pinkerton man he was purposely riding in the cab because the Wells Fargo car was heavy with a gold shipment. Specifically on the lookout for trouble he recognized the robbery routine immediately.

The detective jumped from the off-side onto a steeply banked roadbed, pulling his five-inch barreled Colt from its holster. Fighting for footing in the loose rock and gravel he managed to stay in the steam cloud while scampering back to the opening between the tender and the first car. Before he could see the riders, he heard angry shouting from the old hogger, Tom Fiser — demanding to know who, why and what these men on horseback wanted. The answer came with multiple gun shots and the scream of the fireman — which was followed by a shotgun blast … and silence, save for the hissing and ticking of the 2-10-2.

Knowing that life might be over in a flash of gunpowder and wishing he had grabbed his Winchester before bailing out of the cab, Bartlett vaulted over the coupling between the cars shooting at the first rider he saw. Not waiting to learn of his marksmanship, the Pinkerton man wheeled and fanned at least three shots at other men on horseback now visibly painted by the light reflected from the steam. At least three because there were so many shots being fired he wasn't sure how many were his. But, he was sure one of these muzzle blasts caused his left arm to violently twitch. Bartlett tried to vault back over the coupling, but this left arm gave way and he crashed to the roadbed striking his head on the rail. Luckily his momentum carried him over the bed and down into the tumbleweeds and protection of the night.

An explosion ripped the air and produced a flash that silhouetted the entire train. These guys are good, he thought. They've shot the engineer and fireman fought off my return fire and blew the door off the money car in a very timely and precision manner. But how much time had elapsed?

Lying on the down slope of the raised roadbed, he knew his first priority was to reload. Even with the now searing pain in his left arm, he managed to eject the spent cartridges and stuff the cylinder with six fresh.32-20 rounds. Normally he only loaded five in the six shot single-action revolver as it wasn't safe to carry with the hammer down on a loaded round, but this was a firefight and not carry conditions.

Wide-eyed and ignoring the wound, he crept up the embankment fully expecting gunfire. Nothing. Dead quiet—even the engine. Had he passed out? Where is everyone—robbers, brakemen, Wells Fargo agents, horses? Staggering to his feet, he sought the safety of the engine and what light it provided hoping to retrieve his rifle. At the cab's ladder, using his good arm, he quietly climbed aboard. His rifle and ammo belt were as he left them, though he quickly realized with a bum arm the rifle would be of little use. The fireman, a boomer who was on his first trip firing for the S.F, lay across a pile of coal at such an odd angle it was clear he was dead. Tom, however, appeared to have propped himself up against the firebox, but looked slack jawed. Kneeling down, Bartlett could see the stain of blood on Tom's chest, surely a mortal wound.

He had met the hogman on a previous and uneventful run back in '98, when they were a little younger. They had gotten along well, neither man was married, but both had strong family ties and a formidable sense of fairness. Though Tom, ten years his senior was pushing 40 back then, they had bonded through discussions of family life and treatment of their fellow man. Their first meeting was one of Bartlett's early cases for the renowned Chicago based private detective agency. A thieving brakeman on Tom's train had been surreptitiously tightening select wheel brakes to cause hot boxes. When the conductor ordered the train onto a siding to investigate, the brakeman would slip into a loaded box car and throw out crates of freight to be picked up later by his gang. Bartlett suspected the rouse and was able to catch the crook in the act. That was the easy part. More difficult was tying the yard dicks into the act. The two railroad policemen had claimed they investigated the freight loss but couldn't explain it or catch the culprits. Bartlett, using various methods of, shall we say, persuasion, convinced the brakeman to tell how the Santa Fe railroad police were in on the thefts.

Not seeing any sign of the robbers from the vantage point of the cab windows, Bartlett untied the bandana from around the engineer's neck and wiped his friend's face while asking the obvious "how ya doin'" questions. The only response Tom could muster was a pleading look and a beckoning finger. Bartlett leaned close as the old hogger took a breath and whispered, "Will you see to it that my nephew, Thomas, gets my watch and what benefits the S.F....." He didn't finish as his eyes closed and his fingers relaxed.

No time for bereavement, he had to find the conductor and check the damage and inspect his own wound. Opening the firebox door for light, surprised that the fire was so low, he pulled his shirt off and stared at the bloody upper arm. Using the knife he always carried in his boot, he cut the good sleeve from his shirt and made a bandage as best he could. He was able to move his fingers and the arm, but only with intense pain.

Climbing back down, the first bodies he found were strangers—possibly robbers shot by him due to their proximity to the tender. Hoisting himself aboard the severely damaged W.F. car he found both agents had been blown into the next life by the blast that took the door off their car. The safe had also been dynamited, but Bartlett couldn't remember a second blast—or was this the only blast he heard? These were ruthless men.

"You all right mister?" The voice stunned Bartlett and he dropped, twisted and drew the Single Action Army revolver.

"Don't shoot. We're just bos. Been ridin' in the empty hopper just aft o' this money car," the man dressed as an obvious hobo pleaded.

"How many are you? Where did the robbers go? Where's the conductor and brakemen?" Bartlett demanded, holstering his gun and jumping back to trackside.

The bo, terrified and flustered stammered, "You a rail dick?"

"Not likely. I work for Pinkerton. I'm not out to arrest, thump or toss you. Now, where are the others?"

"Back at the end, sir."

By the light of the caboose lanterns, Bartlett came upon an eerie scene that sent a chill through him—the conductor, brakeman and rear brakeman all lay shot dead while some of the hobos were rummaging through the trainmen's pockets. For the third time the detective drew his handgun as he ordered the bos to line up facing the waycar.

Only after asserting they were just trying to get back the four bits each had paid the conductor to ride to Seligman, Bartlett holstered his.32-20. He then discovered there were a total of six men who, hidden in the hopper car, had escaped the slaughter of the robbers. They all had different opinions as to the direction the robbers departed. Additional questioning determined that two of the men were boomers. One, Johnson, a squat looking tough had been a brakeman for the U.P. and the other, Smitherman, a tall gangly kid, was a hostler who had just quit the Needles yard and hopped this special.

"Johnson, you're now the acting rear brakeman. Grab two torpedoes and the red lantern from the dog house and protect the rear of this train. Do you know how to do it?" Bartlett ordered.

"Yeah. I jest go back 'bout a quarter mile an place the bombs on the track 'bout ten paces apart and set the lantern along side."

"Almost right. After you set the torpedoes, you stay there and wave the lantern at any approaching train. Don't come back until you hear our whistle. You got that?"

Turning to assume his task, Johnson mumbled a "yes sir."

"Smitherman. Do you think you can move this train if one of these other men fire for you?"

"Yes sir." It was only this here morning that I built the fire in this here very engine and moved her onto the main line."

"Okay, I'm commandeering this train—I'm now the conductor and assume full responsibility. You there," Bartlett said pointing to one of the bos, come with me and Smitherman. You'll fire the engine. The rest of you men load the bodies into what's left of the Wells Fargo car and then you can ride the rest of the way into Seligman in the caboose." Almost as an afterthought, he added, "There's two more in the cab. They were all good men. Treat 'em with respect.

"Once at the station all of you are to stay in the waycar until I say it's okay to leave. That means until after the Marshall in Seligman and I have had a chance to question you. That's an order."

As soon as steam pressure returned to the engine the crippled train and impromptu crew limped the remaining 40 or so miles into the station at Seligman, Arizona.

Bartlett S. Listner (he was never called Bart) had grown up along the Chicago and North Western Railway where his father's life ended in an all too common coupling accident. Pappy Listner, as he was known, was a good father and for as much as Bartlett knew, was a good husband, too. Sometimes, though, even good guys die young. For the younger Listner, detective work was also an accident—that of being in the right place at the right time. His father, a C&NW brakeman, had gotten him a job as a call boy for the road. Bartlett's duty was to locate and notify boomers and others on the call board when needed to make a train. He seemed to have a natural ability to find people and the discretion when to not find them plus the physical grit to drag them in when necessary. On a day with a building snow storm he was able to round up, in a most timely manner, the required men to make up a special train. This special just happened to be for a Pinkerton operative who, recognizing Bartlett's abilities, immediately offered him a job.

Arriving at Seligman, the first thing Bartlett did, even before tending to his wounds and reporting to the Trainmaster, was to telegraph Pinkerton headquarters with a preliminary report. Finally, after all reports had been filed, the marshal notified and the men interrogated, he stopped by the barber shop to have his injuries tended. The bullet had passed through his upper arm, just chipping the bone. His head wound, which he now saw in a mirror, was ugly, covered in dried blood and would leave a nasty scar.

Hungry and tired, he took a room at the Harvey House Hotel. Here, after a few hours sleep, he cleaned up and settled into a back corner of the restaurant. Peggy, a vermillion haired Harvey Girl, was first to serve him. She remembered Bartlett as not only had their career paths crossed many times over the years, but they were from the same neighborhood. Their mothers had been friends. She was at least ten years older than Bartlett and had been a real looker — maybe even a dance hall girl — sometime in the nineties. Now, however, her figure gone and in a bland, food stained dress, she was just pudgy dumpy. Friendly, kind hearted, good at her job, she was a mother image for the other girls, but pudgy dumpy.

"Hi honey. Long time no see."

"Hello, Peggy. It's only been a month or so since I was here last. You doin' okay?"

"They keep me plenty busy. What can I getcha?"

While waiting for his food, he wrote a short note on the Harvey House postcards to his mother to let her know he was okay. With the release of the boomers and bos from the official investigation he was sure the story made front pages all across the nation and he didn't want her to worry. Sipping coffee after enjoying his steak and eggs, Smitherman the hostler/boomer, entered the room, looked around and when he saw Bartlett, headed straight toward him.

Without so much as a nod from the detective Smitherman sat down, and in a low voice, revealed, "It really ain't none of my business, but ol' Tom Fiser was a friend o' mine." Looking around as if worried about his backside, he continued, "I seen three men in the Golden Spur Saloon ah woopin' it up. On the bar in front of them was a Wellsl Fargo pouch — you know the kind they ship gold nuggets in."

"How many horses?"

"There were four tied up right in front of the Spur. But, I only seen three men at the bar."

Wow, this is a break. The robbers weren't even smart enough not to head to the train's destination. Seems these criminals had more dollars than sense. Bartlett thanked the man, paid his bill and kissed Peggy on the cheek before heading for the saloon.

Over confidence, not having a plan and being in a hurry can yield catastrophic events. Luck, however, can negate many such blunders. Bartlett's first mistake was of the self-assurance nature. The second was not securing the help of a posse or even the Marshall. He walked into the bar, stood directly behind the three men with the nugget pouch, drew his Colt and said in a commanding voice, "I'm Pinkerton detective Listner. You are all under arrest for robbery and murder. Place your hands on the bar."

The three men complied at once … the fourth—the one Bartlett failed to notice and sitting at a rear table placed *his* hands on a shotgun. The blast wounded two of the three robbers, but good guy Bartlett, who had not formulated a plan or waited for help, caught the mass of the charge. Like his father before him, sometimes even good guys die young.

Last Knight

In the beginning was Elvis and Smokey
the Everly's Richie and Fats
four-on-the-floor or three-on-the-tree
and DARLING COME SOFTLY TO ME.

The young man, in his late teens, pulled into the driveway, eager to show his father and great grandfather his latest acquisition, a '32 Ford. Almost at the same time a delivery man arrived with a package. Taking the carefully wrapped box, with the word "FRAGILE" stamped in red on all sides, into the library of the ancient tudor style house, he approached a much older man seated in a leather wingback.

"Pop." Then a little louder, "Grandpa, come outside for a minute I want to show you my new car. It's got all the extras."

The old timer knew cars. He had studied, and in some cases rubbed shoulders with, the best of the early engineers, customizers and racers. Men with the immortalized names of Iskenderian, Duntov, Barris, Fangio, Vukovich.

After the ritualistic inspection of the male bonding medium the two men returned to the den where the younger remembered the package. "I almost forgot, Pop, this came for you a little while ago."

"What is it Sonny?" the old man asked, settling into his overstuffed chair.

"I don't know Pop. It's from some law office back east and it sounds like it has liquid in it. You getting your Geritol by mail now?" The great grandson joked.

Staring at the proffered package the old man pushed back further into the cushions of the chair as if trying to distance himself from it. His mouth dropped open... "oh my God", escaped in a barely audible, raspy whisper.

"Grandpa, what's wrong? Are you okay?" The young gentleman crossed the room to take this ancient man's hand and search his frightened stare. "What is it, Pop?"

As recollections of events, forever melded to the sentimental portions of his mind, were forced to the present, the great grandfather's eyes soon began refocusing to a new intensity. "Get a couple of glasses and some ice, Sonny—and call your Dad in here. I've got a story to tell you."

A man with graying hair and his teenage son watched the great grandfather, in his 96th year, carefully and ceremoniously unwrap the package. Inside, sealed and encased in a solid wood box with a glass front panel, was a bottle of whisky. Attached to the outside of this shrine was a small brass hammer and a pouch. From this pouch he pulled a sheet of paper containing a list of names—names that had lines drawn through each, save one.

It was a very long time ago that they had met for the last time—a sort of reunion and farewell to one of the members who had but a short time to live.

Pretensions and pressures were checked at the door that night. Whatever problems they faced outside seemed far away and not important. Maybe it was seeing a "best" friend for the first time in two or three decades or just that deep feeling that only comes from the knowledge that to this group each truly belonged. They all knew that this assembly was just this night only and never again would they all be together. Maybe it came with the understanding that these were their roots and the distinct sensation of having come home again. Perhaps it was the familiarity and companionship of old friends, whose dues were also paid in full. It was a most memorable occasion.

It wasn't a large gathering, but 21 men out of a possible 36 wasn't too bad for an informal reunion. Some had died, some couldn't be found, most were graying and pot bellied, but all had, at one time, belonged to the Knights of the Twentieth Century. Born so many years ago in a back alley garage of a Midwestern American city, The Knights hot rod club was not unlike other clubs of guys of that era. Back when rock & roll was in its infancy and fast cars had to be built by hand, the members bonded together to learn, help each other and talk engines, cars and speed. It was exciting being the center of attention during this era of historic automotive and musical upheaval.

> *Three-twos and spinner caps, drive-ins and glass packs,*
>
> *James Dean and Yakety-Yak and a screamin' tenor sax.*
>
> *In the beginning those times were ours, the words, the music,*
>
> *the clothes and the cars, hot rods and puppy love*
>
> *and guardian angels up above.*

"Here, you do it Sonny," the old man said handing the brass hammer to his great grandson.

Uncapping the bottle, which had been freed by breaking the glass front and without lifting his eyes from the list, the old man in his articulate way, began to pour forth a tale as if he had been rehearsing it all his life.

"Moonie, that's what they called me because I was the first to have Moon wheel covers on my rod, a '34 roadster that I had stuffed a Caddy engine into. It had a dropped front axle, chopped windshield and sported three-duces on the engine. Though I never got it completely finished it ran one-oh-four point six in the quarter mile. Not that this was the fastest in the club, but still very respectable. I didn't drive the roadster on the street much because something was always breaking so I kept a stock '39 Ford as my everyday car. The '39 was battered and shabby and second gear was stripped but, it ran quite reliably—those old flatheads would just run forever. The only thing I hated about that old relic was the hot, scratchy mohair seats. I got my share of carpet burns on my elbow trying to put my arm around a girl.

"Ah...the girls. It seems that we built and raced the cars to impress the girls and then whenever one of the guys had made enough of an impression she'd up and marry him and that would be the end of his hot rodding. Brides and all the 'comes-with' things associated with marriage probably contributed more to the demise of hot rodders and their clubs than anything else.

"You boys should have seen my bride! She was just about the prettiest thing that ever rode shotgun in an open roadster. I met her at a club dance—a sock hop we called it. She wore dungarees with

32

the cuffs rolled up, in giant folds, almost to her knees. Her oversized shirt must have been her daddy's white dress button-down which also had huge folds of the sleeves all the way up her arm. The shirt tails were tied in a knot at her tiny waist, the slightest view of smooth soft skin barely visible. She wore her hair in a flip and she just had that fresh scrubbed look about her. Quite the opposite of me with my axle greased ducktails and form-fitted pink shirt with string tie and pleated slacks of charcoal gray. We rocked and rolled to the likes of Fat's Domino, Dale Wright, Buddy Holly and Larry Williams and when she put her head under my chin to 'Sixteen Candles' I knew it was something special. It was. Last week it would have been our 72nd anniversary...if she were still alive."

"Grandpa," the impatient teenager interrupted, "What about the bottle?"

"I'm comin' to that, Sonny. Don't rush me. Like I was sayin', it was at this gathering when we all got together for that one last time to say goodbye to Freddie. Now, nothing lasts forever, and by age 50 Freddie had developed a terminal case of cancer. Knowing that he was a short timer he kept himself busy hunting us down and planning this assembly to unite us for one last time and to establish his gift as a tontine—the bottle from which we are drinking at this very moment.

He said he won the fifth at a club dance and being a teetotaler, just put it away. Freddie was Jewish and for that solemn affair he gave us a little insight into these ancient teachings. It was such a somber and commemorative occasion that I still remember his final words to us. Here was this dying compatriot, frail and weak, who looked each one of us in the eye as he decreed: 'In our faith it is believed that on Rosh Hashana, the New Year, it is written; on Yom Kippur, The Day of Atonement, it is sealed:

> How many shall pass on,
> How many shall come to be,
> Who shall live to see ripe age,
> And who shall not,
> Who shall live,
> And who shall die;

and so it must be, that only the last surviving member of The Knights, The Knights Of The Twentieth Century, may toast his fellow members with—and savor the nectar of this—this last man bottle.'"

With a sigh of finality his still steady hand, rough, dried and cracked like a cheap paint job that had crystallized, picked up the small doubles glass. Using both hands, and not unlike how one would make an offering, raised the glass to just slightly above his head whispering, "I'll see you soon fellahs, keep 'em tuned up."

Warmed by the energy of the aged whiskey the old man rose from the security of his wingback and shuffled to the leaded windows overlooking the springtime embraced driveway. Just for an instant he was sure he saw Freddie waving from his NINETEEN thirty-two Ford, the one with the hopped-up Chevy engine and the plaque that said Knights, dangling from the back bumper. But, a deliberate wipe of the hand across his tear filling eyes revealed it was only his great grandson's…brand new TWENTY thirty-two Ford.

Flashing Blue Lights

The first shot tore through his upper leg exiting just below the hip.
The second and third shot hit ....

~~~~~~~~~~~~

He lay on the extra firm, queen sized mattress under a sheet and light wool blanket listening to the sounds of the city. The bike ride had helped but he still felt itchy. It was almost midnight, and all he had done for the last hour was stare at the dancing lights on the ceiling. Somewhere close by emergency vehicles' sirens wailed and yelped. They passed his apartment causing the beacons—the blue flashing beacons—to play tag with the other lights that bounced off his ceiling, walls and mirrors. The tough ex-cop/private detective/motorcycle rider closed his eyes and fought the twenty some-odd-year old nightmare ....

~~~~~~~~~~~~

Keying the mic and activating the roof lights all with one movement, Sergeant Travis Tarvon calmly gave his car number, "Four-John- Eleven."

"4-John -11," the dispatcher echoed.

"Possible DUI, farm-to-market, four-three-two, four miles west of eight-twenty-one. Older model Ford sedan, blue in color, bears Texas Tom-Adam-Sam-nine-nine-eight."

"Eight-William-Eight. Car 8-William-8."

"8-William-8."

"8-William-8 are you clear on 4-John-11's location? Possible DUI?"

"Affirmative. I'm south bound eight-twenty. Be about fifteen."

A jack rabbit, highlighted by the headlights of both vehicles, scampered across the highway as the patrol car's spotlight lit up the interior of the losermobile. The blue flashing lights were swallowed in the pitch black of the West Texas prairie. In the grimy Ford he could see three subjects, two males and a female. The driver slowed and put two wheels on the gravel shoulder kicking up a cloud of dust. Nobody was making any frantic moves like they were trying to hide contraband or weapons. It looked like a routine stop.

Just before exiting his car the radio broke squelch, "4-John-11, no wants NCIC, Texas Tom-Adam-Sam-nine-nine-eight."

"4-John-11 okay. 2-7."

"2-7, 4-John-11. Oh-one-forty-four hours. KQA-two-three-oh."

At the open window, the experienced officer noted the distinct odor of alcoholic beverage on the driver's breath and a half empty whiskey bottle on the back seat. The occupants, dirty, scruffy and smelly all appeared to be in their thirties. The female, in a tube top and seated in the shotgun seat, seemed to be spaced out. The small framed back seat passenger watched with intense but dilated eyes.

"I'm stopping you, sir, because you drove off the road in two places back there. May I see your operator's license, please," Travis commanded in a firm but polite tone.

The man with a two day's growth of beard said his name was Tom Hickey. After a few minutes of fumbling in his wallet and scattering the contents of the glove box all over the front seat, he claimed he couldn't find his license or registration. "You're going to have to step out of the car, sir," Travis said, opening the driver's door while trying to watch everybody's hands at once.

He led the man, who was about his size, to the rear of the cruiser and well out of view of the passengers. Travis ran the driver through a series of divided-skills evaluations and horizontal gaze nystagmus for documentation purposes in case of a contested court hearing. The Sergeant had an uneasy feeling. This man was more than just drunk. He could have stalled until his back-up arrived, but he felt if he could just put the cuffs on him, he and the others would be easier to control. "I'm going to have to arrest you for driving under the influence."

"Aw, c'mon man. I can handle it. You've seen worse. C'mon let me go," Hickey whined.

With a sigh of capitulation, the arrestee turned to place his hands on the trunk of the cruiser as the deputy tucked his flashlight under his arm. Then sort of as an afterthought the rotted tooth, whiskey breathed bully turned back. "Aw man, officer," he said looking at Travis's name tag. "Sergeant Tarvon, how 'bout …."

Before he even finished the sentence, sans any warning, and before Travis could react, the brawny man was on him. The flashlight fell as he raised his hands to ward off the attack. The assault was so sudden and from such close proximity he didn't have time to move out of the way. Juiced up on drugs and booze some men can act faster than a Bob Cat in heat.

Squeezed into a bear hug Travis knew instantly he was in trouble. Rocking, twisting, kicking, they fell into the ditch next to the roadway, with Travis on the bottom. He immediately felt sharp pain in his rib cage area. They rolled long-ways in the culvert, but Travis was quickly able to pin the man with his left arm while he reached for his portable radio, hoping it would reach from this remote and desolate location.

"FOUR-JOHN-ELEVEN! TEN-SEVENTY-EIGHTY! FOUR-JOHN-ELEVEN," he barked loudly into the mic, trying not to sound panicky.

The dispatcher, in an even and professional voice immediately responded, "4-John-11 … 8-William-8."

"8-William-8, in route."

"Okay 8-William-8. 4-John-11."

When he received no response, the seasoned dispatcher continued a monotone monologue with run-together words and sentences that only cops can decipher. "Attention all cars all departments unit 4-John-11 requesting a 10-78 last twenty is farm-to-market four-three-two four miles west of state route eight-twenty-one involves Ford sedan blue in color bearing Texas Tom-Adam-Sam-nine-nine-eight 4-John-11."

Travis heard only the heavy breathing and grunts of the man named Hickey.

All across the county every officer with a radio, on-duty or off, began speeding toward the dreaded officer-needs-assistance call. None acknowledged the call or asked permission, fearing that their transmission might override additional information from 4-John-11.

One patrolman, in the middle of writing a ticket, suddenly and without a word let the astonished motorist go before racing, code three, to help his brother officer.

Hickey retorted with what could only be described as super human strength. Travis, all two hundred and ten pounds of him, was suddenly thrown across the ditch. Dazed and still trying to get his feet under him, he saw in the strobe light syncopation of the blue flashing emergency lights the foul smelling brute pouncing and screaming, "I'M GOING TO KILL YOU, YOU DIRTY BASTARD!"

~~~~~~~~~~~~~~~~~~~

Travis had begun to perspire. He hadn't faced his demon in a long time. Maybe he could put it behind him if he looked at it in an objective way. Fat chance. The emotions were and probably would always be too strong. He should have; no, no he wasn't going to play the shoulda, woulda, coulda game tonight. It was pointless. Tonight he would be human, a fallible human being who is not perfect. Tonight he would try to forgive himself. Because if he didn't, how could he expect anyone else to.

~~~~~~~~~~~~~~~~~~~

As the assailant pounded with his fists, Travis hammered his face with the radio until it shattered. The two men fought for survival in a blackened, muddy ditch lit only by the intermittent flashes of the blue lights. They rolled in the damp mud as Hickey clamped a headlock on the officer with one arm while his free hand ripped Travis's hair. Travis broke the hold when he grabbed Hickey's crotch, squeezing with all his might while biting the heathen's forearm. The taste of blood and sweat fed his animal instincts, intensifying his need to survive.

Suddenly free of each other, Hickey struggled to get up, spewing death threats, while Travis scratched at his holster. To Travis the surrealism of the pseudo time deception phenomenon, tachyinterval, only made the onset of panic more pronounced. He was amazed at how much information his mind could process at a time like this. "Why was it taking so long for his gun to come into battery? Why was his arm taking so long to block the foot that was coming at his head? Where was his back-up? Did the 10-78 call get out? Where were the other occupants of the car?"

The kick, only partially blocked, knocked his service revolver out of his hand and somewhere behind him. The force of Hickey's full leg kick temporarily caused the man to lose his momentum — time for Travis to scramble for the gun. Frantically probing the weeds and debris, he found the weapon and rolled on his side at the instant Hickey leapt on him raining blows to his face. He knew he had to shoot this crazed superman before he lost consciousness but this scumbag, like he read Travis's mind, grabbed the three-fifty-seven with both hands and turned it toward the Sergeant's face. The two adversaries, now literally nose to nose fought for control. Travis, aware that his finger was exerting pressure on the trigger, maneuvered his left hand to clamp the cylinder and prevent it from being fired. Hickey twisted the magnum into Travis's chest and, still eyeball to eyeball spat, "I'm gonna kill you!" Summoning all his dwindling strength, Travis forced his knees up and with a mighty thrust catapulted gun and man over his head.

Exhausted, arms trembling, Travis clawed at his pants leg and the .38 snub-nose back-up gun strapped to an ankle holster. Eyes riveted on Hickey, highlighted by the eerie glow of the cruiser's taillights, he watched in horror as the big brute leveled the magnum at him. Struggling to bring the small stainless steel revolver into battery Travis heard himself screaming, "NO! NO! NO!"

At less than six feet apart and almost simultaneously, the two weapons spit fire at each other blinding the shooters in brilliant flashes of white hot death. Hickey's first shot tore through Travis's upper leg exiting just below the hip. His second and third shot hit the dirt to the left of the deputy's head. Travis, eyes locked on a shirt chest button, emptied his five shot Chief's Special. Hickey stood stock still.

Completely baffled, Travis thought, "I couldn't have missed him!" The wide-eyed man, the one with the three-fifty-seven, then jumped out of the ditch and ran across the road and into the darkness.

Injured, exhausted and with an empty gun Travis fought to control the onset of panic. Fishing for his pocket knife — his last line of defense — he searched the roadside fearing he'd catch a glimpse of Hickey returning.

Now large numbers of blue flashing lights uniformly lit the area as the back-ups started to arrive. When you're down, out and in need of help nothing, absolutely nothing, is more comforting, even to a cop, than the presence of a fresh, clean and bright-eyed uniformed officer. Fellow knights in blue with brightly colored arm patches, shiny badges and lots of guns covered the scene. These calm and organized keepers of the peace applied first-aid to Travis, took care of securing the other occupants of the sedan and ordered the ambulance. With flashlights and riot guns at the ready they fanned out and searched for Hickey.

Of Travis's five shots, four struck the intended target. Two of the one-hundred-twenty-five grain semi-jacketed hollow points had ripped the man's heart apart. His body, pumped up on adrenaline and high on alcohol and drugs, had powered him for over a hundred feet into the prairie. He never even knew he was dead.

Travis was drenched in perspiration, his heart beat hard and fast. The dancing lights on his ceiling were gone. He touched the scars on his leg to reassure himself that they were in fact long healed. In the bathroom he rinsed his mouth with Scope to take away the taste of blood and sweat.

He hadn't gone through the whole scenario in a long time — it seemed easier like maybe his mind was also healing. The face that grimaced back at him from the mirror told him that the guilt that had been eating at him all these years was gone. Tonight for the first time he faced the fact that, although he had killed a man, his action was excusable and justifiable. Tonight he could forgive himself and tonight, for the first time, he was certain that God had forgiven him.

~~~

Train Run

He drove a hot rod Ford
That could lay a fat black patch
That punk was a fool
Whose daring had no match.

Bonnie Sue knew, deep down, that he wasn't a "bad kid," but some of her friends and especially her mom didn't see it that way. Tommy, she felt, was just frustrated, though she wasn't sure what it was that he was so antsy about. He didn't do well in school, but he was very smart. He had, after all, figured out, without any help, how to take his car motor all apart and put it back together again. Besides, he had said he loved her. True, it was only once and in a fit of passion. It was on a Friday night, last month, at the drive-in. It was one of those Francis the Talking Mule flicks. The movie was boring so they just made out. Tommy kept trying to touch her where she didn't think he should. They fought, she cried, and Tommy said, "I really love you, Bonnie Sue, I mean it."

Bonnie Sue was sure that if only they could both finish school, get married (and Tommy in a good job) she'd be able to change his fast driving ways and other things that might need adjustments. Right now all she wanted was for her man to be here.

Tommy, at 16 and a half, was one of the more dedicated and speed crazed hot rodders in his sophomore class. Though he had never applied to one of the hot rod clubs for membership he was always thinking about joining—if they would take him. That was the rub. He'd already had two tickets for speeding and he had a reputation for fast driving on city streets. Hot rod clubs frowned on "squirrels," as they called them. He had never shied away from a traffic light race even when Bonnie Sue pouted about his high speed drags. Trouble was, he couldn't figure her out. She was pretty enough but she was always talking about love and all that mushy stuff and she only sometimes seemed to enjoy the drag racing—legal or otherwise. On their first few dates she had been all excited about his races even going so far as to taunt one of her girl friends because this friend's steady drove a stocker.

But he was really burned up that she had so little regard for the fact that he held the record for the Train Run and now must defend that honor. Johnny Medford, with his Daddy's brand new '55 Olds 88, had bested Tommy's record by at least 50 yards. For Tommy to let this go unchallenged would be like wearing your sister's bloomers or something equally unthinkable.

The troubles with Bonnie Sue culminated last night as they sat sipping Cokes in the lot of the West Chester Pike Bun Boy. Removing his arm from her shoulders to light a Lucky, Tommy asked, while trying to make it sound like a casual mention, "You want to ride with me when I go for the Train Run record tomorrow night?"

"Oh, Tommy, you're not going to do that again are you?" Not waiting for an answer she continued while tossing her pony tailed head in a dignified affront, "Tommy, I swear you're going to kill yourself one of these days with all this crazy…."

"Come on Baby I just have ta do it, ya dig. I'm not gonna to be no chicken hearted punk. I'll be the coolest cat in town if I beat that harry-high-schooler in his daddy's stocker."

"Oh Tommy, it's so dangerous I just worry that you'll be killed and I won't have you. I think you're the coolest guy at North Anderson anyway. Winning The Run can't make you any better in my eyes. Please, just for me don't do it," Bonnie Sue pleaded, all pouty faced.

"Aw, don't cry honey. I know you dig me and all, but this is something I just have to do. Besides it should be a snap. The last time I ended up backing off before the tracks, I had so much reserve power. And since then I've added dual points. And, hey, I'll put in new plugs in the morning to be extra safe! Don't worry," Tommy boasted, flicking his butt over the trunk of the flopped top of the faded black '51 Ford.

The object of his non-romantic desires, the '51, sported two-deuces with chrome racing air cleaners and glass-packed dual exhaust. It was not only fast but it sounded cool. In addition to the Mallory distributor he had recently added he was planning to install

Offenhauser high compression heads and maybe a Clay-Smith cam. His after school job at Wylie's Pure Oil Station didn't allow for many luxuries even though he was top paid of all the part timers at $1.10 per hour.

The rest of the evening was like, no-wheres-ville. They ended up, as they always did after a date, parked at the old abandoned army base down near the feed mill. Every time he tried to put the move on Bonnie Sue she'd scrunch up closer to her door and whimper about how she just wasn't in the mood. Chicks! Who could understand them? What kind of mood could she be in parked in a lover's lane? He took her straight home, not even walking her to the door. Then he pealed out because he knew it would make her angry.

Saturday, Train Run day, was chilly for September in Texas. Tommy had managed to install the new plugs between pumping gas and oil changes at Wylie's service station. The powerful flathead was running cherry and sounding very sweet. The soon-to-be nosed and decked rod had even gotten a wax job, compliments of the kids who hung out at the station. Kids, of course meant anyone who wasn't old enough to have a drivers license. These kids, in hopes of being able to get a ride to the race area would do almost anything for the privilege of seeing one of their idols in a run against death.

Just before quitting time, Johnny, riding in Delbert's straight eight Pontiac because his dad had stripped him of his driving rights upon finding out about the Train Run, stopped in at Wylie's.

"Hey Mr. Cool, I hear tell that you're gonna try to beat my record tonight?" Johnny sneered.

"Yeah, that's right sonny and I'll do it in a rod I built myself, not in my daddy's stocker," Tommy shot right back in a menacing tone.

"Why, I ought to climb out of here and…."

"Okay, Okay, punks. Enough of this tough-guy talk. Do you guys wanna belly-ache or race," Delbert demanded, taking control of the pre-race details. "Now listen up: me and Harry as witnesses, plus about a dozen kids, watched Johnny here, beat the train from the no passing sign through the intersection. Now if you want to beat this record you must start at the end of the guard rail. Ya dig, Tommy?"

"Well, I was thinking about starting halfway between the sign and the rail and...."

"No, no that won't do. You have to use a permanent fixture, dig. Otherwise cats would be claiming to have started at all kinds of locations and the record would be muddied. We talked about it and that's the way it has to be. So, unless you're yellow we'll see ya five minutes before the eight-three-eight," Delbert stated.

Curling his lip, Tommy spat, "I ain't yella—I'll be there."

He didn't have time to be nervous only time to shower, change clothes and chow down with his mom and sister before heading for Bonnie Sue's.

She wouldn't get into the car unless Tommy promised not to race the train, almost tearfully pleading—promising "anything" if he wouldn't make The Run. Too late. Even the thought of "anything" with Bonnie Sue didn't change his mind, though for a moment or two he had his doubts.

Tires squealing and defiance in his eyes
With his girl he had a fight
he cut out for the showdown as she cried,
"I know I'll grieve if you race this race tonight."

They were waiting for him, a dozen or so classmates, buddies and kids all lined up on the grass strip that lay between the road and the tracks of the mainline. Some of the kids, seeing the empty passenger seat, offered or begged to ride shotgun for this run for the record.

By 8:47 no sound akin to a train had been heard—the eight-three-eight was late! However, all was well and tension was relieved within a few minutes as the sound of number eight-three-eight, out of Wichita Falls, pierced the cool evening air. Without any discussion two of the spectator cars pulled onto the concrete blocking the highway so that no other vehicles could get in the way. Tommy moved the '51 to the point adjacent with the end of the guard rail, rapped the accelerator a few times and stared down the straight-away.

44

A little over a mile away the slightly curving tracks met and crossed the highway. All he had to do was beat the train to this point and he would again be top rodder at North Anderson High and surely Bonnie Sue's faith in his abilities would be returned.

The plume of thick gray smoke could be seen superimposed on the clear twilight sky from over a mile away and long before the west bound express itself was visible. Tommy raced the engine again and again wishing he had a tach to more accurately gauge the speed of his mill. Some of the kids were jumping up and down with excitement. Delbert stood slack jawed and Johnny sat, wide eyed, glad it wasn't him this time.

The importance of the lateness of the eight-three-eight didn't register with Tommy as he readied himself for a good clean start. Glancing over his shoulder to the tracks he timed the dumping of the clutch to the exact moment the locomotive was even with him and the guard rail. The huge 4-8-4 iron monster, oblivious to its place in the destiny of that night, overshadowed the gathering of children playing with their toys.

Tires spinning, the little flathead strained in first gear, as the train roared by. A speed shift to second brought a chirp of rubber and Tommy felt a twinge of pride as the force of acceleration pushed him into the seat back. Just when it seemed that the engine was about to explode he power shifted into third. Now topping 70 miles per hour he dared a glance at the rushing sound to his right—the sound of a death knell?

Tommy was horrified to see that he was just now beginning to pass the speeding train. He was sure he should have been equal to the engine by now, but he was at least one car plus the tender behind. He pushed harder on the gas pedal and strained to hear if his engine had a miss or something. Ninety, 95, the needle swept past the 100 MPH mark and still he was not in front. The convergence, the intersection of death, was dead ahead. Where was the miscalculation? Did someone move the guard rail? Was the train running faster than its usual 60 MPH? Yeah! that's it. The train was late so they're running faster to make up for lost time. Flashing through his jumbled mind were thoughts of clamping on the binders and turning into the double barbed wire fence to his left—taunts of chicken—yellow—Bonnie Sue.

He slammed the massive locomotive
that was doin' better than 70 per
and when they pulled him from the carnage
his last thoughts were of her.

Escape From A Terrorist's Cell

He had worked two years in deep cover to reach this point—the place where the clandestine terrorist group headquartered. Confidence can be scary knowing there are members of this gang who might have recognized him from past encounters. However, the friendly face of Drake, a fellow cop who was instrumental in bringing Chad into the terrorist cell, met him at the door. The cell believed the only way to rid America of the Islamic threat was to take the fight to them. They were well-connected and had a plan to take-out any and all Muslims in the USA.

Drake and Chad had met at a car show, both having an interest in vintage Corvettes. Drake, a city kitty, was restoring a '63 split window while Chad, a deputy sheriff, was now driving his renovated '59, 290 with the factory RPO 684. When their friendship continued, Drake casually brought up the cell belief and Chad readily agreed to the concept. Chad, of course, reported this information to his contact with the FBI—and a covert infiltration plan was established.

"Hey Drake, how's it goin?" Chad grinned.

"Just monitoring the T.O.O.P.s"

"Monitoring toops? What's that?" Chad asked, hoping to string out the conversation a little longer—to allow his mind more time to formulate questions.

"Tee double oh pee, toop, as in temporarily out of prison. Since the bleeding hearts and certain minority cry babies have been down on our case for using more graphic terms of endearment such as 'dirtbag', 'scumball', 'sleezebag', the Captain, last night, came up with more descriptive nomenclature to identify those who are, shall we say, recidivistic."

"I like that. Very cool."

It was standing room only for the fifty or so men—an eclectic gathering, sort of a cross section of America. Some decked out in camouflage, others like they just climbed down from the cab of a combine. Many were in business suits and still others in casual sporting attire.

All stopped their small talk as the General's contingent entered. The General walked to the podium while the cops good naturedly elbowed their way to a side wall.

"It's so nice to see so many of you ...."

"That's him! That's the sombitch that I toldja was takin' picters of this place last week with that FBI guy." Billy Ray Cusper shouted. His words cut like a knife through the hushed throng. All eyes followed the accusing finger that was pointed in the direction of the plain-clothes officers. Confused, astonished and embarrassed, Drake turned to Chad, his mouth slightly agape.

"What does he mean, Chad? You been lying to us? YOU AN INFILTRATOR?" Drake roared.

"Hey, man, it wasn't me...." Drake hit him hard in the gut doubling him over as another in the crowd brought a knee up catching Chad's nose with bone breaking force. He went down and tried to ball up, but the crowd, sensing blood, surged in so close he only fell against the legs and feet that were now kicking at him.

In what seemed like enough time to beat three men to death he finally heard The General pounding a gavel and calling for order. Drake began shouting not to kill him as they needed him conscious for interrogation. As far as Chad was concerned, it took far too long to restore order.

Bloodied and hurting, he slumped to the floor when the legs and feet moved back. His kidneys felt like a vice had been clamped on them and his ears rung from the kicks to his head as he fought nausea and unconsciousness.

The room grew quiet except for Billy Ray's broken-record accusations. The General came over to where Chad lay and nudged him with his foot, only it was more of a kick.

"What do you have to say for yourself, Chad? Are you not one of us? A faithful witness will not lie, saith the Lord."

"But a lie well told and stuck to is as good as the truth," Chad thought as he tried to right himself. He could only roll his head and even that hurt.

The General placed his hand on Drakes' shoulder, saying, "Check him for weapons, empty his pockets and throw him in my office."

Roughly they stripped him of the ankle holstered snub nose revolver, car keys and badge case. Chad, to say the least, wasn't looking forward to the inevitable interrogation. But first he had to assess the damage. Nothing seemed to be broken. He could move all of his extremities without excruciating pain. His nose might be broken and, well, there wasn't much he could do about bruised kidneys, if in fact they were only bruised and not ruptured. The good news was that if something was ruptured he might die before they had the pleasure of torturing him to death.

Time. Everything always comes down to time, and Chad knew he had very little of that precious commodity left. A quick glance showed the General's office to contain the one door they had brought him through and a window that, to Chad's natural sense of direction, opened to the woods which backed up to the graveled parking lot. He strained to his feet and was surprised he could walk as he moved toward the window. It opened just as the door opened. He dove through the black hole slamming into a small shrub that thankfully broke his fall rather than his bones.

Half running, half hobbling he stumbled through the tree line toward the car. Almost across the paddock area, flood lights suddenly illuminated everything—and the sprint was on. Reaching the Vette, he frantically bent the rear license plate, tearing at the tape on the back side, for the hidden key. Suddenly, the front door opened and a man stepped out, turned back and yelled, "He's out here!"

Too late for a clean escape. Chad leaned over the open roadster thrusting the key into the tiny horizontal glove box between the seats. The man was running toward him; fifty feet... forty... his fingers locked onto the Sig Sauer P230 hide-out gun he always kept in the box—thirty...twenty—the man raised his gun hand.

Chad, from point shoulder arms, doubled tapped the assailant, watched him hesitate as the shots took effect and then shot him again. Dead on his feet, the thug's forward momentum drove him into the side of the passenger door.

The injected engine caught with a roar as he dumped the clutch, thankful that he had backed into the parking space. The vintage sports car shuddered for a moment then fish-tailed away, spraying gravel and producing huge plumes of dust.

Grabbing second gear and feathering the throttle to control spin, Chad, out of the corner of his eye, saw a figure running for a plain dark sedan parked off to the side. Halfway down the straight stretch he chanced a look at the rearview mirror. Through a billowing cloud of dust he saw headlights swinging in line just as the tach reached red line. He had just gotten into third gear before having to clamp on the binders as his headlamps picked up the sweeping bend that led to the county road. He cranked the wheel hard over, inducing an understeer that pointed the front end at the edge of the road while heal-toeing back down into second. With the timing of a practiced race driver he fed fuel to the hungry 290 horses, setting up the classic four wheel drift, a trick he had learned from years of police chases. Only this time he was the chasee!

The gravel turned to blacktop and the car straightened out. Chad chanced a look over his shoulder — the dust fogged headlights were just entering the bend.

Now in third the Vette rocketed onto the north bound Interstate on-ramp as the trailing headlights cleared the dust bowl. At the top of the ramp the engine crested 6500 and he pulled down into high gear. With a moment for a breather and clear track ahead he scanned the instruments. Fuel: half; Water temp: 190; Tach: 5200 climbing; Speedometer: 115 climbing; Amps: steady on the mark; Oil pressure unwavering at 60; Mirror: pursuing headlights clearing the ramp!

His mind ticked off options as he realized that anything that had stayed this close to him had to be a police-packaged scout car. And anyone who could handle a special vehicle like that had to be a cop.

At speeds ranging from the sixties to the nineties the two men with years of police chase experience diced in and out of traffic, but the headlights never got closer than half a mile. Weaving through a line of interspaced cars, Chad switched off his taillights, making it harder to be seen from the rear.

A youthful driver in a late model T-Bird thought it was a game and tried to keep the trained sheriff's deputy boxed in. Seventy miles per hour, nose-to-tail to the car in front, Chad executed the Precision Immobilization Technique by nudging the T-Bird's rear quarter panel with his bumper. Terror filled the young driver's face, as his car spun out of the way and onto the infield. Once clear of the small pocket of vehicles the road appeared unobstructed and he really let her eat.

Topping out around 140, all the engine would allow with a 3:70 rear axle, he was finally pulling ahead of the headlights, but he knew he couldn't expect to maintain this kind of speed for long on a public road.

He also knew what he had to do as his hand searched under the dash, this time for the brake light switch. The decision, the reaction, was instantaneous when the high beams picked up the distant reflection of the "no-U-turn" sign that indicated an upcoming median crossover. Fighting exhaustion, the LEO stood on the brakes trying to keep the tires just short of locking up.

The metallic linings ground into the drums rendering them red hot. The speed dropped, 130...120...110. Chad crammed the shift lever into third, the engine shrieking in protest as the tires continued to chirp at the pavement. Still too fast! He spun the wheel to the left, hoping to gain a few feet from tire scrub, 90...80, he momentarily released the brakes to point the car toward the infield.

The little two-seater, fighting for traction, entered into what would appear to any but the practiced, an uncontrolled skid. With the calmness of a Formula-I driver he bounced half onto the hard-packed dirt crossover and half onto the gravel apron. Wrenching the wheel for control, the skilled driver trounced the throttle realizing too late he was one gear too high. He smacked the southbound tarmac spinning out right behind an air-horn-blaring, double-bottom, eighteen wheeler that had just roared by.

With another semi-truck bearing down on him Chad managed to get the car pointed south and wrestled the shift lever into second. He once again got on it hard while studying the northbound lanes for those headlights. The brake light kill switch had done the trick as he watched the dark sedan overshoot the turnaround.

Though he hadn't completely cracked the case, he was sure he had enough to secure search warrants … and live another day.

The Pick-Up

From some quarry deep in Wisconsin, via cavernous ships, came the iron ore. Compounded, mixed and incorporated with other raw ingredients from mines as far away as the continent of Africa; the River Rouge's open hearth furnaces formed the very heart of America's rolling stock. But it took the conscientious and loving care of the meticulous assembly line workers to collate these unique organs and create the real soul of each vehicle.

Early in January, 1937, number 3846, a pick-up truck, received its "soul". She came down the line and under the tender guardianship of the day shift, was bestowed the larger 85 horsepower V8 engine, Vermillion Red paint with black stripe and black "solid" wheels.

I felt good and rode proud and tall on the train to St. Louis where an elderly gentleman gently drove me to the show room at the Ford dealership just west of downtown. I didn't have to wait long, like the plainer coupes and sedans, some of which had to remain out in the rain and cold. On January 22, Number 3846, that's me, became the property of Mr. Silas T. Wentworth, a lanky and muscular farmer from up-state Missouri.

Silas T., his wife, Priscilla, and their son, Jamie, took pride in their first "new" car. The depression had been difficult but through hard work and very austere living they prospered. I heard Silas T. talking about how I, as their new addition to the family, would enable him to increase his market deliveries three fold over the horse and wagon.

Even hauling hogs to market was no strain for my powerful flathead engine, and return trips, empty except for a few supplies, made life easy and enjoyable. Silas T. changed my oil and greased me on a very regular basis and Jamie kept me clean. The missus even made seat covers for me.

Things changed in 1940. Jamie turned 16 and began driving me to school and other places. Silas T. bought a heavy duty, dual-rear-wheel truck who soon became the pride of the family. Jamie was hard on me with all his quick starts and fast driving, but I knew I was having a better life than some of the others I'd see stuck by the roadway or—in junk yards! Once, when we went to town, I saw a sedan that had been right behind me on the assembly line. That sedan was now a police car with a spot light and a two-tone paint job. And, even though she was just a sedan, she turned up her nose at common pick-ups.

Jamie had a special girl and they often went out for rides together, only they spent more time parking than actually riding. They talked of marriage and how he was sure his dad would give him the pick-up and sign on a note so as he could buy the old Potter place.

We had a lot of fun, the three of us. Jamie and I once raced a Chevrolet out on the East River Road. We sprayed gravel all over that snooty looking Chevy and beat him by a country mile by doing almost 90! Mabel, that's his girl, made him promise never to do that again because they would need me for farm use.

It was in my bed, on blanket covered straw, during the summer of 1942, they got engaged. Mabel was scared but Jamie promised to love her forever. They talked about the kids they wanted and how they would fix up the old Potter place, even a stall in the barn for me, when he got back.

It all seemed so perfect except that I was getting tired and one of my springs was starting to sag a little. Jamie sure looked sharp in that uniform with all those shiny buttons. I don't know why everyone was crying, even Mabel. The two men drove me to town. They shook hands, hugged, and Jamie patted me on my fender before he got into a bus. Silas T. brought me back, parked me in the lean-to where the surrey used to be, and disconnected my battery.

It was a long time before anyone opened that barn door again. Silas T. Wentworth, on that cold and windy day, looked gaunt and sad. A plump pimply faced kid, Mr. Wentworth called him Butch, kicked my tires, shook my fenders and looked me over then handed my first master a check. The next day Butch returned, winched me onto a trailer, and took me back into the big city.

Much to my surprise Butch began cleaning me and showing me off to his friends who came to visit the garage. It seems the garage is the headquarters for the Piston Busters Car Club. It wasn't long before Butch and friends had yanked my old and tired engine and with a little drilling, grinding and welding—the welding hurt—installed an almost new Corvette engine! Wow! Butch sanded off the old faded paint and applied a bright yellow primer, converted to hydraulic brakes and added fancy chrome wheels with new white-wall tires. Boy, if only my old assembly line mates could see me now! I'll bet even the police car would be envious.

Every time we went to the Big Boy drive-in all the other guys would gather around and admire me. Sundays, we'd go to the drag strip, and though it hurt to have that much pressure put on my rails, I loved it. Sometimes we even brought home a trophy! The speeds we reached were far more than Jamie and I had ever dreamed. Things weren't all that great though. A few of my body mounts were wearing out and the high output V8 engine, twisting against my rusty frame, gave me a lot of pain. I was sure that someday I wouldn't be able to keep it together.

Other than that, life was pretty good—at least I didn't have to haul any smelly ol' hogs or dusty hay. But I did carry a few kegs of beer and a bunch of club members more than once. Butch always kept me in a garage and never let anyone else drive me, 'cept Carrie, his girl, and that was only on one occasion.

Late in the spring of '60 we were coming out of a high speed turn on the new subdivision road when one of my shock mounts broke. It caused me to loose control and we slammed into a stone wall bending my front axle and crumpling one fender. Butch broke my windshield with his head and leaked a sticky red oil all over my cowl and hood. He lay there for a long time before one of those stuck-up police cars and a shiny new ambulance arrived. Then things happened pretty fast and next thing I know they tow me to, of all places, a junk yard!

With a half century's worth of the formerly new and proud modes of transportation to trade stories with, I was never lonely. And though I was not happy with my situation at least I had had a more complete and exciting life than most of the other "junkers". But, I still had a lot of life left in me and I didn't want to spend forever with these rusty heaps.

Oh, sometimes somebody would come and look me over—shake me or kick my now flat tires, but mostly they just wanted my parts.

As the years rolled by I lost my steering wheel, the good front fender, my radiator, engine—it was only a Chevy—and other items. My interior rotted away and the faded yellow primer—Butch never did get around to that metal flake paint job he had promised—rusted through in many places. At least I had the other cars to keep me company not like being shut in the Wentworth barn all alone. A once majestic LaSalle, the leader of the yard, because of the shade from a Maple tree that grew out of his trunk, became my best friend. He loved to tell of the times he chauffeured the Mayor and his important guests and friends around.

Sometimes you get lucky. I had never resigned myself to the junk yard mentality of my fellow prisoners as I always believed I'd be rescued. It was hot, late in the fall of 1989, when I winked a goodby to the huge LaSalle. Craig, a jovial man who looked to be almost as old as Silas T. had looked the last time I saw him, carefully loaded me onto a trailer.

My next home was, well, better than the factory. It was clean, brightly lighted and had some very sophisticated tools and machinery. I just knew Craig and I were going be the best of friends. It took over two years, but in that time I was reborn! Even my assembly line mates would hardly recognize me. Craigie —that's what his wife calls him—took me all apart, I mean every nut, bolt, flange, bushing—everything. He stripped my metal bare and then what he didn't primer and paint he chromed. I also received new fiberglass fenders, a new dropped front axle, a chopped top—it only hurt a little—rolled & pleated naugahyde interior and—ugh—another Chevy engine, but complete with supercharger. I loved it. I wanted to go by the junk yard and show-off.

In no time at all Craigie sold me to a man who I'm ashamed to identify. A man whose smile never reaches his eyes. Almost every weekend he loads me into a closed trailer and tows me to a car show. He ropes me off so none of the countless admirers can caress my 27 hand-rubbed coats of lacquer or fondle my cute little stainless and wood steering wheel. Ah, this should be the life, no more hauling of any kind, frame stressing races or even getting rained on. Only trouble is I hate it. My engine, even though it's not a Ford, has never been started. Once when he had me sitting in his driveway a few of his friends came by in "real" hot-rods with engines that worked—I was so embarrassed. I long for just sitting at a Big Boy and maybe a few wheel spins in the lot, the wind at 100 per or the pleasure of a master who knows how to handle a street rod.

Say…if you see me at one of those frilly, pseudo-hot-rod, indoor car shows, make my owner an offer he can't refuse, put some guts in my mill and lets do it! I won't let you down.

The Vette

As it got closer his suspicions were confirmed—it was a vintage Corvette. Too bad he wasn't driving his old Vette. It could be a fun run over these delightfully twisty and hilly country roads in the outback of the great state of Indiana. Within minutes, on a long straight stretch, the red, with white inset, fifty-nine/sixty two-seater made its bid to pass.

The familiar rumble of the twin-pipes only made the longing, the recollections, even stronger. What surprised him was that the driver was a lady, a smart looking young lady with long, flame-red hair that trailed out over the rear deck of her open roadster.

Memories of another redhead in a Corvette, back when the Vette was new, quickened his pulse and flooded his mind. She gave a quick look and a smile at mid point, just as she smacked third gear and dumped a set of quads. And with a chirp of rubber she was gone.

A glance at his speedometer told him that the little excitement had caused him to push his seventy-two El Camino to well above the legal limit. Ah, there was a time when he would have relished a high speed run, but at fifty-three years of age and driving a "stocker," Jack Cambry knew better.

Twenty miles on down the road he still couldn't shake the memory of Natalie. It came back in a rush overwhelming his mind—everything from her in-bred sophistication, to the time in the back seat of her fifty-five Bel-Air; strains of "their song," the Crew Cuts, Angels in the Sky, playing softly over the radio. He hadn't thought of her in a long time and was confused as to why her familiarity—the longing—was so strong. Perhaps it was the guilt that ground the spider gears of his mind.

She had a long pony tail the first time they met. He had just transferred to a new school and she had come over to him during that first recess. He was lonely and scared but she flipped her pony tail and just said, "Hi, I'm Natalie and I hope you like it here," or something to that effect. Her hair was a soothing deep auburn not the fire red of a Rita Hayworth. They were standing under the pavilion watching the sixth graders in a game of kickball.

She was nice and very pretty but he never let on that he thought so...must have been afraid of getting teased or just too young or something. Funny how some recollections are crystal clear and others are hazy.

Their first date hadn't been for four more years until they were sixteen and he had wheels. Now that he thought about it she was his first real date. Oh, he'd met girls at the Saturday matinee and even kissed a few at games of post office or spin the bottle. But Natalie was the first real date. He couldn't remember how they came to go out; maybe it was when a gang of kids were all standing around the soda fountain at Richter's Pharmacy talking about the up-coming sock hop. Yeah, that was it. She said to nobody in particular, but she was looking at him, that she wanted to go but didn't have a ride.

He laughed to himself remembering that first date. Why she ever went out with him again after he made a total fool of himself was a mystery. He had tried to ace some cat in a '52 Olds away from a light but stalled by dumping the clutch on an under revved engine. Not very cool on a first date. But, the car was cool, as only a Corvette could be.

She was some dish. Not only was she tom-boyish good-looking, but she had a `55 Chev. She had removed the hood and trunk ornaments in preparation for a nose and deck job on this Power-pack stick and had installed spinner hubcaps and a chrome air cleaner herself. She knew more about cars than most guys. She was perfect. Even at sixteen and until they parted at eighteen they fit together, like a valve to a keeper or a connecting rod to a wrist pin.

They had such fun together, he, Natalie and the Vette. They almost never missed a Sunday at the drag strip. He'd be stuck in "B" Sports Car against a lot of usually faster machines and she'd run his Corvette in the Powder Puff class and pull trophy most every time.

How'd it happen? They'd dated—gone steady actually—broken up, then got back together just before his car club's annual dance. Yeah, it was the evening of the Knights' big dance when he got pulled by Herb's '57 Fury that everyone had said was a dog. It was no stocker. To this day he was sure Herb had an Isky Five-Cycle cam and maybe more cubes than came from the factory.

He was angry all evening and when they all stopped at Spooner's drive-in for an after-dance Coke he had tried to put the make on Herb's date. That was also the night Natalie had picked to tell him her Dad had been transferred out of state. He had only meant to get back at Herb for goading him into a race that was a set-up in the first place.

Though they saw each other a few more times before he left for college and she for Chicago, he never really got a chance to apologize or anything. The next year was a little hazy. He had gotten involved with some chick at OSU, rushed a fraternity and flunked out of school. Next thing he knew he was in the Navy.

Wow, the parade of memories from just seeing an old car — an old Corvette — driven by a red headed honey! Oh, he'd thought about her, especially when the loneliness of military life had almost consumed him and again when he committed himself to marriage.

He believed he had really been in love with Sue Ellen, but, Natalie was always somewhere deep in the reserve fuel tank of his mind. When Sue Ellen left him (maybe he never was really and completely committed to her) he had hunted for Natalie. The search only lasted until he learned she was married.

~~~~~~~~~~~~

The yellow diamond shaped sign indicated a right followed by a left, both with a suggested safe speed of forty. He knew he wasn't in a Corvette and he wasn't in his twenties, but the urge was too great as he set the classic pick-up into the first bend at a little over 70. He rode it through on rails pretending it was a four wheel drift, getting hard on the gas at the apex of each turn. It felt good, engine, speed, noise and…memories.

Daydreaming sure does help while the miles away. Already he was over halfway to Chicago. It had been such a beautiful day that he had driven the old way through the countryside of farm belt America, the route before the Interstate.

Slowing for a small burg he noticed the red and white Vette parked at the side of a Shell station. Well, he needed gas anyway,

60

and Shell was one of the cards he carried. It sure wouldn't hurt to take a few minutes to look at the vehicle of the past hour's recollections.

A cursory exam of the sports car yielded the knowledge that it was a 1959 model and had a 6500 RPM red line on the tach which indicated it came with a factory 270 or 290 horsepower engine. Absorbed in a world of automobilia he didn't see her until she was standing right next to him.

"Excuse me, sir. I'd like to get into my car."

She couldn't have been much more than twenty-five and could have passed as Natalie's twin if it were thirty plus years ago.

"I'm sorry. I was just admiring your Vette. Had it long?"

"Well, we've owned it for about five years but it was only in the last six months that we've had the time and money to get it into running shape," she said with a smile that showed a slight over bite.

"You are a credit to Corvette owners of old by the way you handled it back there on the open road. Drove like a pro or your daddy owns the road," he joked, trying to expand the moment.

"Wrong on both counts, mister. I'm not a professional and my daddy died last year. So if you'll excuse me…."

"I'm sorry for intruding. It's just that this car stirred thoughts of another Corvette and another red head too many years ago. The car got traded and the red head…I guess she's lost forever."

She reached for the door handle, stopped, turned toward him and said, "No, I'm the one who should be sorry. I'm not in a good mood. I just broke up with my boy friend. I know you old timers get all twisted out of shape at the sight of machines like this. Uh, the car has the original two-eighty-three engine, bored sixty thousandths over, twin four barrels and an oh-two-seven, solid-lifter, Duntov cam powered through a four-speed transmission and four-eleven, Posi-traction rear axle.

"Say, you do know your stuff. Learn it from your dad? He asked, trying not to sound conciliatory.

"I learned mostly from my mom. It's her car and we made a project of rebuilding it. We had the mechanical work done at a shop in Cincinnati, that's where my mom's from. We did the interior and all the body work ourselves, except the final paint," the red haired beauty stated proudly.

At the mention of Cincinnati and a widow who knew cars, a chill with the speed of a small-block Chevy, swept over him. An intense smile exposed a face full of age lines as his clear hazel eyes studied her features—red hair, the slightly up-turned nose, the high cheek bones and that slight overbite with very small teeth.

"Why are you looking at me like that? Are you going to hit on me, pal? Come on, let me get into my car I've got places to go," she scolded, brushing past him to vault into the drivers seat.

"I'm, I'm sorry," he stammered. "Was…is you mother's name, Wilson?"

"No, Her name's Minderman. Now please let me go." She twisted the key firing up all eight cylinders with the unmistakably familiar throaty roar of the short-stroke Chevy.

With a rap of the accelerator that sent the little engine revving past three grand she lifted the "T" handle and slapped the lever into reverse. He stepped back, smarting from the false and brash accusation, still overwhelmed by the memories and similarities. He looked at his shoes waiting for her to back away.

The Vette, engine loping at seven-fifty RPM, didn't move. He snuck a glance. Maybe he was still in her way. Boy was he embarrassed. The girl with Rita Hayworth hair and the features of a teenage lost love was staring at him, mouth agape.

Barely audible, over the rumble of the two-seventy, he heard her say, "Yes. You mean my mother's maiden name? Yeah, it was Wilson. Did you know her?" She turned her head as if checking the rear view mirror then turned back again, eyes wide. "Oh wow! If your name's Jack then my mom's been looking for you."

Sometimes Ya Get Lucky

Convertibles are great, sports cars even better, but a motorcycle is best for pure motoring fun—and a Harley Davidson is the most fun of all. Decked out in torn, ragged denim work pants and a sleeveless shirt, Sander Rackman looked and felt like a hardened outlaw biker as he followed the old highway to Warsaw, deep in the mountainous hills and valleys of Kentucky.

"Hi. Where can I find Eve?"

The bag boy glanced around while bagging groceries for a matronly looking farmer's wife who covered Sander with a disdainful stare.

"I'm not sure. I don't think she comes in 'till eleven. Ask the manager—he's over there," the kid said, nodding toward the bread racks.

Eleven it is. Maybe a cup of coffee at the Bun Boy across the street and a few phone calls will help kill some time. Rackman had gotten a tip that the target's girl friend, Eve, worked at this IGA. The target was the guy named in the summons in Sander's pocket. He wasn't privy to particulars of the case; his job was to serve process.

A few minutes before the hour he parked his Hog in the back of the IGA lot where employees would usually park, sat on the ground leaning against the MC and watched. The bike fit Sander's image: scruffy and rough—not some shiny, primped sissified bad-boy-wannabe's ride. Right on time an old beater with a woman driver, you could hardly call her a chick, drove in and parked two spaces to his left. Take away the clean, starched uniform and she'd look like she'd seen a few too many miles from the back of Harley.

"Hey, Eve baby, how ya doin'? It's Char," Sander said to her quizzical frown. Making up stuff as he went along in hopes of gaining her trust, he continued, "You know, we met up at the Roundup a while back. I'm looking for your old man. Where can I find him?"

With her lip twisted and a squint, she replied, "Char? Wasn't you at the pig roast up to Cecil's place back a couple of months ago?"

"Yeah, I was there too. But I thought I also saw you at the Roundup," he ad-libbed.

"Look, I'm gonna be late for work, ah what …."

"I was just wondering where I can find your old man."

"First off, I ain't got no old man no more, and second, I don't know, much less care where the hell he is. Nice bike you got."

With the knowledge that she and Knueson were on the outs he put on his best smile. "Well, if you ain't seein' him no more maybe you and me could toss a few down sometime?"

She turned toward him thrusting her hip out, "Yeah, maybe we could at that … Char. Why don't you stop back around nine when I get off work?"

"I can't tonight baby. But ah, I'd like to take a rain check. Where can I find Bobby? He promised to put me on to his main man."

"Have you tried his farm? And he ain't got a main man. He's the main man if you catch my drift. He grows the stuff his self right there. But don't tell him I told ya or he'll kill me. Know what I mean, honey? The farm is down around Bee Camp Hollar—over to Switzerland County. The name on the mailbox is the name William Cusper—that's the name he uses."

She smiled through chipped, nicotine stained teeth as the P.I. smiled back thinking he wouldn't' take her to a dog fight—even if she was the main attration.

Some clouds, along with the humidity, had begun to roll in, but as long as he kept the older model FLH moving, it was comfortable enough. At the only gas station in town he learned that Switzerland County was right across the dam bridge in Indiana. It took a stop at the Vevay police department to learn the location of Bee Camp Hollar and that William R. Cusper was only known as such. A check at the courthouse provided the information that a William Cusper did in fact own 178 acres on Bee Camp plus another 40 in Posey Township. Neither of the properties was encumbered by any liens. There was no record of Bobby Knueson. The man might be a drug manufacturing, biker-sleeze bag, but he was smart enough to keep his real identity secret from the locals. Even though the subpoena in his pocket only had the name of Bobby Knueson, it would still be good as long as he added the a.k.a..

The hollar looked just like the name sounded—down-home, unsophisticated good 'ol boy country. The rusty mailbox with the crudely hand painted name, Cusper, was perched atop an old stump. The farm house, if you could call it that, was visible back a short gravel drive. The house was really an older double-wide that could use a little sprucing up. A polished Harley Sportster and a dusty, but well cared for, late model Ford F-150 pick-up truck were parked off to the side and in front of a weathered, wood-sided barn.

Sander secured his bike near the mailbox and walked to the trailer. The door was standing open so he called, then yelled for Mr. Cusper. Dirty dishes were scattered throughout the kitchen and living room as were articles of clothing, beer cans and an empty pizza box. What really caught his attention was the AR15 or M16 rifle, he couldn't tell which, and handfuls of ammunition lying on the stained, sun faded sofa.

The barn was also void of any living creatures, disturbingly quiet save for the sound of a tractor. He walked in the direction of the noise which came from around back of the barn and a stand of cedars. In the adjoining field was a man on a red and silver trimmed Massey Ferguson diesel tractor pulling a sixty-inch bush-hog. The operator, a man of about forty, throttled back as Sander approached. Above the din of the tractor and rotating blades he shouted, "William Cusper?"

"Yeah, what do you want?" the man hollered back. He was a burly man with large, dark eyes and curly, black hair that was matted with sweat. On his upper arm was the tattoo of an eagle. He pulled a blue bandanna from a hip pocket and wiped a neck that was as thick as a tractor tire.

Producing the court paper from a back pocket, Sander handed it to Cusper, saying, "Thanks, you've been served."

Before he could back away, the man shoved it back shouting, "I ain't Mr. Cusper. I thought you was ah askin' if this was his place. He's gone for now but will be back around sundown."

Since Sander didn't have any physical description of the man and no other way to identify him, he had to take the subpoena back or risk a bad service. Before he could ask any more questions the tractor had been set into motion again, forcing him to step out of the way.

Serving process was always an iffy proposition. Sometimes he had had to resort to elaborate scams and cover stories in order to be able to swear that the named person had in fact been served. In past cases Sander had employed various pretexts, including posing as an electric company employee in a uniform he had purchased at a yard sale and as a sweepstakes front man. The latter had been cruel because the target's wife had really believed they were about to share in the Reader's Digest jackpot.

His favorite had been "the auto accident." His client in a divorce case lived out of state and wasn't available to help identify her ex. The matter was complicated by the fact that the ex had a twin. The man lived with his girl friend but, on Sander's first attempt at service, the ex and the girl friend both denied he was the correct twin.

The ex drove an old pick-up with more dents than a golf ball. Sander grew a short scruffy beard to change his appearance, then bought an old junk car with part of the wife's retainer. Next, he staked out the man's truck. When the subject got in the vehicle and pulled onto traffic, Sander maneuvered in front of him. When conditions were right he slammed on his brakes just hard enough to cause a slight rear-ender.

Fearful of a police report and a mark against his insurance, the ex readily agreed to exchange information and settle the matter right there. When the man produced his driver's license, bearing the name and photo of the ex, Sander served him with the divorce papers.

Other times things can get hairy. Private investigators usually only get the summons or subpoenas when the Sheriff's office can't locate the person. Working alone and without any form of radio backup, finding losers who don't want to be found can lead to dangerous conditions. Sander was never without at least one handgun.

At the county road the detective fired up his Harley and rode on back the hollar while his mind worked at trying to come up with a new pretext or a different twist to an old one. About a quarter mile away, a middle-aged woman in overalls was tending a large vegetable garden in front of a neat, clean frame house. He stopped at her gravel drive and, while fighting the chipped stone to secure his kick-stand, the lady approached. "May I help you?"

"Yes, thank you. I'm looking for Billy Cusper. Do you know where I can find him?"

"Why, yes. That's him on that tractor over there," she said, pointing to the field he had just come out of.

Sometimes ya get lucky. By the time he'd turned the heavy bike around on the narrow one lane road, cruised back to the rusty mailbox and secured the kick-stand once again, Cusper was standing next to the pick-up. Leaving his bike running, Sander, subpoena concealed in his left hand, strode right at the 250 pound tractor operator/biker.

"Did you find him, man? I tell ya he won't be back 'till much later. I'll tell him …."

In mid sentence, Sander, now within striking distance, stuffed the court order in the man's shirt pocket, spitting out, "You're Knueson and you've been served, Bobby!"

The roundhouse blow was easy to duck because, like any good cop or P.I., he was ready for it. Now all he wanted to do was get out of there with the minimum amount of damage. Mr. Knueson/Cusper had different ideas. Most perpetrators, once you've beaten them by either placing them under arrest or serving them with process, would curse and yell, call you a few choice names and sometimes take a half-poke at you just to show that they went down swinging like a real man. The guys who don't say anything are the perps you have to look out for. Knueson was silent.

Recovering from the missed punch, Bobby stepped back then forward, cocking his right arm just as Sander buried his fist in the big man's gut. The blow was followed by a pirouette and a side-leg kick to the knee. It was all one movement, but the kick missed, only striking the dirtbag's upper leg. However, the force of the impact did slam Knueson against the truck. Without a moment's hesitation, Bobby grabbed an iron bar from the bed of the pick-up and raised it above his head as he again advanced.

"Look man, I don't want no trouble. I'm just doin' my job," Sander growled, as he backed away and into a scrub tree he hadn't noticed before. The action shifted into slow motion, a pseudo time deception phenomena known as tachyinterval. Frustration is rampant under this unique condition when events appear to occur in slow motion because the brain is processing more information than the body can react to in a timely manner. He knew the iron bar was coming, knew he couldn't back away in time, knew he had to get his gun out and that the man meant to kill him. But he couldn't understand why it was taking so long to extract the 2 ½ inch barreled Diamondback from his hip holster. Both combatants knew, tachyinterval or not, that once the gun cleared the scabbard and came into battery it was going to explode with flesh tearing, lethal results. Like most important events in life, timing is everything.

At the instant before the revolver, stuffed full of Hornady 125 grain hollow points, reached the point-shoulder position, the thug let the bar fall. The look in Knueson's eyes signaled only temporary surrender as his vengeful stare locked on the vent-ribbed blued steel instrument of death still pointed at him. Slowly they backed away from each other, he toward the double-wide where the rifle and ammunition lay ready on a couch, Sander toward the still idling bike.

Thankful that he had left the bike running while fearful of stalling the engine with a nerve tingling clutch hand, Sander turned and ran for his Harley.

II TRUE ESCAPADES & EXPERIENCES

Close Encounters Of The Heart-Stopping Kind

KA-POW, KA-POW, KA-POW the sound of the .357 Magnum reverberated off the walls of the family room. I reached for... the remote to terminate the inane slaughter of television violence.

Killing... the room lights brought instant darkness to compliment the deafening quiet as I stepped out onto the deck. Now the only sound to penetrate the solitude of our secluded haven on the shores of Goose Creek Bay, was that of a Great Horned Owl and the light rustling of leaves from the wisps of a soft summer breeze.

Complacency and tranquility could only describe my feelings as I followed the planking surrounding this picture-windowed cedar home, nestled among the trees of our 144 acre Hoosier farm. Admiring the view of the Kentucky hills across the Ohio River and its smattering of manmade lights, I walked the length of the deck to our bedroom.

After undressing in preparation to shower, I moved back outside to gather some towels that had been left to dry on the rail earlier in the day. Turning to retrace the two steps to the bedroom's sliding-screen door, I was stunned to see the outline of a man, his feet firmly planted, standing halfway down the deck. A quick glance was all I needed to see that this invader of placidity was about my size, had heavy, dark, bushy hair and ... AND he had something in his hand, AND that something, was pointing at me!

Having been a police officer and a private investigator I've been in tight spots before, but standing naked on my own property, this guy really got my attention! With my eyes riveted on the thing leveled at me while struggling to reach the door, I yelled, "WHO ARE YOU ... GET OUT OF HERE." He didn't say anything and as best I could see his expressionless blank stare didn't change.

Stumbling, crashing, running into the house, slamming the screen door closed behind me, I saw out of the corner of my eye, that the trespasser was now advancing toward my end of the deck. The thoughts that went through my mind as I raced to the bureau where I kept a gun ran from ..."Surely it's a friend playing a joke on me and he's going to burst out laughing any second," to ..."this could only be a sleaze bag from some past arrest or investigation who had sworn to get me."

In what seemed like an inordinate amount of time, I reached the dresser—hang on now—just give me half a second. The muscles in my back tensed in preparation for the bullet that was sure to come as my brain strained to scan all enemies, past and present.

Snatching the pistol from a drawer full of socks, I whirled around, dropped to the floor behind the bed and came up with the classic two-hand hold directed at the screen door whose frame was now filled by the stranger. The silent stranger with something in his hand.

Again I hollered for the man to leave or tell me what he wanted or who he was—anything. No response. He just stood there in the shadows while the harsh incandescence light from the bathroom spotlighted me. Now I could detect that the ominous object in his hand had something sticking out of it—like a barrel!

I waited, listening, looking for the flash of fire that was certainly only moments away. Maybe the screen will deflect the bullet, maybe he'll miss, maybe .... The years of police indoctrination took hold as I resigned myself to empty my gun into this intruder before I died. I strained to see, almost hoping to discern a flash of fire that would bring this confrontation to a very climatic and final end. My death threat didn't move, didn't make a sound. The screen rippled. It might have been the wind. The hair on the back of my neck stood up.

I had to think, go over my options, form a plan, I couldn't take my eyes off the thing in his hand. Surely this isn't real—too much TV!

I didn't have to shoot unless he shot first or unless I was sure it was a weapon he was holding and he gave some indication that he was going to use it. Since I was home alone I could even allow him to enter the house, and as long as he didn't try to get too close or actually assault me, I could just play this thing out. I really wanted to know who he was ... and, why?

The bed afforded enough cover that I didn't want to risk trying for the phone to call the sheriff or a neighbor—the nearest being over a half mile to the west. Besides the police would be at least 20 minutes away since there was only one on-duty officer for the entire county. I could make a dash for the hallway where I could hide, but if he shot me as I ran I wouldn't be able to return the favor. Besides he could hide too and wait until I went to bed or my wife and sons came home and then attack.

Half lying, half sitting, still undressed, light shining on me and my legs beginning to cramp, I continued to shout, "WHO ARE YOU... WHAT DO YOU WANT...GET OUT OF HERE OR I'LL BLOW YOU AWAY, MAN!"

My imagination was running wild. Maybe he was just guarding the door so the real perp could slip in the front and sneak up behind me. I tried to be cognizant of my peripheral vision, lest I take my eyes from what has to be some form of lethal and instant destruction hidden by the screen. I held my breath so not even the sound of my breathing could mask another invader.

Then, still without so much as a word, he turned and started back down the deck. In a flash I killed the light in the bathroom and pulled on a pair of shorts then ran toward the hall. I don't know why I took the time to put on my briefs, but it made me feel better, less vulnerable.

Reaching the entrance way, I saw through the kitchen window, that he had made the end of the deck. He froze as I covered him with light from the driveway floods while opening the door and taking careful aim. He was less than twenty feet from me now and I could see what was in his hand. It was a pencil and pad of paper.

He could have been killed. I might have shot him. My head felt hot and at the same time a chill came over my whole body. I'd had men in my sights before, but this was different. I was just doing my job then, this was personal—this was home to my wife and children!

I motioned for him to come over where he displayed a message on the pad reading, "My Father says I'm a very special person". The stranger was a mentally handicapped, deaf mute!

Keeping my distance I put the gun down and took his pad. After writing notes back and forth he finally told me who he was. He seemed shy, so I invited him in the kitchen for a Coke while I telephoned his family who promised to send someone right up. I learned from further note writing that he had often admired our house from the road and just wanted to see it up close. He had driven his car only part way up the quarter mile driveway, with his lights out, and had walked the rest of the way.

End of story? Not quite. The next day I learned that he was a walk-away from a state mental hospital, committed by his family because he was prone to violence and had attacked people during previous encounters. On this occasion he had savagely beaten his aged father before stealing the car he used to visit me. His brother told me the family wouldn't have held it against me if I had killed him.

I was relieved that the taking of a human life hadn't been necessary, but I was also comforted that I had subscribed to the old country adage: "The door might not always be locked, but the gun is always loaded". Maybe he had wanted more than just a look, but the gun scared him. What if the gun hadn't been available or what if the kids or my wife had been home and one of them had been the first to encounter him, what if ….

Corvette Escapades I

At 50 +/- MPH, it had to appear that we were hurtling straight for the telephone pole...then at what must have seemed like the absolute last possible moment—as the tires chirped on the hard dirt in a full panic stop—she was thrown forward, her knuckles white against the black "chicken bar." Now, and suddenly realizing we weren't going to hit the pole, the pony-tailed blond surely believed we were going to roll. One hand came free as she was slammed against the passenger door, the open roadster making a very hard left while the rear end swung out and the engine revved tight. Surviving all that, and as we headed into the straight-a-way, the 15 year-old was now pinned to the seatback—a prisoner of acceleration.

After three times around, I pulled into the infield and grinned at my passenger, a reen-age honey. She was wide-eyed and as white as my Ermine White Vette. "I, I, I...was never so scared. I thought we were going to hit that pole...and roll over...lets do it again," she stammered. Stop watches in hand, my buddy and the 5/8 mile dirt track owner were striding over excitedly proclaiming that I had broken the track record.

This was spring, 1960, and I was just getting the feel of my combination 18th birthday gift and high school graduation present, a new 230 HP, 3-speed (close-ratio) Corvette (with options of AM Push-Button radio, White-wall tires and heater, the cost was $3433.01). The track, laid out in some farmer's field, was near Middletown, about an hour north of Cincinnati. It was the only place around that allowed anyone with a driver's license to race. Passengers were also allowed—this, in the days long before the proliferation of lawyers got into everything. I loved road racing, but being only 18, SCCA was out of the question for three more years.

Post graduation, and against my parent's wishes, I took a job instead of going to college. I needed money to build my Vette—I mean what's more important, playing Joe College with a stocker or having a fast machine?

During the rest of the summer, as funds permitted, I added: Marchal headlamps, quick steering adapter, HD shocks, metallic brake linings, 4-speed transmission, HD clutch, three two-barrel carburetors on an Offenhauser manifold, Duntov 097 cam with solid lifters, dual points and a Mallory 50K volt coil. The last item was one of the most significant improvements—in relation to other hi-performance 283 Chevys. When I first installed the coil, the engine developed a miss. I figured the coil was bad, but before taking it back, for some reason, I thought to turn the lights out in the garage and watch the engine run with the hood up. There were sparks all over the place.

Though I had replaced the factory graphite spark plug wires with stranded type wires, voltage was leaking everywhere. I took some neoprene fuel hose, slit pieces to match each plug wire and then sealed the wires in the neoprene with electrician's tape. Now, there was no leakage and performance was significantly enhanced.

Sure, this stuff was expensive and it took every dime I earned, but I was living at home and had a pal whose father owned a garage. He had given me the garage's venders number thus allowing me to purchase all Chevrolet parts at a 40% discount. By late summer, I discovered three problems: hot days and/or racing produced vapor lock, hard cornering sometimes caused loss of power due to the carburetor float remaining closed because gas was jamming it in the up position and progressive linkage was not conducive to racing.

The solution to the last problem was easy, I rigged straight linkage, but idled on the center carb only. The fix for the other problems came to me in an inspiration. I bought an extra fuel pump (electric) and fuel block. Then I drilled and tapped a hole into the base of each float bowl where I threaded in a ball-check valve inline with a flow valve. I ran a fuel line back to the fuel tank from the new pump. Now, I had one pump pumping gas into the carbs in the normal fashion, while another pump sucked gas out of the carbs—though restricted by the flow-valve. It took some experimenting with float levels and flow-valve settings, but after I got it worked out I never had vapor lock or "ran out of gas" in a corner again.

On return trips to the Middletown dirt track, sporting all these goodies, I was not able to equal, much less, exceed my previous and still unbroken track record. The cause, I figured, was due to gear ratios. First gear in the 3-speed was a perfect for that track inasmuch as I never had to shift into 2nd. With the 4-speed, 1st gear had a lower ratio and thus I had to either back off or shift (time wasting) into 2nd (and back into 1st again, later).

The 3-speed transmission, like most cars back then, didn't have synchronizers in 1st gear. Of course, having learned to drive on a Crosley that had no synchronizers in any gear (called a "crash-box"), I knew how to double-clutch. Before replacing the 3-speed with the fully synchronized 4-speed, I made a few bucks off other kids by betting I could shift the Vette into 1st at 50 MPH and without using a clutch. It was easy: I knew 50 MPH equaled 5000 RPM in 1st. Therefore, at 50 MPH, all I had to do was pull the shift lever into neutral, rev the engine to 5000 and the shift lever would slide into first like a thrust bearing onto a greased shaft.

Other Sunday's found me at the local dragstrip. As stock 230, I never had a chance because sports cars ran according to displacement—not HP. Thus, I would be up against 270s and fulies. However, by the time I had hopped up the engine, I was in contention. The bad news was there were a bunch of contenders. The good news was, since I was no longer "stock" I could choose to run modified sports car or altered coupe (with my hardtop on). The really good news was, there were fewer contenders in these non-stock classes and I got my share of trophies.

The Copyright

Finally, after forever writing, rewriting, editing, proof reading, submitting — waiting — celebrating the acceptance — more waiting ... at long last you see your creation published. Grabbing a cup of joe, settling comfortably in an easy chair, you casually read your in-print masterpiece. Somewhere between the "he said and then she said" your head begins to heat up and your midsection tightens as this text — with your name on it — reads, *"she said and then he said."* The publisher not only changed the wording, but in doing so, changed the entire meaning — the trick ending you so intricately wove.

Now, much to your chagrin, this nonsensical piece, under your by-line, is in the public domain. Aside from the embarrassment of knowing family and friends will read this, publishers/buyers of your future material might consciously or subconsciously refuse you legitimate honors as well as monetary gains.

Even if you had a written contract with the publisher allowing them the right to "edit for typos, spelling, syntax or clarity" they do not have the right to change the meaning or substance of "your" material. What to do? Sue? Sure, but where, state or federal court?

In most instances of "contract" violation, such as delivery of goods or services, your remedy is in state court where you will be required to prove damages, i.e., what the violation actually cost you in real money. In matters of intangible "goods", such as writings, unless you can come up with someone who will testify that they denied you funds because they found the subject piece to be poorly written, you might be out of luck. However, our Federal Government realized this almost insurmountable burden and wrote the Federal Copyright laws to require the publisher to prove they had NOT caused damages. In other words, the damages are assumed. All you have to prove is a violation of the Federal Copyright Law — the publisher then must prove their violation was not harmful to you.

A few years ago, I received an e-mail from a person claiming to be the editor of a major publisher. He was inquiring about including one of my stories from my book of short stories in their anthology. I've had such request before and many turn out to be from someone just trying to get a free copy of one of my books. I suggested to this e-mailer that he contact the publisher and get back to me about a specific story. I didn't think anymore of it. Six months or so later, I heard again from this de facto publisher, Voyageur Press, requesting my story, Last Knight, for their book, The All-American Hot Rod. This is one of my best, as it had been reprinted a number of times since the original publication about 10 years before. We agree to a price ($500) and they sent a contract which I signed and returned. I also sent them an electronic copy of the story to facilitate their typesetting and to make sure they didn't make any errors. Nowhere in this written contract was there any mention of THEIR right to edit or change my writings.

Another year or so and I received a check and my "author's copies" of this significant coffee table book of early hot rod stories and articles. Upon checking their treatment of my story, I was outraged to read they had screwed it up.

The opening lines of Last Knight are: "The young man, in his late teens, pulled into the driveway, eager to show his father and great grandfather his latest acquisition, a '32 Ford."

At the onset, the reader is thinking this is 1932 (the story was written and first published in 1991). The story seems to use flash backs to the '50s allowing the reader to, at least subconsciously, wonder what time period the story is taking place — but not to the extent of confusion.

It isn't until the final paragraph that the reader is surprised to learn when the story is actually taking place in the future — in the year 2032, to wit:

"Just for an instant he was sure he saw Freddie waving from his NINETEEN Thirty-Two Ford, the one with the hopped-up Chevy engine and the plaque that said KNIGHTS, dangling from the back bumper. But, a deliberate wipe of the hand across his tear filling eyes revealed it was only his great grandson's ... brand new TWENTY Thirty-Two Ford."

The publisher, without my permission, had changed the wording by deleting the terms NINETEEN Thirty-Two and TWENTY Thirty-

Two. In place of these words, they substituted an apostrophe and the numbers, 3 2 ('32). Thus the respective lines read, "… his '32 Ford, the one with …." and "… brand new '32 Ford." The reader could only scratch his head and wonder the gist of the story.

I immediately contacted the editor via e-mail (written proof/evidence) suggesting they "Tip-in" a label, with the corrected type, over the offending paragraph. Having been in our family printing business, I was aware of this tactic of printing a gummed or pressure sensitive label to cover mistakes. Voyageur had about 4000 (of the 5000 first printing) copies in their warehouse at the time and it couldn't have cost them $500 to make this correction. The editor told me they weren't interested in doing a tip-in, but they would correct the errors in a second printing. Big deal! This cavalier attitude led me to seek advice of my attorney, who referred me to Barbara Bison Jacobson, a specialist in Copyright Law.

We decided to wait for the second printing before taking any action. This next publication not only didn't get the dates correct, but they took additional liberties with my writings. Ms. Jacobson immediately sent the editor a letter citing their violation of Federal Copyright law. The reality was there was nothing we could do about the printed and distributed copies of The All-American Hot Rod — our only option was monetary. Since I didn't have to prove I'd lost any money — damages — the issues were: did the publisher violate my copyright, and if so, how much would I be entitled to.

Within a few months, the publisher had their lawyer contact Ms. Jacobson with an offer of $5K contingent upon my signing a confidentiality clause. In other words, they realized they were wrong and were willing to pay for their mistake, but they didn't want me to divulge this fact or the amount of the settlement. As a writer, there was no way I'd agree to these terms and it was back to negotiating.

At this point, I would have settled for $7000+/- and no restrictive covenant. Time, and their refusal to drop the covenant, forced us to file suit in Federal Court seeking the full amount provided by statute — $150K. As the court date approached, the publisher clearly recognized his position and finally agreed to drop the confidentiality clause. Now, all that remained was how much they were willing to pay. Of course, I could demand a trial, but trials are never a sure thing and any finding by a trial court can be appealed — which can be very expensive. In other words, even if I won a huge amount from the courts, I might end up paying attorney fees exceeding this judgment. In the end, I accepted a one-time payment of $30K and no restrictions.

Somewhere out there are thousands of copies of a book containing a confusing story under my by-line. I can't do anything about it, but I am content that I have been fairly compensated and I am able to enlighten my fellow writers about potential Copyright violations.

Summary: Copyright protection is one of the few laws enumerated in the Constitution (Article I, Section 8.) In addition to establishing monetary damage scales, your copyright is, for all intents an purposes, established immediately upon creation—you don't have to register it with the Copyright Office. However, it is recommended that you do. Finally, though it seems simple and clear-cut, Federal Law is complex and requires the expertise of someone experienced in this highly specialized field. Therefore, if you believe your copyrights have been violated, seek the counsel of an attorney practiced in such matters.

Truckin'—Circa 1960

Nineteen-fifty-eight found me sixteen and in possession of a driver's license, an automobile and a girl friend. Life doesn't get any better than this. However, within two years I had contempt for the automobile, the police and the girl ... well; maybe it was she who held the contempt. All was not lost. I now longed for the coveted Chauffer license. With that, I could operate semi-trucks—not that I knew how to drive one. As a youngster, I had always fantasized being one of those real men handling these big rigs—backing them into tight spots, squeezing down narrow alleys and, air horns blasting, high-ballin' on the open road.

Ohio Drivers who held the Chauffeur license (now called a Commercial Drivers License or CDL) were required to wear a 1 3/4" badge in a prominent location (usually on one's cap) when driving for hire. In 1960 there were no classes of drivers, if you passed the exam you could drive for hire a taxi, straight truck, semi-truck & trailer—anything legally licensed. The exam consisted only of a written test that asked mostly questions about weights, sizes and vehicle running lights. Medical exams or demonstration of ability to operate a truck were not compulsory. One only had to be 18 years of age and possess a valid Ohio operator's license to qualify.

The week I turned eighteen, I scanned the state booklet, memorized some statistics and, eureka, I'm a truck driver. Immediately thereafter, I stopped by my father's medium sized manufacturing company and told the general manager I was available should they need a backup truck driver. The company, The Progress Lithographing Co., had a 1951 International semi with 32' single-axle trailer. He did ask if I knew how to drive it and I assured him, with fingers crossed, I did. He didn't ask how I learned, but since I was the owner's son and had cut the grass of the factory's 12 acre site for the past six summers with a side-sickle bar cutter equipped Farmall, he obviously gave me the benefit of a doubt.

Within a month the G.M. called to ask if I could make a rush-job run to Lebanon, Ohio. They needed to deliver about 10 tons printed material in a hurry. It was early morning and I was working on a term paper for my college history class when the call came. Guess who didn't do well in history that semester?

I quickly sought out the company machinist, Obe, who had been most helpful in supplementing the mechanical skills I learned in high school shop classes. I knew Obe had driven the semi in the past, but had purposely allowed his chauffeur license to lapse because he didn't want to drive the truck after spending all day rigging machinery and such into it. The regular driver was only part time as there wasn't enough work. Our Cincinnati based paper convertor did most of its business at distances where it was more economical to utilize commercial haulers. Trucking with the company truck was usually just between the company's four plants, all located within 50 miles of each other.

Though the chauffeur's test required knowledge of weights and size limits, I really had no firsthand experience or understanding of how much 10 tons is and what it was like to propel a 32' trailer so loaded.

The tractor had just been serviced and this required hooking it up with the all-steel single-axle trailer. After sliding the fifth wheel onto the king pin, Obe showed me how to attach the glad-hands, where to plug in the trailer lights and how to retract the dolly. It was a rainy afternoon, making my first attempts to back the trailer into the unlighted loading dock more difficult. I did find it easier than backing the short utility trailer behind the company Farmall tractor. It seems, the shorter the trailer, the harder it is to back up.

As soon as the shipping clerk waved that the rig was loaded, I started for the cab, only to have Obe hail me back to the dock. In a fatherly, but firm tone, he told me that it was I, not the loading party, who was responsible for the safety and security of the load. If the load shifts and is damaged or causes an accident, I will be the one held accountable. We walked into the trailer where Obe pointed out how loads should always be placed against the bulkhead in the front of the trailer and skids should be touching each other, nose to tail.

Obe, riding shotgun, joined me on this, my maiden voyage. He was along because we would have to load and return with some machinery. Following Obe's instructions, I pulled out of the dock in low 2nd and then came to a stop on the level apron. Here he told me to set the trailers brakes — a chrome handle attached to the steering column — and then climb out to close the trailer doors.

There were no freeways open then requiring us to take U.S. 42 with its undulations and numerous traffic lights. I wasn't complaining, as this gave me a lot of shifting practice. Because the highway was wet, I followed Obe's advice to always first gingerly apply the trailer brakes before stepping on the cab brake pedal — this to avoid a jackknife. It was raining even harder on the return trip and loaded with bulky, but light weight machinery (secured with chain and nailed to the wood trailer floor rails), I got another lesson. Starting down a long hill and with no other traffic in sight, Obe told me to slam on the cab brakes just short of locking the wheels and watch the rear view mirror. Cool. The trailer began coming over the center line as if trying to catch the tractor. Releasing the cab brakes brought everything back into line. Now he had me lock up the trailer brakes only. Though not as rapid deceleration when used in tandem with the cab brakes, the rig slowed and stayed in a straight line.

The rig had the standard 5-speed crash box transmission and optional 2-speed electric shift rear axle. Today, every stick-shift transmission includes synchronizers to slow the gears and keep them from grinding during a shift. A crash box has no synchronizers — just cut gears. Thus to keep from grinding (crashing) the gears double-clutching is required. To change up, you have to shift into neutral, let the clutch out to slow the transmission gears down, shove in the clutch and move the shift lever to the higher gear. Down shifting also requires a move to neutral, but while the clutch is out (in neutral) — engine speed must be increased to match the transmission gear speed before again pressing in on the clutch and shifting to the lower gear. Utilizing a tachometer you can make perfect shifts (even without using the clutch!). But, a practiced ear and a "feel" will produce good enough shifts and at a much quicker pace. I had learned to drive a crash box with my first car, a 1952 Crosley which I converted to a fiberglass bodied sports car at age 15 — but that's another story. The '51 International was equipped with the optional 150 gallon, saddle style, diamond-plate fuel tank and west coast mirrors. Power steering was not even an option, but air brakes were standard.

To shift to a higher rear axle ratio, after tripping the switch, entails only letting up on the throttle momentarily — the use of the clutch is not necessary. To shift to the lower rear axle speed while under a load, keep the gas pedal to the metal while quickly disengaging/reengaging the clutch. If not under a load, push the button in while double-clutching into the lower gear, but slowly. Shifting these old rigs is not so much the mechanics of engine/vehicle speed or the grade of the road as it is based on a feel or sense of when to shift.

Changing transmission gears and axle ratios at the same time is called split shifting and is tricky as it requires all of the above directions to be done at the same time and in a most timely manner. If you try to hurry the axle shift you could end up in "nothing gear" a potential disaster if heading down hill.

I don't know now, and surely didn't know then the load limits of the rig, but I'm certain those limits were greatly exceeded more than once in the years I acted as relief driver. Because inter-plant shipping didn't require weighing loads, how did I know? Most trucks are geared so low and have more torque than horsepower; they can usually start in second gear/hi-range. However, I hauled many loads so heavy that first gear/lo-range (bull-dog low, aka granny gear) was necessary to pull out of an up-hill loading dock. Sometimes, even on level roads, I could not even get into low 5th.

I joined the company full time in 1963 as a salesman. Though we now had an everyday driver he only drove the straight truck, thus if full loads or heavy machinery were involved, I had to double as the semi-driver. By now, the clutch was slipping and the king pins were worn causing a shimmy. I had also noticed on trips in the '51, the air pressure gauge indicated a higher than normal reading. We worked a trade for a new 1963 Chevrolet tractor. On the '51s final voyage to the Chevrolet dealer, sans the trailer, the air pressure kept building toward the danger zone. As old as the truck was, I was indeed worried that an air line could burst so I drove in the outside lane just in case … and in-case happened. Starting down a long hill into the city, I heard the unmistakable sound of a abruptly opened air line. Fighting panic and assuming the brakes had failed, I began edging toward the guard rail while split-shifting from high 5th to low 4th.

As the engine screamed, I reached to yank on the emergency brake ….

Flashing through my mind was the Hollywood "in-case" version of oil spray covering the windshield as the truck slammed cars and barriers before upending and bursting into flames. My imaginative thoughts were all for naught. In a few seconds, the "open line" stopped blowing air as I realized there must have been a pressure relief valve that was designed to pop before the air lines did.

H-Modified Sports Car

In the early portion of '57 I truly awoke. Rock & Roll music was in full control, girls were suddenly of interest, and for my fifteenth birthday, my father bought me a car!

The car, a 1952 Crosley two door sedan with its tiny four cylinder engine that barely ran, was a real dream to me. The dream being to convert this slow, top heavy, unattractive little old lady's car into a screaming, low slung sports car. To accomplish this would require replacing the metal body with a new, racing style fiberglass shell and hopping up the engine or maybe stuffing a V8-60 between the rails.

The magazine advertisements for the plastic body declared the average installation time should be fourteen hours. They lied. My father must have known this because what could a fifteen-year-old, sans license, do with a real sports car? Of course, not having a license didn't stop me from putting a few "test" miles on the stocker during post midnight joy rides when all were asleep. Once actual construction began, the car would be totally undrivable except in the various stages when tests were "required"

By late spring, I had the body off and faced the grinding task of cleaning the remains. The drudgery of this work was mind numbing and the dirt and filth was so heavy that I had to spend a good portion of each day just cleaning the garage. The garage was surrounded by shade trees and the area remained quite cool in the summer as the house was not air-conditioned. On one outside wall, under the wood double hung windows, was the heart of the workshop; a large work bench, some eight feet long. We made this bench from wood my brother, Willie, and I had swiped from some of the new houses under construction in the area. This creation was made of plywood and two-by-fours and held together with nails, since by that stage of life we hadn't discovered threaded fasteners. It was sturdy enough with a full length shelf under and eye-ball level to a floor. In those days, we were never short of nails and building materials for making tree houses and jitneys. Mostly we used scrap lumber, but the 4 x 8 plywood and interior grade eight foot 2 x 4s used for the workbench was a significant "requisition".

When the fiberglass body arrived from Almquist a quick check of the dimensions showed that there was no way it would fit and look right. There weren't any instructions, just a shell, two curved pieces that had to be fitted and made into doors, and a copy of the invoice showing that the amount of $295.00 had been paid. A quick check of the body to frame/engine alignment made it clear the engine would not be in the center of the hood opening and the car would have a very high center of gravity if mounted to the stock frame. Definitely not the low slung sports car I imagined it should resemble.

For the finished car to look right and handle correctly, the frame would have to be "Z'd" and "C'd" and the engine would have to be moved back and down, alterations I had only read about in hot rod magazines.

The end of fall found everything ready for a road test. All that was required for this trial was weather conditions of least thirty-plus degrees and dry. Not normal for this time of year, but I had faith that the Gods of high speed would smile on me. Sure enough, I got the bright sun-shiny day only it happened to arrive on a school day. All I could think about the entire morning was the test drive, and by sixth bell, I could resist no longer. I cut Biology and quickly thumbed home.

Exchanging my school outfit for the warmest clothes I could find, I headed for the garage and a date with excitement and apprehension. Without wasting any precious fair weather, I fired up the now souped-up engine. Listening to the idling four-banger was music to my ears, as I familiarize myself with its every sound for reference after the test run.

My plan was to drive to the area of streets across the main road that ran through our small village. The quick steering was perfect, a result of the lengthened pitman arm. It took less than one full turn for lock to lock. At the entrance to my "test track," I doubled clutched into first gear, listened to the engine, took one more look at the frame welds, and mashed the throttle. That instant the tires spun, and the car rocketed forward almost causing me to lose my grip on the steering wheel. By the time I backed off the mufferless rod it was half on the grass shoulder of the road. Holy cow, I could get really hurt, I thought, as I lined up for another try.

Calming myself, I gripped the wheel with renewed strength and felt a rush of adrenalin as I dumped the clutch while tugging at the cable. This time I held the little beast in a straight line. I reached about fifty in second gear and noticed the main frame section was bowing out, but the front end was very stable and I pushed on, taking the first turn on rails. It hugged the road like oil on concrete. Now I was sailing down the short, flat straight to the second turn where I applied full power half way through and promptly spun out, narrowly missing a tree. This was like, crazy man! I loved it!

The thought of disturbing any of the people living on this normally quiet street never occurred to me, at least not on the first trip around. The only negative observation I had was that the engine seemed to flatten out well before it should. Maybe the stock carb was not enough for the hot cam. At the end of the first run, I was enjoying it so much that I decided to go again, this time trying for a little more speed in the corners.

Heading into turn one, I tried what I had only read about; the four-wheel drift. Just before the apex and at about thirty miles per hour I jerked the wheel hard left which, as it should, started the front end sliding. At this attitude, if I did nothing else the car would plow off the road. If I backed off the gas, I would spin out. However, I forced myself to do what I had read about; I opened the throttle full sending the little sports car into an actual four wheel drift—if only for a second. I over-corrected and did a complete one-eighty right in the middle of the street. It was exhilarating. Here I was doing what I had only dreamed about doing and doing it with a car I had made. I got straightened out and headed for turn two where I was determined to master the drift.

This time I got it right. However, unknown to me old lady Fritz, who lived just past turn two, had had time to get her broom ready when she heard me start my second trip around. Now here I was, coming out of a controlled slide with no place to go other than into a tree or right past the edge of her drive where she stood, broom in hand. She was either crazy or had more faith in my driving than I had because the line I was taking was going to put me within inches of where she stood. She didn't budge and as I got within swinging distance, she gave a round house swipe at me, knocking the tiny, single Plexiglas windscreen loose from its retaining bolts. I ducked and didn't get hit, but I could hear her screaming something as I slammed into third gear. Enough! Get me back to the garage.

I hadn't been home long enough for the engine to cool down when the police pulled up. I approached the open window of the scout car just as Officer Bloomfield was saying into the mic, "Twenty-one, two-seven the Klein residence."

"Two-seven, Twenty-one. Advise the subject if I catch him racing that thing, he's going straight to Juvenile," came the voice over the radio.

Uh oh, I was in big trouble now. I could just see my chance of ever getting a license fly right out the window.

"Chuck? It's Chuck, isn't it?" The uniformed cop asked.

"Yes sir."

"Maybe I better take a look at this thing you've been terrorizing the neighborhood with. Is that it?" He said, nodding toward the garage.

I stood over to one side as he walked around my pride and joy which was squeezed between parts boxes and the work bench—the one made from stolen lumber. Maybe they were still looking for the thief, I thought, sweat beginning to form on my forehead. He didn't say anything for the longest time, just peering into everything. Finally, the officer reached back to where his handcuffs were. I looked out the door at the woods. I could run and hide in one of the old tree houses, and when it got dark, I could thumb to Texas or someplace, anyplace. Thoughts of prison raced through my mind as he casually hitched up his pants and said, "Did you build this yourself?"

"Yes sir," I replied with a voice that resonated with guilt.

"Pretty good. I wish I'd had been able to do something like this when I was younger. You've got quite a place here, with that work bench and all."

He did know! Now the axe is going to fall. If I made a break for it, he might shoot me. I had visions of my body lying spread eagle on the driveway. I wondered if the bullet in my back would hurt more than the falling on the blacktop. I suddenly had an over-powering urge to fess up, but my throat was all choked and I couldn't speak.

"Can I take a look at the engine?" Officer Bloomfield asked, without commenting on my total silence. He reached for the leather straps that held the hood down while I hurried to assist, still unable to talk. Maybe the parts I got off old man Crifield were stolen, This is crazy. I've got to get hold of myself and start acting cool. I grabbed the straps on my side of the car and helped the officer lift the hood.

"Looks like you've done a lot of work on this, fellah," the cop commented, admiringly. Silence. "I'll tell you one thing, Chuck. You're pretty cool. There's no question that this engine has recently been run, I can feel the heat from here, and there's no doubt in my mind that this is the car Mrs. Fritz described as almost running her down. However, since I didn't see you driving it and you have had the presence of mind not to admit to anything, there's nothing I can do other than let you know that if we catch you, it'll be a citation at least. And if Sergeant Prince catches you, well, you heard him on the radio; he'll haul your sorry tail to Juvenile Hall. Is that clear, son?"

I couldn't believe my ears. "Yes, sir," I said, in as normal a voice as I could muster.

"I'm not going to give you a ticket or even tell Prince, but I would like to know, just for the sake of truth: How fast were you going around that corner at Mrs. Fritz's? She said you were going at least fifty, but I don't think any car could go that fast around that narrow corner."

"You mean no matter what I say, I won't get into trouble?" I asked still not believing my good fate.

"That's right. Off the record."

"Well, I don't really know as the rod doesn't have a speedometer, but I'm sure I was going at least forty, sir."

"You can cut that `sir' bit too. The official investigation is over. I'm impressed. Your car looks like it should be something you can be proud of, and from what you tell me and what Mrs. Fritz said, it must handle better than anything I've seen."

"Thank you. Do you want me to fire it up so you can hear it?" I offered, but still afraid to call him by his first name.

"Maybe some other time. I better get back on the air or the Sarge will come looking for me himself." I followed him to the cruiser and listened as he called in.

"Twenty-one, two-six."

"Two-six, Twenty-one. Were you able to catch the little whippersnapper?"

"Negative. Subject vehicle was in garage, and I was unable to determine who the driver was." Tony hung the mic back on the dash and said, "Look Chuck, you better take it easy here in the Village. Even a dog knows not to dump where he eats, if you know what I mean."

"You're right, Tony, I'm sorry. I'll try to keep my testing to the strip."

As the cruiser drove away, a wave of exhaustion swept over me. My emotions had been on a wild roller coaster, and I was too whipped to think about anything, even the flatness of the engine at high speed. I went inside only to be questioned by my mother.

Post Script: Because I was too young to race SCCA, my only legal racing was done on a drag strip where I took trophy in H Modified Sports Car many times. In 1959 the oil pump failed causing a burned rod bearing and I tired of putting money into it. I then sold it to a used car lot specializing in sports cars. The last I heard, mid-60s, my Almquist bodied Crosley was in North Carolina racing in SCCA events. Sure would like to have it back!

Early Police Experiences

"Chief? What can I do to help? I'm available day or night."

"Do you own a handgun?"

"Yes sir."

"Wear it, along with dark pants and a blue shirt and be in my office seven o'clock tonight." Cool!

Wow! This is going to be way cool. Here I was a junior executive with our family paper-converting business and not too many years from my last encounter as a hot-rodding chasee. Now, I was about to become the chaser. Living in Amberley Village, a small bedroom community contiguous to Cincinnati, I had phoned the police chief to volunteer my time.

It was 1968 and cities all across the country were under siege from riots, looting and burning. No one knew what direction the rioters would take—stick to destruction of their own neighborhoods or branch out to the mostly white suburbs. All white Amberley, under a county wide mutual-aid agreement, had already sent two of their officers to augment the city where the crux of the rioting had been taking place.

Before leaving my comfortable and secure home, I made my wife strap on a holster and gun, telling her not to open the door to anyone. And if someone breaks in—shoot him. Don't talk to him. Don't warn him. Just empty the gun into him, reload and try (lines might be jammed) to call the police.

Arriving at the station, in my black wool trousers, blue button-down, oxford cloth shirt and a snub-nose .38 in a hip holster, I was shown to the Chief's office. With a glance up to me, Chief Krueger reached into his desk, produced a badge, and with the command to 'pin it on,' said, "You're now a deputy police officer. Tell the rest of the men to assemble in the squad room." Heavy!

With all police officers crowded in the office, the Chief told what he had learned from earlier meetings with other area police chiefs.

Rumors of mass black invasions of white communities were rampant, but no one was sure which way things might go. Krueger sent us out to patrol the five-square mile village with these words: "I don't want any of my men hurt—if any of those rioters (might have used different word) so much as touches anyone of you—kill him." Heavy, my kitty! I rode with a sergeant until about midnight and again the next night. This was fun and somewhere in the back of my mind a light began to glow.

With my life-long interest in guns/shooting, I worked on a novel concept, instinct shooting with a handgun. These experiments coupled with a new found ability to write resulted in my first paid article in Law & Order Magazine (this brainchild later led to a book on the subject—now in its 3rd edition and continuous print for over 25 years). Krueger encouraged me to pursue a career in LE and helped by sending me to one of the first NRA Police Firearms Instructor courses and by writing a letter of recommendation. The Chief indicated he would hire me if I moved out of Amberley, but I wanted more action than a nice quiet bedroom community. Krueger also gave me a significant hint as to what police work is all about. He reiterated what one of his officers told him that cemented his hiring. This, then candidate, told the chief he liked being in a position of being able to help people. I realized I felt the same way and is the reason I became a police officer and later a volunteer fire fighter and a member of Kiwanis International.

Though the family business was busy and I was making good money, I was disillusioned with the direction of certain aspects of our country. I didn't see myself as a placard carrying protester— and being cannon fodder in Nam was also not an option. Police work seemed like a way I could make my contribution to society. In 1971, I found full time employment with the Village of Woodlawn, Ohio Police Department.

> *Everyone should have at least one job in his or her lifetime*
> *where they start each day with the revelation,*
> *"You mean they pay me to do this"?*

Applying to police agencies, my biggest worry was my juvenile record. During the late 1950s, and between the ages of 15 and 18, I had been involved in a number of... ah, not too bright endeavors—

such as moving traffic violations and "disagreements" with my father. Some of these activities resulted in trips to Juvenile Detention. On one such occasion, I was handcuffed and hauled to the Amberley station where, after cooling my heels for a short while, then Captain Krueger, without saying a word, approached me, removed the cuffs, walked to the door, opened it, removed his service revolver, snapped it open to make sure it was loaded and finally said, "We don't have to take you to Juvenile. Go ahead; you can walk out that door. But you better run fast, because I'm going to shoot you in the back if you do." I looked at my shoes. This was big time and I was just a punk. The Captain then said to the Sergeant, "Take him to Juvenile and if he tries to run, shoot him." Very heavy, my kitty!

A night in the "cooler" and my heels were frigid. I was beaten and ready to kowtow to authority—at least until I got my bravado back. In court the next day, and with my parents present, I apologized for my recent behavior and promised to be a good boy. The Judge, Benjamin Schwartz, in no uncertain words, told me he never wanted to see me in his court room again.

As fate would have it, and on another day, there I stood in the same court room. After the proceedings were over it was obvious the Judge had forgotten his threat. I approached the bench, hat in hand, and said, "Excuse me your Honor, but the last time I was here you told me you never wanted to see me in your court room again." Judge Schwartz broke out into a huge grin, climbed down from behind the bench and shook my hand. It was 13 years later and I was the arresting officer of a young juvenile offender.

This kind of "anti-social" behavior might have deterred others from pursuing a career in law enforcement. However, for me, I was lucky to have Bill Krueger as my captain/chief. He was the type of man who could look beyond juvenile pranks and difficult father/son relations to see the good in individuals. He also had a unique perspective about life experiences. On a later visit to his office, he told me of a candidate for one of the department's openings who had an exemplary high school record. Not only did this young police officer hopeful excel in class, but he had never been in a fistfight or had even been sent to the principal's office for any sort of transgression or trouble. The Chief didn't hire him citing the reason that such a person might not be able to deal with, and empathize with persons he would have to confront as a police officer. My resume didn't lack for negative experiences.

Woodlawn was exciting work resulting in the opportunities to make felony arrests for crimes ranging from gun dealing to rape to armed robbery to murder. But one of the most horrific events I witnessed, ironically, occurred in Amberley. I was on my way home after working the 2nd as the Amberley fire trucks rolled onto Ridge Road. Still being in uniform, I followed, thinking, they might need me to help with traffic. It was a house fire in the new part of Elbrook. As the men fought the fire, I made a coffee run to Frisch's. Officer Currens was injured when he used his bare hands to break the window where the children slept—all three died. Though it was traumatizing to know children were in that house, there is no word for what I later learned.

A day or two after the fire, I visited APD. Krueger played the interview tapes of the home owner (I knew him personally) and his wife. He explained how he tried to fight the fire and told his wife to call the fire department after getting the children out. She talked about how she chased their dogs trying to save them and then said, "All is not lost, I still have my dogs." It was difficult to conceive how she cherished her dogs more than her children. The fire department was called by a neighbor—well after the home was enflamed.

Meanwhile, in less than six months on the job at Woodlawn, I was told by Sgt. Paul Roddic that he, the WPD chief and others were part of a theft ring and if I didn't play along they would shoot me in the knees. This all happened while I was working my first 3rd with Roddic. During these late night shifts I witnessed him using his collection of keys to local businesses to steal things. Knowing I couldn't go to my chief, I visited Krueger—a man I knew I could trust. He made notes of our conversation and set up a meeting with the FBI. They told me to keep a record of the sergeant's transgressions and report back weekly. After the criminal officer's girl friend turned him in, my reports were part of the evidence used to help convince him to plead guilty. Former Sergeant Roddic went to prison. The WPD chief knew that I knew he was involved. Then, based upon a letter from Lt. Webster which said in part, "Klein would be better off with his own kind of people," I was terminated. Though the chief showed me the letter, he refused to allow me to copy it and when my attorney asked, the letter "disappeared." To say the Lt. was a bigot and made life for me difficult, would be a gross understatement.

I was broken-hearted, but felt I needed to clear my name and thus applied to other police agencies. The Village of Terrace Park, Ohio had an opening and Chief Hiett told me if I can pass a polygraph test, the job was mine. I passed as I had done nothing wrong at Woodlawn. Though my reputation was clear, I wasn't making enough money to live on and I resigned before completing a full year.

By the late 70s I began a search for an old-time, small community to raise my family. I found a 144 acre farm in Switzerland County, Indiana. Here, my sons enjoyed shooting, hunting, riding motorcycles and I began new careers as a Private Detective and writer. I also spent seven years in the 80s as one of Sheriff J. D. Leap's reserve officers and ten years as a state trained volunteer firefighter for Patriot.

Corvette Escapades II

Late on a summer night, I noticed my buddy Howard's '57 Chevy in the lot at the White Castle drive-in. Pulling up next to him, I said, "Hey man, I see you finally got that junker runnin'."

"This "junker" will dust you off any time you're ready," came the reply from Hard (as he was known, 'cuz that's how the Kentuckians he worked with pronounced Howard).

Before I could think of a good come-back, Louie Wolpa walked over saying, "It's about time you two smoked one off." Howard and I looked at each other and grinned.

"I'm ready, if you are," he said.

"Wait a minute. What have you got in this thing? You're too eager. Pop the hood and let me see," I demanded.

"Okay with me. It's just a stock two-seventy."

"Bull! You never drove a stocker in your life."

He opened the hood, but all that was obvious were two-four's. Anything else had to be hidden in the engine. "Fire it up one time, Hard," I insisted.

When the engine caught I could tell by the sound that it had a hot cam, maybe an Isky 5-cycle? "How big did you bore it and what's the cam?" I said, probing for information.

"Now look, do you want to talk or do you want to race?" Howard took a hard line and I knew it was now or never.

"Okay. But no standing start. We go from a roll. I'll take Louie and you get a passenger to count."

The rules were made and we pulled onto north bound Reading Road, leveling off side by side, between twenty-five and thirty. I rolled my window down to hear the count, as Howard's passenger shouted above the din, "One…two…three!"

At the sound of the magic number, I stabbed the throttle and hit the high beam switch, the big Marchal's lighting up all of the four lane road. The sudden acceleration slammed me back in the seat and I fixed one eye on the tach and put my full attention into hearing the engine. I got the jump on him, the three-two's and a lower first gear ratio, having the advantage on the low end. The recent tune up had not been in vain.

In my second gear (a ratio between his first and second) my lead increased, but once into third and as we neared the top of the hill, just before Langdon Farm Road, he began to close the distance — his two-four's and whatever else he had, now had the edge.

Cresting the hill, abreast of each other and at a little over a hundred, the powerful French headlights picked up the reflective decals of a city police car waiting for the light at Langdon Farm. It was too late now. I could see by the condition of the "walk-wait" signal that the light was about to change to red for our north bound cars. We went through the red light together at something over fifty, hand on horns, high beams on and engines revved tight. The cop didn't waste anytime in turning on his bubble gum machine and pulling out around the line of cars waiting with him. Howard stopped in front of the high school, but I kept right on going while reaching over in front of Louie to hit the switches, turning my tail and brake lights out. I took the first right and got on it all the way to where it curved around and backed into Langdon Farm. Approaching this intersection I set up for a four-wheel drift — after seeing that there was no other traffic. The big Vette slid around the bend in perfect control, smoke billowing from the wheel wells as I poured the coal to her. From Langdon Farm we wound our way through the back streets of suburban villages. The last time I saw the cop, he was about a half-mile behind me and losing ground. I wasn't worried about a road block because the city and the villages were on different radio frequencies.

Once at home, I put the Vette in the garage and found a key to my sister's car, which we took back to White Castle. Howard was waiting for us, grinning from ear to ear. He explained how John-law pulled next to him, told him to wait, and took off after me. As soon as the cop was out of sight, Howard merely turned around and drove back to the drive-in. The cop, obviously a rookie, had failed to copy license plate numbers or even get a good look at Hard and we were now both scot free.

98

By the spring of 1961, I was tired of working (college has to be more fun) and itching to travel. I quit my job, packed some necessities and headed west.

Hero Enough

"Four-six-eight. Car 4-6-8, person injured, Woodlawn Food Market, Marion and Wayne. 4-6-8."

"Four-six-eight, okay," I responded to the dispatcher's detail. The time was late afternoon in our small southwestern Ohio village. It had been a quiet Saturday afternoon—one of those lazy spring days when cops do more waving and smiling than anything else. I turned my cruiser around, swung into traffic, and headed toward the food market.

Almost simultaneously my partner, 4-6-9, and I arrived to face a group of bystanders, some with coats, others in jackets and still others in shirt sleeves. It was that kind of day. In the morning it had been downright cold, but by mid-afternoon it was almost hot whenever those windows of ever-shifting and towering cumulus clouds parted enough to let the sun burn through.

"He's walking up there, on Wayne," one of the women in the crowd shouted, before we could even get out of our cars. Off we drove, not knowing who or what we're looking for. About a quarter mile away on this tree lined, narrow, two-lane road we came across a man carrying a coat and walking away from us. He had a nasty gash on the back of his head and blood had stained his shirt collar. We hit the roof lights to warn traffic and got out to talk to him.

"What happened?" I asked.

"He hit me with a bottle, almost killed me."

"Who hit you?"

"The man back there at the store. He stole my money and hit me in the head."

"Is he still there?" I asked becoming embarrassed that one of us should have stayed at the store to begin the investigation.

"Yeah, he's still there."

"Do you want me to call the life squad?"

"No, no. I ain't going to no hospital."

My partner, sensing the back-up of traffic and realizing someone has to return to the store to investigate a possible armed robbery took control.

"Patrolman Klein, why don't you take the gentleman back to the station for a statement and I'll return to the scene of the crime."

The heavy set man, about 50 years old, and still clutching what appeared to be a thick winter coat, reluctantly made himself at ease in the front seat of my almost new 1971 Dodge patrol car. During the five minute ride to the station, and after advising the dispatcher of the situation, I made small talk trying to learn more about my passenger. Said he was retired, though he didn't look that old, and was living with his daughter in Lincoln Heights, an adjacent suburb.

Pulling into the station lot the radio broke squelch. I recognized my partner's identification as he broadcast, "Four-six-nine. Advise 4-6-8 his signal 22 is a signal 30. Request 4-8-4, signal 2, code 2 our office — assist 4-6-8."

My partner had told me the injured party was a wanted person and that it was serious enough that he was requesting assistance from another community! In retrospect, I guess I should have waited for the back-up to arrive. But hey, I was young and tough and besides the perp was already getting out of the scout car when the call came in.

Since he was bigger and he wasn't aware of his new status, I thought it might be better if we went inside. Entering the deserted squad room of the 1950's era police station, I ushered the perp to a chair on the pretext of wanting to apply first aid to his scalp wound. At the same time I began assuring him that we'd get the guy that attacked him.

Once seated, I knew the tactical position was mine. I reached for his coat that was now crumpled and lying on his lap while saying, "Let me take this. It will make you more comfortable, sir." As I pulled at the heavy wool material, I could now see the man's hand was wrapped around a revolver!

Instinctively I grabbed for it, he shoved at me with is left arm then everything seemed to be happening in slow motion. I could see my hand going for the perp's gun as the barrel slowly rotated toward me. I was trying to balance myself for the thrust of the perp's free elbow all the while my right hand raced to my service revolver. At the same time I was aware that my mind was screaming, why is it taking so long? My right hand clawed at the security strap on the Jordan holster. I seized the custom gripped three-fifty-seven magnum, again wondering why it was taking such an inordinate amount of time to clear leather. I heard my voice hollering, "LET GO! LET GO! LET GO!" I had what I hoped was a death grip on the gun-in-the-coat. The man was strong, I wasn't gaining an advantage, my Smith & Wesson started toward his throat, trigger finger tightening. The pending explosion of one or both weapons was imminent.

"LET GO! LET GO!" I knew as soon as my Model 19 reached battery it was going off. The magnum slammed into the perp's neck, my souped-up mind was telling my unreasonably slow trigger finger: PULL, PULL, PULL.

The man relaxed, his gun hand released, he stopped shoving … and in that nano-second, through my mind flashed: kill him, he tried to kill you, they'll make you a hero, blow him away, kill him. But over-riding this subconscious speed-of-light musing was a deeper inner articulation: American police officer, fair play, the rule of law, the right thing to do.

By the time I had the assaulting weapon secured and was ordering the perp to lie face down on the floor the backup had arrived. We searched and cuffed him and threw him in the holding cell. My partner walked in as I began telling the sequence of events. He picked up the signal 30's revolver, opened it, looked at the loaded cylinder and said as he showed it to me, "you're a lucky guy."

The primer that had been under the hammer was dented—it had been struck by the firing pin. The man had pulled the trigger in an attempt to shoot me. But, because either the coat or my hand had impaired the fall of the hammer, it was a few ounces shy of striking hard enough to cause detonation.

I think it was then my knees got a little weak and irate thoughts raced through my mind of how this dirt bag had tried to kill me. This was followed by anger at myself for not blowing him away when I had the chance. If I had put the scum two-seven, I would be hailed a hero for taking a potential cop-killer off the streets and for surviving, for all intents and purposes, a firefight.

Turns out the perp, a walk-away from a mental hospital, had tried to steal goods from the food market and when confronted by the store owner, pulled the revolver on him. The proprietor, in self-defense, grabbed a pop bottle and hit the robber on the head. The store owner yelled for someone to call the police. A customer, who had only seen a bleeding man walking out of the store, called to report what she'd observed, merely, an "injured man."

There were no newspaper reports of the incident—like confrontations happen to police officers every day. My scrapbook doesn't contain any commendations of heroism, but I know, inside myself, I did the right thing and that's hero enough.

Corvette Escapades III

The sun has riz,

and the sun has set,

and we ain't outta Texas yet.

The big square trademark radiator filled my outside rearview mirror. He looked like he was going to run over the top of me—and I was running 90 miles per hour! The dark blob in my mirror had been gaining on me for at least the past fifteen minutes. At first I thought it was a cop, but the rate he was closing was steady and not increasing as if it were the police. Besides, 90 was not really considered speeding west of San Antonio. Speed limit signs were seldom encountered and actual "speed limits" in many parts of the west were whatever was "reasonable and proper."

I had left Houston early that morning with limited funds advanced by the Show Winds Theatrical Company. It was early summer, 1961, I was nineteen and had started a dream job as the front man for a live stage show company that produced one-night stands in small towns across the southwest. My first stop-over was Pecos.

I edged closer to the berm and again checked my instruments: Tach, 4000, engine temperature 185°F, oil pressure…. It was a huge silver and black Rolls Royce and it was now abreast of me. The mustachioed driver, black cap atop his head, didn't even acknowledge me while the passenger, in the rear seat, couldn't be seen from behind the newspaper he was reading.

This is not happening. This is Texas, USA, and I'm driving the most powerful American made car—the 1960 Corvette! I can't let this go down—this is for the honor of America. I fed a little more fuel to my three Rochester, two-barrel carburetors and matched the interlopers speed—110. After a few minutes in his slipstream, I moved over into the east bound lanes and shoved my foot in it. The little roadster responded with push-you-back-in-the-seat acceleration while the twin straight-thru mufflers resonated off the side of the

Rolls. I topped out at a little over 125 and then settled back to 120 — a nice easy two-mile-per-minute clip. I gleefully watched the Rolls growing smaller in my mirrors.

It was hot, maybe 90 or so, and even the rush of air at such a high speed didn't help much. My cheerfulness quickly faded upon glancing at my gauges. The engine temperature was approaching 220 degrees! I had removed the thermostat prior to beginning the trip knowing the little 283 engine would need all the advantages it could get in the hot south-west summer. The engine was basically the 270 horsepower version to which I had exchanged the two-four barrel carbs for three-duces on straight linkage. The reason was for better response during high speed cornering and improved fuel economy — it got 14.5 MPG at a cruising speed of 90 per. Other attributes included metallic brake linings, quick steering, 4-speed transmission, heavy duty shocks and a 3.70 rear axle.

I had been running all day at 90 without straining the engine, but the extra 30 MPH had been too much. I cut back down to 90. Sure enough, 15 minutes later here came the Rolls with the haughty chauffeur and oblivious passenger — 110, steady as she goes. Well, we don't have to tell anyone — obviously they won't — they didn't even know they had slighted an American icon.

Hot, dirty, tired and coming down with a cold, I stopped at a Pecos hospital where I conned the resident into giving me a shot of penicillin. Then twelve hours in an air conditioned cabin at Jim Bob's & Mary Beth's Tourist Haven and I was ready to begin work. The agreement was, I was to deliver and post bills in common places of the city. I was also to visit any and all local radio stations and newspapers with publicity releases and offer interviews. Posting the flyers was without incident. However, the radio stations and the only local newspaper were reluctant to give me an interview or a promise to plug the upcoming show — seems they had heard my company's song before.

I was allowed two days to complete my work before moving on to the next municipality. At each town the Company was to have waiting for me a money order, care of general delivery. On the morning of the third day there was still no letter at the post office. I called Houston and was told some long tale that I should not worry they'll make it up to me in Farmington, New Mexico, the next scheduled stop. Boy was I naive. They didn't send me out completely without support. They gave me $30.00 for gas money, which, at .20/gallon was good for about 800 miles.

Around noon the next day, I rolled into Roswell just as a local parade was mustering on the main drag. I flopped the top and, hand waving to the crowds like I was one of the floats, got into line behind what turned out to be the mayor's car—a '61 Chevy Convertible. About the time the parade got to the center of town, a motorcycle cop pulled along side of me, signaling that I should follow him. Oops. At the police station, I tried to tell them I was just following traffic when I somehow got mixed up with the parade vehicles. That was almost truthful inasmuch as a cop, way back at the beginning, asked me if I was in the parade and I nodded yes. Since they couldn't get the mayor to forgo his parade and ceremonial affair to hear my case, the sergeant ordered that I be escorted out of town. Sometimes ya get lucky. Now I was on my way to Route 66 and Albuquerque for dinner and a night's sleep.

The next day, I gassed up and inquired of the best route to Farmington. The locals at the gas station, while admiring my car and asking if I was on the Route 66 TV show, advised I should stay on 66 to Gallup and turn north there as the roads running north out of Albuquerque to the four-corners area were not all paved. I didn't tell them I was on the show, but I didn't tell them I wasn't, either. On my way out of town, I noticed I had picked up a few followers—kids from the gas station who had tried to goad me into a race. The leader of the pack, driving a maroon 1957 Chevrolet with louvers on the hood, lowering blocks and a shaved nose and deck, kept riding up on my rear bumper. Once or twice, when traffic permitted, he pulled along side, shoved it into second gear and goosed it a few times while his shotgun called for a race. After a few miles of this, the taunts and threats became abusive and it was clear I needed to do something.

Picking a stretch of Highway 66 that looked to have a sharp curve with a clear view at the end of a short straightaway, I changed down into third and opened the throttle full. The '57, taken by surprise, lagged a hundred feet back by the time I had entered the hard right hand turn. One of the other attributes I added to my Vette was a panel that included switches for my brake lights, tail lights, left tail light, four-way-flasher (not a factory option yet) and under-hood lights. The tail light switch was in case I was being followed, at night, by someone I didn't want to catch me—such as a cop. I could turn out the tail lights making it very hard for him to see me. The left tail light switch was for the same purpose, whereas if a cop was chasing a car with two tail lights, but after a few hills and dales, the only car in front of him had one tail light, he would think the car he was chasing had turned off. It did work, but that's another story.

Hurtling down the highway at close to 90, and with the '57 coming on strong, things got very busy. Just before trouncing the binders, I flipped the switch cancelling the brake lights. With a quick heal-toe maneuver I jammed the shift lever into second gear red-lining the engine. The car shuttered as the speed dropped. Tires howling in protest, I induced an under-steer setting up a four wheel drift. As the right front tire, just over the edge of the pavement and on the dirt berm fought for adhesion, and just before the apex, I poured the coal to her while straightening the wheel to compensate for drift. Once clear of the corner, I stole a glance at my rear view mirror. The Chevy driver, obviously thinking that if I could take the corner without braking, he could too—learned to late something wasn't right. I couldn't see exactly what happened, but there was a lot of dust and I never saw them again.

Farmington was void of any hotels or motels, but I did find a nice home that offered rooms to rent—$3.00 per night including breakfast and dinner. That was after I checked the post office—no mail here either. I couldn't help being an optimist; my mother was a Pollyanna. I began the next day calling on the local radio station. Here, a kindly, older DJ/station manager took pity on me and told me how, after the town had been excited about and helped promote the theatrical company's promise to come last year—never showed up. When I told him that I hadn't been paid he offered to treat me to dinner at his lodge in Durango, Colorado.

The trip through the mountains to this old west town, nestled down into a valley amid jagged mountain peaks, was the most beautiful scenery I had ever seen. The "one dog" town was right out of a Louis L'Amour dime novel as was the rustic Moose Lodge, complete with hand hewn, exposed rafters and, of course, a giant, moose head mounted over a huge stone fireplace. The western attired members, in their scuffed boots and sweat-stained hats, were authentic — not fancy fringed-shirted Hollywood cowboy wannabees.

Arriving back in Farmington, I found a parking ticket on my windshield. It seemed that everywhere I went, cops were attracted to my Corvette. Not, I'm sure, as enthusiasts, but because they assumed sooner or later the driver was going to race, speed, spin his tires, make noise or all of the above. Their concerns were not without merit. The $3.00 ticket became $100.00 if not paid within 24 hours. Twenty-four or a thousand hours, I wasn't about to pay it. It wasn't the principle of the thing, I just didn't have three bucks to spare!

Early the next morning, I headed for the post office. That was, of course, after I paid my room bill and had a full breakfast. The matronly, middle aged, everybody's-mom-lady-of-the-house, in her gingham dress, wished me good luck. The postmaster told me the mail truck wasn't due for about an hour. I walked to the corner drug store, ordered a coke at the soda fountain and read a three-day old copy of the local paper.

The mail contained nothing for me. Then it was back to the drug store where I used the pay phone to place a collect call to the producer. He refused my call! Well, at least I got gas money to get me this far. California here I come.

As I hit the town's western limit the red light on the police car that had been following me came on. I stopped, got out and walked back to the cruiser.

"You gonna pay that ticket, boy," the rotund, red faced cop spat.

"Not right now, sir. But I will."

"Looks to me like you're leaving town — and that's another crime iffins you gotta outstanding ticket."

"Uh, no sir. I was just going to run a mile or two on the highway. My plugs were beginning to foul from all that town driving I'd been doing and I thought I'd blow 'em out a little. I can't leave until I do the radio interview tonight," I lied.

"Well, go ahead, but if you ain't back in ten minutes, I'm gonna radio to Shiprock to stop you and lock you up. Ya hear?"

It was 25 miles to Shiprock and then another 25 to the Arizona border. Approaching the turn-off to this final town, at my normal

4000 RPM cruising speed of 90, I could see two police cars, lights flashing, on the right shoulder. A uniformed officer was standing in the middle of the road, his hand held up, palm forward. I slowed to about 35, shifted to 2nd to wait for the on-coming pick-up truck to clear the road block. With the left lane now open, I moved across the yellow line as the officers began waving their hands and shouting. I had to put two wheels on the dirt shoulder to keep from hitting them as they watched, dumbfounded, America's only real sports car rocket away from them. It was a gamble, but I figured the chances of another cop being between me and the border to be slim.

I'd never experienced 106°F—and neither had my Vette! Arizona—hot, dusty and hotter. At those daytime temperatures, I couldn't hold much over 55 and the air blowing on my feet from the cowl vent was so hot I had to close it. Gripping the steering wheel caused my hands to sweat, but sticking them out of the window to dry them was even hotter. Back on Route 66 at my first gas stop, I learned most cross country drivers only drove at night—when the desert cooled the air. Long before Flagstaff I found a rarity, an air conditioned restaurant, and hunkered down till evening. Because everyone traveled at night, the traffic was the most I'd seen since leaving Houston.

Somewhere in the early morning hours I started down the mountains from Barstow into the San Bernardino valley. The temperature plunged so much I had to stop to paper my radiator with a road map so the engine could generate enough heat to warm the interior of the cockpit.

He Shoot Me, Too

It started out quiet enough for a Friday when my partner, John Campbell, and I began our Midnight to eight tour of duty. I was four-six-eight, the first-responder car, and John, the senior officer was car 4-6-9, the backup. We're police officers, our bailiwick is a small village adjacent to Cincinnati. Being a pint-sized community, we don't have the luxury of having our own dispatcher and thus rely on the County for all radio messages as did thirty-three other like towns and villages on the network. With this much radio traffic going through one dispatcher on one channel, all transmissions were on a very professional level with superfluous talk almost non-existent. To talk to another car or give detailed information to the dispatcher, the officers were to use the telephone, or if that was not practical, radio channel two could be used—but only with the dispatcher's permission.

The early part of the shift was consumed by checking the business areas and watching for drunk drivers with very little radio traffic, for us. The rest of the county was having a regular Friday night with many calls for bar fights, domestic trouble, and an occasional burglary report. About 2:00 AM, our quiet night became history as the dispatcher put out an all-county broadcast with run-together-words and sentences only cops can decipher.

"Attention all cars all departments armed robbery just occurred the King Kwik Market Route 4 and Connersville Road Fairfield, wanted are three black male subjects wearing ski masks and armed with a sawed-off shotgun and blue steel revolver, last seen south bound State Route 4 in an older model Chrysler sedan, black-over-white in color, bearing Ohio six five three Charles David."

State Route 4 ran through the middle of our beat, and even though Fairfield was ten miles and one county north, I positioned myself at our northern boundary. After half an hour of waiting, I moved on, assuming the get-away car wasn't coming my way.

Soon the Dispatcher radioed our department to advise that the subject license was registered to a William Pilder of 11457 Shelter Road. That address was in our village and in a basically decent neighborhood. The Pilder family was not known as a harbor for criminals or trouble makers. Perhaps the person who copied the license number got it wrong — as often happens under stress.

My partner advised that since he was near the location, he'd check it out. I didn't hear anymore and when 4-6-9 and I met a little later he advised the Pilder place was a dark house on an empty driveway.

Back out on patrol I watched an older model black-over-white sedan approach me from the opposite direction on SR 4. I caught a glimpse of the license plate as we passed — it matched the one from the earlier broadcast and there were three occupants in the vehicle. As I started to turn my police-packaged Plymouth around, they took off at a high rate of speed. Fumbling, fighting, wrestling with the gear shift, steering wheel and emergency light/siren switch, I did my best to begin pursuit while keying the microphone:

"4-6-8, emergency traffic."

"All cars stand-by. 4-6-8, your emergency traffic."

"4-6-8 I'm in pursuit, black over white, Chrysler sedan bearing Ohio six, five, three, Charles David. We're south bound Route Four approaching Snyder Road. They've killed their lights"

"Okay 4-6-8. Four-six-eight are you aware these subjects possibly wanted armed robbery reference earlier broadcast?"

"4-6-8 affirmative. They're now running over 80."

"4-6-9, 4-1-7, 4-3-2, Four-six-eight in pursuit black over white Chrysler sedan south bound Route Four at Snyder. Subject vehicle believed wanted reference earlier broadcast for armed robbery. Be advised subject vehicle has no head lights."

My scout car was barely keeping up with the perps; I darted my eyes to the calibrated speedometer — 95! Then suddenly they slammed on their brakes and turned onto Rickman — a dead end residential street in a heavily wooded area.

"4-6-8 they just turned west on Rickman."

I knew the dispatcher and other cars heard me and were responding, but I was now totally focused on the Chrysler as it crested a small hill. Unexpectedly, the black over white slowed to a stop. The interior light briefly lit. The significance of this didn't register, though I slowed thinking perhaps they were going to run into the woods or make a stand. But the car took off again toward the dead end.

The Chrysler, having reached the road's limit, was now sliding to a halt. I locked the brakes up and cranked the wheel over hard to the left bringing the cruiser to a jolting stop abreast of the sedan. Training the spotlight on the perp's car, I opened my door, drew my service revolver just as the driver jumped out and made for the woods. Half laying over the windshield, I hollered as loud as I could, "FREEZE. DON'T MOVE." The man in the back seat quickly took my advice. My gut contracted and my arm muscles tensed as at any moment I expected to see muzzle flash from the woods.

Using the scout car as a shield, I began a series of shouted commands to try to control the situation. "ALL RIGHT NOW LISTEN UP...YOU, IN THERE ... STICK YOUR HANDS OUT OF THE DOOR AND DON'T HAVE ANYTHING IN THEM. KEEP YOUR HANDS WHERE I CAN SEE THEM OR YOU'RE DEAD MEN."

All the while this was happening I knew the back-up cars were arriving by the sounds of their sirens, but split seconds seemed like hours. Upon my command only one man climbed out. Where was the third and where were the guns? I had the man out of the car and lying on the ground as the area filled with police cars in this normally quiet, dark, wooded, residential neighborhood. The robbers with the scattergun and handgun could be anywhere just waiting to blast any one of us at any moment. At times like this, the safety of the officers is primary to the rights of the suspects, so I knelt down next to the now handcuffed dude and placed my revolver at his head, saying, "If I or any other officer is shot by one of your buddies, I'm going to pull the trigger before I die ... now tell me, where is the third guy and where are the guns?"

"He got out at the top of the hill—he took the shotgun."

"How 'bout the driver?"

"No. No. The handgun's in the back seat."

Quickly, I got on the PA and announced, "All units on the scene, there's two additional subjects in the woods—one armed with a shotgun."

Within minutes the canine unit from neighboring Blue Ash P.D. arrived and in short order found one of the missing robbers—the driver. The third man and the shotgun were still unaccounted for. The Chrysler was quickly searched, turning up only the blue steel revolver and a wallet, but no money. The wallet contained the identification of one Jerry Curtis, a two-time loser, who was out on parole for armed robbery!

The captured suspects were separated and transported to the station while LEOs from other departments inventoried the black over white sedan before having it towed to our impound lot.

Meanwhile at the station, the suspects, when confronted with the wallet, admitted to the robbery and that Curtis was the third man. They both stated Curtis had instructed the driver to stop just over the crest of the hill so he could get out, with the shotgun, and shoot the officer who was chasing them—me! Now it dawned on me why the interior light came on. I felt a chill at the visualization of the squad car window shattering as I took a full charge of buckshot. For whatever reason, he booked it into the woods letting his compatriots fend for themselves.

The driver, one Elliston Whitson, last known address, Chicago, was also on parole for armed robbery. The back seat man was Emanual Pilder who had let Whitson drive the car belonging to Pilder's parents.

Jerry Curtis' parents lived within a mile of Rickman Road. Somewhere after 4:00 AM, with a couple of officers from an adjoining agency watching the back of the house, John and I rang the front door bell. A sleep-eyed Mrs. Curtis opened after we identified ourselves. We told her that the house was surrounded and that we believed her son Paul had been involved in an armed robbery and we had come to arrest him. She said she was sure he was asleep in his upstairs bedroom as she had heard him come home a few hours ago. Mrs. Curtis then led us down the narrow, dimly lit hall to the stairs. I called up for Jerry to come down—twice. No response. Turning to Mrs. Curtis, I said, "You go up and get him." Her reply set my adrenaline flowing for the second time this night: "Hell's fire, I'm ain't goin' up there. He shoot me, too!"

Summoning all the authority I could in my voice, I hollered up the steps: "JERRY CURTIS, POLICE OFFICERS … IF YOU DON'T COME DOWN BY THE TIME I COUNT TO THREE, WE'RE COMING UP AFTER YOU. WE KNOW YOU HAVE A SHOTGUN AND THE HOUSE IS SURROUNDED … ONE … TWO … THREE. There was no sound or movement. John whispered to me, "You go high, I'll go low." I nodded. It was time to do what only police officers get paid to do.

With handguns at the ready, my gut squeezed tight yet again, I stepped around the corner and into that stairwell … prepared to shoot at anything that moved. Starting up the steps with the full expectation of gunfire, a resigned voice called out from above, "Don't shoot, I'm coming down."

By 6:00 a.m. it was all over, the vehicle impounded, the prisoners in lock-up and the paper work under control—time for a cup o' joe at the Country Kitchen. As I held the mug to warm my hands, I noticed they were shaking. Only then did I realize that I was scared. When it was happening—the chase, the confrontations, I didn't have time to think about what might happen. Now I had the shakes. The feelings of fear, which didn't last long, were a good sign because it made me appreciate life a little more.

Jerry Curtis and Elliston Whitson went back to prison for 10 to 20 stretches. Emanuel Pilder, due to his co-operation and no prior convictions, got probation. The money and shotgun have never been found.

Corvette Escapades IV

Seeing her at her Mother's funeral forced memories
forever melded to the sentimental portions of my mind.

~~~~~~~~~~~~~

In my 13th year, the summer of 1954, the Cooper's moved next door. I was just starting to notice girls and Suzan—Suzie—got my attention when she beat me at a game of mumbly-peg. And, even though she was a tom-boy, she was a very good looking tom-boy. Nothing was ever said, but my best friend, Carl, knew that the looks between her cyan and my hazel eyes meant a destiny that didn't include him. Our families became close in many ways. Suzie and I were the same age, her brother and I swam on the school team together and our mothers became the very best of friends.

Throughout high school, I was on the wild side—a hot rodder—and only dated "chicks." I was embarrassed to call Suzie until I'd sowed my oats. I re-noticed her when she came over to swim late in the summer of '61. Now, I was enrolled in college and more mature—and she was so pretty. Somehow I talked her into a date for that Saturday night. I then spent an entire day cleaning and polishing my 1960 Corvette. The Vette was rigged for road racing with the quick-steering adapter, HD shocks, metallic brake linings and 3" x 6" galvanized pipe welded to the exhaust header pipes. The only external change to the car was the addition of Marchal head lamps to replace the outboard standard sealed beam lights.

Temperature wise, it was a perfect Cincinnati evening and I had the top down and soft music playing on the RCA 45 record player I had installed on the "chicken bar" ('cuz the radio was all static due to the solid spark plug wires). She wore something white and was so pretty—wait, I already said that. Slowly, so as to enjoy the music and not disturb her with the loud exhaust, we motored to Sorrento's restaurant, turning every head we passed. Though Corvettes weren't common and car aficionados would always look, everyone noticed a beautiful blonde.

We spent a lot of time together that late summer — swimming, dancing, movies and other fun stuff. One warm night, while watching an Elvis Presley movie at the drive-in, The King sang "Can't Help Falling In Love." At the line, "Take my hand, take my whole life too ...." we instinctively reached to hold hands. I don't remember the song being "our song," but whenever I've heard it, I've thought of Suzie. The end of September found her returning to the University of Colorado at Boulder and our courtship continued via mail.

In mid January, exams over and during a conversation with my friend and fellow hot rod club member, Kookie, I suggested we run out to Boulder. He didn't have anything else going on and was game, especially after I promised Suzie would fix him up with a real honey.

We picked up U.S. 36 in downtown Indianapolis, a reprieve, after following mostly state highways with their inherent undulations, stream-chasing routes and long, wild grasses growing over the edge of the pavement (expressways yet to open). West of the city the traffic thinned out and we were able to return to our cruising speed of 90 MPH. The Corvette had three Rochester 2-barrel carburetors on straight linkage and at that speed the engine was running 4000 RPM which was well into the power curve of the Duntov cam. In other words, it was a comfortable clip that produced over 14 miles per gallon.

Somewhere around 5:00 a.m., in a dense fog, a wheel came off. Kookie was driving and did a great job of keeping the Vette on the road. There was no damage to the car, but, due to the thick fog we never found the tire and wheel. We took a lug nut from each of the other wheels and used those three nuts to hold the spare tire on. Limping into the next town we found a Chevrolet dealer and after a two hour wait for them to open, we were on our way again.

Deep into western Kansas, running the usual 90 per, a semi-truck emerged about a half mile ahead. It appeared we would pass the truck, maintaining the present rate, in the middle of an intersection. The land was flat and the cross road was clear, so I just held her steady at 4000 RPM. Halfway around the semi and over the double yellow line, I was startled to see a state trooper on the truck's front bumper! The noise from the muffler by-pass reverberating off the truck was deafening and produced a look of surprised outrage on the trooper's face as we roared past. Not for an instant did I think I could talk my way out of speeding, excessive noise, driving left of center and passing in an intersection.

I went to full throttle while Kookie scanned the map. One Hundred … a hundred and ten … two-miles-per-minute. We were a lightning bolt on wheels. My co-pilot leaned over and shouted that there was only one little town and then about ten miles to Colorado. We had to chance that there weren't any other cops between us and the border. Now my attention was riveted to controlling this 300 horse-powered, plastic-bodied roadster—a land-rocket that was sans power brakes, power steering or steel-belted-radial-tires. At these speeds even glancing at the gauges was forsaken. I had to rely on engine sounds, the feel of the wheel, gut instincts and luck. Billboards and highway signs such as Burma-Shave and Mail Pouch became mere peripheral splashes of color.

Coming into the small burg, a pandemonium of smoke and danger—fire shooting from the open lake-pipes—people stopped and stared, mouths agape. I forced the Vette to just under 60 in second gear to negotiate a hard left turn then got a piece of third before having to shut down for a tight chicane in the heart of town. Once through the business district, I red-lined in third gear before leveling off again at 90. The state trooper was nowhere in sight.

Inside Colorado, with Denver in view, we came around a bend in the road and there sat two highway patrol cars. Both pulled out after us. We got out of their sight over a small hill and slammed to a stop. Having anticipated this from previous high speed runs, Kookie and I were both wearing like-colored shirts. When the officers finally pulled up behind us, we were standing outside the car studying a road map. They couldn't give us a ticket, because they were unable to determine who was driving. However, they let us know that Kansas had called that we were coming and they were going to follow us all the way through their state if necessary. They stayed with us until we turned off at Boulder.

At the university, we found a motel and called Suzie. She came right over and the hug and kiss made it all worthwhile. We got a little shut-eye, Suzie came through with a co-ed for Kookie and we did the college scene. The next day, Kookie wanted to see a mountain and the girls found the way where we took pictures and enjoyed the day.

The home-bound leg was uneventful except for the final stretch in Indiana … where on lazy, sunny, summer days giant deciduous trees over-hang the country roadways, their branches reaching out as if to shake hands. Uneventful: except this was night, the dead of winter and we picked up a cop. I quickly tripped the switch I had installed to cancel the left tail light. A few miles further down this highway that snaked in and out of those towering trees and the officer, who had been chasing two tail lights, now only saw a vehicle with one light and surely figured we turned at a side road—which he must have done as we never saw him again.

The trip out took almost 24 hours due to loosing the tire. Coming back, we covered the 1190 miles in 19 hours, five minutes—a 63 MPH average—all on two lane roads with no side-lines and very narrow, if any, shoulders. I've never been sure the trip wasn't more about the opportunity to road race than it was to see my girl.

I developed some very strong feelings for her and I know she pined for me also, but the timing wasn't right. Both of us had agendas—places to go, things to do, worlds to conquer and commitments were a long way off.

> *It is said that everyone experiences three loves:*
>
> *the one they marry, the one they're glad they didn't marry*
>
> *and the one that got away.*

Suzie and I kept in touch, but with careers and dating others the touch got lighter. Within a few years, Suzan accepted a job in California and … married. Me? As soon as I figured out that it was just as much fun to be the chaser as it was the chasee, I became a police officer.

The Corvette? A few months after the Colorado trip, before I burned the valves experimenting with nitro-methane and sold it to an unsuspecting dealer, I made one last run. They had just opened the six-lane Interstate between Cincinnati and Dayton and nine of us, all in Corvettes—three rows of three—broke in the new road. With seven Vettes to block cops, two at a time would line up, and from a roll, run flat out. I was up against a '59 270 with a higher rear axle ratio. I beat him from 70 to about 130, and then he came on by.

118

Yeah, I know, we were crazy back then. But traffic was light, cops fewer, radar not perfected and we were very lucky. Lucky to survive and lucky to have lived during that era.

Late in the spring of 1996, and now a widower, my second wife, Annette, and I were honored to be treated to lunch with Mrs. Cooper and my mother. Suzie, who has known Annette since grade school, was in town for a visit and also joined us. Both of my wives have known about "Suzie and me." I made certain they did — a tinge of jealousy never hurt any relationship. I always wondered if Suzan, in the same vein, kept Paul on his toes, too.

> *Never being able to satiate aspirations*
>
> *is better than not having*
>
> *any fantasies at all.*

At some point during the luncheon, Suzie and I found ourselves alone … and 42 years since our eyes locked in that game of mumbly-peg, I asked this girl next door, "Did life turn out okay? Are you happy?" She smiled, her blue eyes twinkling, "Oh yes. Surely you remember your mother always telling us, 'the secret to life is the ability to adapt to change.' And you?"

I smiled out of the corner of my mouth and gave her a slow wink, "Can't argue with my mom."

~~~~~~~~~~~~~~~

After the funeral Suzan introduced me to her daughters,

one of which immediately turned to her sisters and whispered,

"He's Klein. He could have been our father."

Beshert

"Hey Mike, wanna double to Spatz's Saturday night?"

"Yeah, but you're not takin' that Sandy chick I saw you talkin' to after 5th bell are ya?"

"Nah, man, I wouldn't take her to a dog fight, even if she was fighting". I was only prying Annette's phone number from her … and I called her and she said Ooookayyyy."

Mike Gehring, his girl Heather, and Annette and I motored from Cincinnati to Hamilton, Ohio, about 30 miles, to the night club, Spatz's—a show place that was known to never request age ID and to feature name entertainment. MG and I had doubled to Spatz's a few other times and always had a great time.

Tonight it was a coolish Midwest summer evening, but MG put the top down on his daddy's almost new '58 Impala. We laughed our way north while I entertained all with my rendition of a Shelly Berman monologue.

"I was on a plane last week and the stewardess told me to fasten my seat belt. I asked why and she replied, 'incase we come to a sudden stop, it will keep you from striking the seat in front of you. 'Sudden stop … you mean … like against a mountain?'"

I wore a Madras sport coat, blue, button-down Oxford cloth shirt and penny loafers. Annette had on a shirtwaist dress and flats. She had high cheek bones, a few freckles and wore her red-highlighted hair in a pageboy cut. Mike, an afterschool salesman for Max's Gentry Shop, looked very spiffy in a Fabian sweater over a white, button-down shirt. Heather, a dishwater blonde, also was dressed in a shirtwaist dress and flats. Most nightclubs wouldn't allow men in without a tie, but Spatz's was a little more relaxed.

Somewhere the parent-scowling side of midnight, I walked Annette, a honey of a girl, to her door while Mike and Heather snuggled in the car.

120

"Do you kiss on the first date, I asked, hungering for her full and slightly parted lips?"

"No. Do you?"

"Yeah," I said moving in for the kiss.

"Well, I said I don't, she said, putting her arms up in a defensive move."

"How 'but the last?" I said, stung by the put-down.

"Is this our last date?" Annette smugly retorted.

"I'll call ya," I tossed over my shoulder as I strolled to the Impala.

Man, she was so good lookin'—and sensual, I'd have done anything for a hug and a kiss—only I didn't know what that anything was! At least I didn't lose my cool.

~~~~~~~~~~~~

Time moved on. I met and married a pretty lass, Patty. We had three children though one died in a tragic accident before age one. After moving to the country in the late 1970s, Patty, and I met and became very good friends with Elaine, another transplant from the big city. The ladies really got along well and I always had a feeling that if I had known Elaine at the same time I was dating Patty...well, it would have been a difficult choice.

The girls were born in Cincinnati, on the same day, in the same year. In their twenties they married out of their religion and to men who were "juniors". Both gave birth to boys as their first born, whom they named after their husbands (making them "thirds"). They each nicknamed these boys, Trey. Patty and Elaine, with their families, moved to Switzerland County, Indiana in the 1970s and worked in real estate. In addition, they both smoked cigarettes, their favorite drink was Tab and they had a cavalier attitude about their personal health.

Elaine divorced her husband, and Patty and I parted after 28 years (it was a very amiable dissolution). We had to sell the farm and now it was back to the city where I found a small row house in the downtown area. In the late 1980s Elaine developed back pain which was misdiagnosed as muscular issues. By the time it was correctly identified as pancreatic cancer, it was too late for treatment and she died within six months.

Meanwhile, and while still in college, Annette married a high school classmate of mine. She gave birth to three children and, by the late 70s, became a divorcee. Being so pretty, she never was at a loss for an escort, but none of these eligibles were marriage material and she remained single.

~~~~~~~~~~~~~

It's 1995, I'm busy dating, writing and conducting private investigations. On a spring evening, I attended a special Cincinnati Symphony Orchestra performance. Special, because a High school classmate, Richard Stoltzman, was the guest soloist. Smiling my way around the enormous hall during intermission, I was hailed by Annette's brother, Herb, whom I had also known since high school. No sooner had our hands clasped in the obligatory handshake than I noticed Annette, three in from the isle. I lost all track of time, the performance and where my seat was. Boy was she stunning. It was 1959 all over again—with her red-highlighted, short up-turned hair and a few freckles she still looked like the same teen-ager to me.

Not wanting to screw this opportunity up, and being a writer, I decided to send her a letter (this is before e-mail):

Dear Annette,

Enjoyed seeing you the other night

You seem like the kind of girl

I would like to get to know

And hopefully make your toes curl.

Anyway, and aside from being a great guy, I am also a staunch proponent of intercourse—wait, wait I left a word out: SOCIAL—it goes before intercourse as in I like talking and listening to a lady who is mentally active. This is just awful! We hardly know each other and already you probably think I'm some kind of sex machine. I'm so embarrassed.

On the plus side: I never lie, cheat or steal. Well, that's not exactly all true; I might steal your heart, if…

122

So if you're still reading maybe there's a chance. Just now, I was daydreaming that you'd visit my historic downtown row house for a little fireside tête-à-tête. Nothing is more soothing in the fall of the year than viewing ancient classic roof tops through floor-to-ceiling, paned-windows from which the likes of the Chimney Sweep, the Fiddler and Mary Poppins can surely be glimpsed. A slight chill in the air while we listen to manmade music as the natural sounds of crackling fire and city…are we in love yet—sorry, I'm getting carried away; romantics tend to do that.

Alright, already we're now coming to final options. You're either going to:

a) Foolishly crumple this up and throw it away;

b) Grab the phone and call;

c) Send me a big giant box stuffed full of gifts & toys & things;

d) Drive to 1621 Main and beat on my door;

e) Call your lawyer.

Chuck

She didn't call—so I called. After three attempts, I finally got to talk to her. The dialogue went something like this:

"Do you kiss on your second date?" I asked

"What?"

"On our first date, you told me you didn't kiss on a first date. So, I want to … "

"What first date? Are you putting me on?"

"We had a date way back in high school. I don't remember the details other than you wouldn't kiss me goodnight and I told you I'd call you. Well, I'm calling—so it took thirty something years, but you can't say I didn't call." I said, hoping I wasn't being too smart-alecky, presumptuous or just plain dumb.

"Hum. I sorta remember listening to you do a Shelly Berman routine in the back seat of a convertible, but I'm not sure where or if we were on a date."

"So, do ya?"

"Do I what?"

"Kiss on the second date?"

"There's only one way to find out."

In that single, short phone conversation, we seemed to jell. Plans were made for coffee at the local bistro.

Upon entering the espresso house, the first thing I did was to hold up my index finger while impetuously grinning, "Kiss my finger."

Her smile broadened as her lips lightly brushed the callouses before she asked, "Why?"

"I finally got that kiss!"

Between sips of licorice flavored herbal tea and in a lifetime measured in short hot flashes, we melded souls in wispy and sometimes intellectual conversation. I'm not sure if the quaint bistro was crowded or if the three-piece jazz combo was in good form as I only saw two brown eyes and heard the concussion of bells superimposed on my mind. The lady named Annette stirred feelings of emotional splendor long since thought lost.

Perhaps it was the tea, or just destiny that caused strong and compelling interaction from the very first encounter. We fit together like a soft playing radio to a padded dash. Before the night ended it seemed, Burns and Allen style, we were finishing each others sentences — sometimes without even talking.

In a tiny booth designed for esoteric confidences we talked, laughed, bantered and oozed vibes far later than we both were accustomed to being out. Somewhere between the late night and early morning hours I told her, "This is fun and I really like being with you. The similarities are startling. The way you talk, look, laugh, well, ah," I stammered, examining my hands. "You really remind me of; let me count…my second wife. Yeah, that's it, wife number two."

I knew her mouth dropped open in indignation, but her voice was smiling. "Your second wife? How, how, many wives have you had?"

Keeping my eyes downcast, I took a sip of tea after which I slowly dabbed the napkin at the corners of my mouth. Then, still suppressing a grin, I touched the back of her hand with one finger, looked up, and matched her smile as I whispered, "Only one."

A month or so into our relationship, I gave her my book, Circa 1957, an autobiographical accounting of the era (It didn't start out that way, it's just that I couldn't come up with better stuff than what really happened). Deep into the book she called one night to say, "The incident where Paul [me, the protagonist] goes to Spatz's Show Bar might have been where we went on our date, and we doubled with a guy named Mike." Maybe, but neither of us were sure.

Annette and I, both second-time-arounders, continued to date for another year before we married. Her sister is wedded to a classmate of mine and her brother and I have been friends since high school. Our children are matched in ages and interests — our families melded as though it has always been.

Patty also attended this marriage as many of our mutual friends were invited. One of these now friends-with-all returned to Cincinnati a year later and the five of us got together for a brunch. I noticed Patty had lost some weight and commented how nice she looked. She said she was on a hi-carb diet and was slimming down very fast. That wasn't like her. She was never slim, and had slowly gained weight over the span of three-plus decades — always trying this diet or that. A month later she called me to meet for lunch where she told me that the back pain she'd been experiencing had been misdiagnosed — it was pancreatic cancer. And just like Elaine, almost six months to the day after the cancer was detected, she passed away.

A few years into this union with Annette; her brother rediscovered a box of her memorabilia he said he had saved from a flooded basement long ago and had forgotten to return to her. She thought the souvenirs and remembrances from her past had been lost. In the container was a journal she kept for only two years. On the page for May 21, 1959 is the entry: "Date with Chuck Klein — went to Spatz's — doubled with Mike G. and Heather." The Jewish people have a word for this, Beshert, which means: "meant to be."

III POLICE ETHICS AND ISSUES

Police & Firearms Nomenclature

FIREARMS NOMENCLATURE: Police officers may be experts at firearms use-of-force, but far too many have misunderstandings of the terms used when report writing about guns. This lack of knowledge is not limited to cops as one noted author penned, "...he grabbed the 30.06 rifle...." The thirty-ought-six is probably the most well know cartridge in the world. However, it is displayed as .30-06. The ".30" is the caliber or bore diameter (in hundreds of an inch) of the barrel. The "06" refers to the year (1906) when the cartridge was accepted by and for the U.S. Military. Another well-known author, when describing a group of men in the early 1970s, had one of them shooting a Glock pistol. Glock didn't make handguns until the 1980s.

Other egregious errors found in news media stories, articles, books and police reports include: "The gun used was a Colt automatic" (Did the writer mean machinegun or the more common SEMI-automatic? Colt has made both). "He took out his pistol, opened the cylinder...." (Pistols don't have cylinders — only revolvers do). "The killer placed a fresh bullet into his gun" (I think he means, Cartridge).

We hear a lot of catch phrases such as "The embassy/military base/etc. is on high/heightened/full alert." Sometimes these terms are military codes and sometimes they're only the news writer's perception of what's happening. Back in the 1960s, the military established a set of color codes to help individual soldiers be alert to the different awareness levels of danger. Over the years most police agencies and training facilities have adopted the same color codes. It is important to have different levels for reasons of mental preparedness to risks and also to stand-down when the danger is less, though not completely gone.

Everyone, police, military as well as civilians, can use and benefit from this time tested system of risk consciousness. These Color Conditions have no time frame inasmuch as you can go from Condition White to Condition Black in a split second.

128

The first level or lowest level of awareness is CONDITION WHITE. This denotes a relaxed state of mind. The condition that most people are in when going about their daily business.

The second level, a raised measure of mental alertness, is CONDITION YELLOW. The person in Condition Yellow will be more cognizant of his or her surroundings. Police officers and others who carry firearms must remain at this level at all times. Others, for reasons of just making sure they aren't caught unawares will be tuned-in to everything that is going on within their arena of observation. Those in Condition Yellow should not only be aware of their surroundings, but their position in relation to these surrounds. In other words, for example, if while dining in a restaurant, your goals might be to observe the people (and their movements), fixtures, and places, while impressing on your mind the locations of exits and possible hindrances to those exits.

OTHER COLOR CODES:

Orange: Next level of awareness. The prudent person should now be on the lookout for an unspecified, but real danger.

Red: This means a potentially deadly assault is forthcoming. You have seen the enemy and he is advancing.

Black: You are now engaged in a lethal encounter.

POLICE RADIO CODES and signals are something entirely different:

Code 2: Respond at once without emergency lights and siren. Used for responding to silent alarm drops so as not to alert the criminals.

Code 3: Respond at once using emergency lights and siren. All stops pulled — get there NOW.

Code 4: No further assistance required. Disregard previous transmission. Necessary to keep the scene from being over-run by police personnel and to not lose coverage in other areas.

Code 7: Out of service (2-7) for a meal break.

POLICE RADIO SIGNALS: Though not uniform by any measure, some signals and codes are almost universally accepted.

Signal **2:** Spoken as Signal-two. In most jurisdictions it means to respond to the station.

Signal **22:** Spoken as Signal-twenty-two, meaning injured person.

Signal **26:** Spoken as two-six meaning in-service as in an officer is on-duty and available for details/assignments.

Signal **27:** Spoken as two-seven. Officially it means out-of-service as in the officer is going off the air to handle a detail. In days before individual officer radios, every time an officer was out of his cruiser (away from the car mounted radio) he advised the dispatcher he was 2-7. Two-Seven also could unofficially denote a deceased person (the perp is 2-7) or a fellow officer who is "not with it" or asleep (shh, the Lieutenant is 2-7).

Signal **30:** Spoken as Signal-thirty. Wanted person, vehicle or firearm. An officer receiving such a radio transmission is being told the person with him (or vehicle/firearm queried) is a wanted or dangerous person.

Signal **44:** Spoken as Signal-forty-four or car number followed by 44, meaning, what is your location (Four-six-eight, forty-four)?

Signal: **10-4:** Spoken as Ten-four. Okay. I acknowledge your transmission.

Signal: **10-78:** Spoken as Ten-seventy-eight. Officer needs help.

ADDITIONAL FIREARM RELATED TERMS:

ACP: Automatic Colt Pistol. The most common guns/cartridges are .45 ACP, .380 ACP,

BALLISTICS: Science of the characteristics of projectiles in motion. *Interior ballistics* cover the time between the start of primer ignition and the bullet's exit from the barrel. Exterior ballistics encompass the bullet's flight from the barrel exit to the point of impact with a target. Terminal ballistics is the study of occurrences after the projectile impacts the target.

BULLET: (aka PROJECTILE) The missile only. The part of the cartridge that separates from the case and exits from the muzzle to impact on the target.

BULLET CONFIGURATIONS: Some common abbreviations include HP—hollow point; SJHP—semi-jacketed hollow point; RN—

130

round nose; FMJ—full metal jacket; JHP—jacketed hollow point; WC—wadcutter; SWC—semi-wadcutter; FN—flat nose; JSP—jacketed soft point.

CALIBER: Refers to a weapon's (land or grove) or bullet's diametrical size—usually expressed in thousands of an inch or metric equivalent. Sometimes includes other information to indicate powder charge (e.g., .38-40) or year of adoption (e.g., .30-06) or special designation (e.g., .38 Special).

CARTRIDGE: A complete unit of ammunition which is comprised of the cartridge case, primer, propellant, and bullet—a loaded round of ammunition.

CLIP: Device to hold cartridges for insertion into a cylinder or magazine See "MAGAZINE."

CYLINDER: Revolving mechanical part of a revolver which houses multiple chambers.

GREAT BODILY HARM: (aka Serious Physical Harm) means ANY of the following;

a) Any mental illness or condition of such gravity as would normally require hospitalization or prolonged psychiatric treatment;

b) Any physical harm which carries a substantial risk of death;

c) Any physical harm which involves some permanent incapacity, whether partial or total, or which involves some temporary, substantial incapacity;

d) Any physical harm which involves some permanent disfigurement, or which involves some temporary serious disfigurement;

e) Any physical harm which involves acute pain of such duration as to result in substantial suffering, or which involves any degree of prolonged or intractable pain.

LE: Law Enforcement.

LEO: Law Enforcement Officer.

LETHAL FORCE: Any force used for the purpose of causing Great Bodily Harm or death or force which the person knows or reasonably should know will create a strong probability that Great Bodily Harm or death will result.

FIREARM: Any weapon from which a projectile(s) is discharged by means of a rapidly burning or exploding propellant.

GRIP: See "STOCK."

HANDGUN: A firearm (revolver or pistol) designed to be operated with one hand and without the aid of extraneous support.

INSTINCT COMBAT SHOOTING: The act of operating a HANDGUN by focusing on the target and instinctively coordinating the hand and mind to cause the HANDGUN to discharge at a time and point that ensures interception of the target with the projectile. Method developed by and term coined by Police Firearms Instructor, CHUCK KLEIN.

INSTINCT SHOOTING: (a.k.a. point shooting) Focusing on the target and instinctively shooting any long gun without the aid or use of mechanical sights.

MAGAZINE: Removable part of a pistol which holds cartridges in such a way as to facilitate the chambering of these cartridges during operational functioning.

MUZZLE: The end of the barrel from which the discharged projectile exits.

NCIC: National Crime Information Center. A computer clearing house for posting wanted persons and stolen vehicles and firearms.

PISTOL: aka: Autoloader, auto pistol, semi-auto. Any self-loading handgun that is not a revolver. Usually incorporates the chamber as part of the barrel. Requires the manually pulling and releasing of the trigger for each shot. After each shot the recoil "automatically" pushes the slide rearward, ejecting the spent cartridge, cocking the hammer/firing pin and, on the return forward movement, striping a fresh cartridge from the magazine for insertion into the chamber. This action/reaction does not disengage the sear, which can only be done by releasing the trigger.

Fully automatic weapons such as machine guns or submachine guns will continue to fire until either the trigger is released or the magazine is emptied.

POINT BLANK RANGE: Distance so close that appreciable projectile deviation of line of flight is negligible.

POINT SHOOTING: See "INSTINCT SHOOTING."

132

PRIMER: Detonating mixture structured to ignite propellant when struck a sharp blow as from a firing pin.

REVOLVER: A multi-shot handgun, utilizing a revolving cylinder as a cartridge receptacle.

SEMI-AUTOMATIC: See "PISTOL."

SNUB-NOSE: Slang term usually meaning any short barreled revolver.

STOCK: Portion of the weapon which is held in or by the hand.

TACHYINTERVAL: Time-deception phenomena. A condition that occurs when, under extreme stress, events appear to happen in slow motion. Events, of course, do not slow down but, the mind seems to speed up due to the brains ability to digest information much faster than the body can act/react. Many people who have been in serious auto accidents or gun fights have experienced this condition.

TUNNEL-VISION: Peripheral-optic distortion/dysfunction phenomena. A condition that can occur during high concentration where one sees (is aware of) only the center of his/hers attention. This temporary occurrence renders the victim oblivious to surrounding events.

Police Ethics

ETHICS: Trust is all bound up in ethics. Not just the trust between you and your fellow officer, but the trust between a police officer and the public. In the old days, cops were low pay, marginally educated and generally selected for brawn not brain. Back then, it was considered part of the compensation package to get half price (or free in some cases) meals, coffee and an occasional apple. The restaurants/stores figured that by allowing this small gratuity the beneficiary's presence would be a deterrent to the bad guys and thus a fair trade-off. All too often it didn't work out so well. Human nature, being what it is, found cops taking advantage by treating family and friends which, in turn encouraged food and retail shop owners to believe they could "stretch" certain laws.

Ethics is described as a system of moral standards or values where "moral" is defined as recognizing the distinction between right and wrong and acting thereupon. In other words, you are an ethical person if you can tell the difference between and right and wrong — and conduct yourself accordingly. The problems arise with the definitions of right and wrong. Ethics do not change — only the definitions of right and wrong and the punishment of wrong or possibility thereof, change. In decades past, one could use racial epithets with impunity. It was wrong then as it is now, only now a variety of real punishments is certain. Yesteryear it was okay to give unlisted phone numbers and license plate information to the restaurant owner who gave free meals. But not today. Violating one's right to privacy had become so blatant that protective laws were passed. This is not to say that unless there is a law against something, it's ethical. Ethical right and wrong is separate and distinct from legal right and wrong. It might have been technically legal to give someone's unlisted phone number away, but was ethically wrong to violate this person's right to privacy.

Someday, if you're lucky, you're not going to be a police officer anymore. And when you're not, you'll quickly be out of the loop — no longer a part of the "you ain't sh_t" crowd. Oh sure, you like to think that by flashing your retired tin, the younger uniformed officer will honor you with full privileges. But suppose they don't. Suppose your grandchild is in a situation that you feel violates his or her constitutional rights and the rookie can only quote chapter and verse of the penal code? Suppose his ethics are not up to your standard and he thinks it's okay to enhance his arrest stats with questionable collars?

PUBLIC SERVICE ATTITUDE: Though some police officers might have the highest of morals and greatest of training, it is attitude (disposition, mind-set) that determines success. Negative attitudes (they don't pay me enough to _____) can break any and all officers as well as their departments. On the other hand, officers with positive attitudes tend to think highly of their job—"you mean they pay me to do this?"

For those in any type of service business, public or private, the goal of a positive attitude is indispensable to success. It doesn't take a psychiatrist to understand that those with a positive attitude are happier, healthier and more productive. Attitude is the sum of morale and knowledge.

ATTITUDE = MORALE + KNOWLEDGE:

MORALE: Positive Morale is the desire to exhibit courage, discipline, confidence, an optimistic outlook and a willingness to help others. Negative Morale is a deterrent that stifles courage, discipline, confidence, optimism and the desire to aid others.

KNOWLEDGE: Positive knowledge is the acquired experience that one must conform to a code of moral ethics while providing for oneself and one's family. Negative knowledge is the acquired experience that *not getting caught* is the guiding rule of ethics.

To succeed in the service industry, it is necessary to have a Positive Attitude and the only route to this goal is through positive morale and positive knowledge. If either morale or knowledge is negative, the result will be negative.

(+) MORALE plus (+) KNOWLEDGE = (+) ATTITUDE

(-) MORALE plus (+) KNOWLEDGE = (-) ATTITUDE

(+) MORALE plus (-) KNOWLEDGE = (-) ATTITUDE

(-) MORALE plus (-) KNOWLEDGE = (-) ATTITUDE

Police officers are a special breed. Our secular one-size-fits-all government cannot just take anyone and make him a LEO by subjecting him to training, no matter how extensive or sensitive the training is.

A cop is one who first and foremost wants to be a law-enforcement officer. He must honestly like being in a position to help people while at the same time having a strong sense of right and wrong, must exhibit ethical leadership and must have a healthy fear of being labeled a coward.

Beyond all that, this cop-mentality person must have a sixth sense, a gut feeling or the natural ability to read other's body language—vibes. LEOS, far more often than noted in the media, face down dangerous men and men bent on committing suicide-by-police without resorting to lethal force. Without this ability to read-the-perp, officers would be shooting down everyone who posed a threat, real or not. Nobody, and no system, is perfect and sometimes by-the-book cops slip through the cracks. These are the officers who end up using questionable degrees of force in controlling a person or situation. Too often the command, in fear of law suits or even just negative publicity, bends over backward to exonerate their sometimes illegal acts.

At the attractive pay now provided for our entry-level police officers, most could not find comparable-paying jobs in the private sector. There is a waiting list for admission to most police academies and at least 100 applicants for every job opening. Supply far exceeds availability of these coveted lifetime positions with generous pensions. Many LEOs go on to secure—in some cases, multiple—college degrees. Though college education is fine for police officers and also makes them very employable on the civilian job market, you can't teach the basic ingredients of a successful police officer: a sixth sense, common sense and bravery.

Individual police (peace) officers—public servants—should have as their daily goal: keeping the peace. A tally of arrests made, citations issued and commendations awarded, i.e., promotion enhancements, is not conducive to public service. A public servant, and that's what a police officer is, should strive to serve the public by protecting their rights and "keeping the peace." Trying to see who can make the most arrests or write the greatest number of tickets, in

136

other words promoting oneself, is not what being a public servant is all about.

We have gotten away from the original intent of hiring police officers—to keep the peace and to provide this country's first line of defense. They were to have been our protectors not only from physical violence, but from orders and actions that are clearly unconstitutional. Today, LEOS, especially on the federal level, have all too often been reduced to being arms of the judicial, executive, and legislative branches of government, which at times use the police for the furtherance of their respective and self-enhancing purposes.

Everybody makes mistakes, however, when police officers make them it usually means someone is physically, emotionally, financially and/or mentally hurt. You knew this, or should have known it, when you signed up for the force. You should also have known that certain mistakes, unlike in many non-police jobs, are career ending. Not only that, but career ending errors are more likely to happen by the very nature of police work. That's why police officers are deployed to long and intense training classes and programs. Very few other professions pay while their members learn, much less encourage enrollment in paid in-service training agendas including such valuable perks as college degrees.

Being hired on at a modern police agency is not a career choice guarantee. Because there are so many opportunities to commit unintentional, career ending screw-ups, police officers should always have an eye on the future. Holding a job that involves snap life or death decisions, high speed driving, possible false arrest charges and surviving departmental politics is a formula for vocation ending ulcers. Career oriented men and women who aspire to public service work should consider their police experience as a possible step to other careers. Long term goals might include becoming a police academy (or other type of) instructor, prosecuting attorney, politician and/or security specialist.

THE FOURTH BRANCH OF GOVERNMENT: While the Constitution specifies only three branches of government—Legislative, Judicial, and Executive—there is a de facto fourth branch. This unofficial, though real entity, is the Enforcement branch. Officially, the Executive Branch is charged with enforcing the laws as explained in the Constitution: Article 2, Section 3 states: "...he [the

President] shall take care that the laws be faithfully executed...." This branch not only is expected to protect "we the people" from ourselves but is required to protect us against constitutional violations — infringements of the other branches.

Evolution, being what it is, has nevertheless produced an Executive branch that spends more time issuing — and enforcing — its own executive orders than it does guarding against constitutional violations. These executive orders have the same weight as legislative laws inasmuch as these orders are enforced by itself — the Executive Branch. This is counter to a U.S. Supreme Court decision that found, "He [the President] is controlled by the law and has his appropriate sphere of duty, which is to execute, not make, the laws." [in Ex parte Milligan (1866) 4 Wall. 2 (118)]. Evolution has also created an Executive Branch that, when it does enforce laws passed by the legislature,, does so selectively and sometimes redefines (puts its "spin" on) the intent and meaning of the law to suit its own purpose.

On the federal level the Executive branch is charged with the duty to see that the orders of the Legislative and Judicial branches are carried out. In county governments that operate by elected commissioners, these commissioners constitute both the legislative and executive branches. A like situation is found in cities operating under a weak mayor/city manager form of government where the city council calls the shots. When the legislative branch on any level also has the power to enforce its own laws, there is at least a conflict of interest and certainly a unique opportunity for abuse.

It's a given that our country's First Professional Line of Defense against crime has always been the local police, Sheriff's Office and other resident constables and marshals. No one has ever questioned that the men and women in blue would fail to be there, small arms in hand, to confront, defend the people and, if necessary, put their lives on the line against an invasion of a foreign power. The question is, where does their allegiance stand when the threat comes from within. Whose side do the local police take when the Executive branch issues an order and orders you to enforce it — especially if this Executive branch "law" is prime facie unconstitutional? To enforce the law might be an act of misfeasance on your part while to refuse to comply with the Executive branch demand could cause, a best, your firing.

This is not a rhetorical question. The answer for a police officer—a member of the de facto Fourth Branch of Government—is found in his sworn oath, first to the Constitution of the United States; second to the state constitution; then to statutes and ordinances. Constitutional provisions are for the protection of the individual; statutes and other laws are for the protection of the government and its interests.

Knowing How To Enforce Laws Against Prohibited Activity
Is A Necessity Of Any Police Job, But Knowing Whom The Law Protects
Is Equally Important And Far More Difficult.

Police Reasoning

Not too long ago a young man was forcibly placed under arrest by a police officer on a major city's downtown street corner. This altercation was videotaped and shown on local and national TV. The incident was inflammatory because it appeared to be a prima facie case of police brutality. Perhaps it's time to look at why police officers react with such compelling force.

The undisputed facts in the case are:

a) The arrestee was placed under arrest;

b) The arrestee resisted this arrest;

c) The arresting officer, in trying to affect this arrest, ended up in a physical scuffle during which he called for assistance;

d) One or more of the responding officers kicked, punched and chemically maced the arrestee;

e) The arresting officer was seriously injured.

There are three reasons why police find it necessary to use force to subdue and contain a subject who resists arrest.

1) Prudence;

2) Bravery;

3) Future Protection.

The first is the official justification and policy of most all police agencies, their governmental employers and society in general. The other two are unofficial and underlying purposes held to and propagated by the fraternity of the police.

1) PRUDENCE: The party line is that use of superior force is needed and prudent for the safety of all. It is imperative that any physical resistance to arrest be brought under control as quickly and efficiently as possible. The age old and obvious reasons are to protect the officer, prevent the escape of the arrestee and to remove the wrong doer from the scene for his protection as well as society's.

It is well established in the courts that police officers may use one step more than what is being used against them in altercations with attacking and resisting suspects. In other words, if a criminal fights with his fists, the officer is justified, in using the next level of weapons at his disposal (feet, baton and/or Chemical Mace). If the offender is armed with a weapon that can cause death or great bodily harm (even a brick) the officer is permitted to use the next level—lethal force.

2) BRAVERY: All officers must prove to their fellow officers that they are not cowards—that they can be counted on to help a fellow officer under any and all circumstances. Cops must never hesitate to jump into a melee lest they be branded a coward. To a police officer there are few things worse than death. Being labeled craven is one such fate. We all, for the most part, are thankful for this machismo as this is what allows and forces them to risk their lives to save ours. Besides, if you were a cop would you want a partner that was afraid to jump into a fisticuff to save your backside? In the above cited case the arresting officer appears not to have used excessive force, but the responding officers, most assuredly, did not. The official report from the police Internal Investigations Section chastised one officer for failing to assist the arresting officer.

3) FUTURE PROTECTION: This is often the only thing that protects an officer—the knowledge that if you assault a cop you're going to have your attitude adjusted. There used to be a time when, if a person assaulted a law enforcement officer, this assailant was going to the hospital before he went to jail—and he did go to jail. However, the courts have become lenient on those who have assaulted LEOSs. This dangerous judicial precedent has, mostly out of shear frustration, caused police, in some cases, to unwisely expand this doctrine of "street justice" to include persons they think need a beating, a la Rodney King. The effect of which has been, justifiably in the eyes of some criminals, an increase in attacks on those charged with providing for our safety. In other words, criminal types used to trust and respect street officers, knowing that if they didn't resist or assault an officer they would be treated fairly.

Today, with cameras capturing most every police action, a person of criminal intentions might feel that if he's caught he is only going to receive, at worst, a sore wrist from the handcuffs so why should he

141

submit peaceably? Besides, added assault charges usually fail to yield real punishment...and therein lies the problem. Until "real" punishment is inflicted upon criminals the danger to society—and especially LEOs—will only increase.

Never steal less than you can successfully hide

and comfortably retire on – after you get out of prison.

The Seventh Sense

PREFACE: Are police officers any different from anyone else? Can any Jane or Joe be an LEO? Oh sure, we hear that all cops have a 6th sense—the real or perceived ability to tell when something's not right or when the interviewee is lying. The 6th sense does exist and is an important asset—but not the only "sense" necessary. Some cops can remember names and faces while others never forget a license plate number or vehicle description. Different attributes are necessary to be able to relate to many peoples and conditions. For example, Mutt and Jeff teams of bad cop—good cop are notorious for working a confession out of a perp.

The real difference, the trait that sets the Jane and Joes from the LEOs apart is the 7th sense—the inborn and intrinsic sense of right and wrong. Like its cousin, the 6th, it can't be learned. You either are of high moral and ethical nature or you're not. Unfortunately, this isn't something that can be determined exclusively by examination. Background checks, written and verbal tests coupled with personal interviews help predict whether the shield will tarnish or shine, but it's usually the agency head that must use his or her 6th sense to determine who has the 7th sense and will make an honest cop.

The threat of terrorist strikes and the new Homeland Security demands are putting increasing pressure on America's first line of defense. Not only do they now have to continue to deal with the common criminal, handle domestic disputes, traffic accidents and other "regular" duties, but the new level of possible massive attacks is heavy on the mind. However, and this is a big however, the beat cops must not—regardless of the pressure—forsake their duty to adhere to their sworn obligations. No matter what the provocation or public opinion American police officers must remain true to their primary responsibility to protect the citizenry—including even the most reprehensible of perps. Part of this sworn duty includes maintaining the highest level of ethical behavior and the commitment to put one's self in harm's way if called upon to do so.

USE OF DEADLY FORCE: Police officers carry firearms and less-than-lethal tools for two reasons: 1) For purposes of self-protection and, 2) To protect society. Ergo, since society allows police to carry these defensive instruments to facilitate the requisites of the job, it goes without saying that officers are expected to place themselves between danger and members of society when so required.

With the best of intentions some police trainers, in an attempt to save officer's lives, have been teaching a mind-set that equates to protect yourself first. Their mantra is—don't take chances—suicide is not in your job description.

A MATTER OF SEMANTICS: Perhaps one of the problems is the definitions of words or phrases. Some have interpreted the notion that "police officers should never act in a cowardly manner" to mean cops must sacrifice their lives for the sake of not being labeled chicken. Nothing could be further from the truth. There is a difference between sacrifice/suicide (purposely giving up one's life to save another) and duty (complying with a moral or legal obligation related to one's occupation or position). An officer's life is of no greater or lesser value than that of any other citizen. However, because of their unique duty they have agreed, by a sworn oath, to place their life—but not to the point of surrender—at risk. In a timely manner and short of sacrifice, a police officer is duty bound to place his/her life in jeopardy to protect members of society.

No one is saying or expecting an LEO to sacrifice his life, but each officer has the duty to protect the public. The very nature of the police occupation is centered on dangerous activity. If the work involved only taking reports, directing traffic and calling in a SWAT team when danger appears, the job could be done by social workers or clerks.

Being afraid is okay. Perhaps the best definition of overcoming fear to perform one's duty is found in the plot and theme song to the early 1950s movie, High Noon. Here, on his wedding day, the town Marshall (played by Gary Cooper) learns a man he sent to prison is returning on the noon train. The officer is torn between leaving on his honeymoon, as planned, or staying to face the perp. His bride (played by Grace Kelly) begs her groom to give it up. She leaves without him as Tex Ritter wails the theme song—the watchwords of police officers of all time:

"I do not know what fate awaits me,

I only know I must be brave,

for I must face the man who hates me,

or lie a coward,

a craven coward,

or lie a coward in my grave."

The bride returns just in time to blow one of the gang members away to save her man, who then out-draws the ex-con. In real life, sometimes the perp wins and sometimes the spouse doesn't come back. But to a sworn police officer either one of those conditions is preferable than being labeled a craven coward.

TYPES OF OFFICERS:

When it comes to dealing with dangerous situations, there tends to be three types of police officers: Fool, Coward and Hero. Fortunately, the hero type overwhelmingly represents the American police ranks. In a small, dangerous minority are the others.

THE FOOL: The Fool is one who temps fate by ignoring training procedures and expertise such as not wearing body armor or, for example, not calling for backup when stopping an armed robbery suspect. While apprehension of criminals is an end in and of itself, per se, only a fool attempts a collar at the expense of officer safety. However, that is not to say that anything short of sacrificing one's life in order to protect/save the life of one you are sworn to serve and protect is not part of the job. This is also not to say that bravado is the same as bravery. There is a difference.

COWARD TYPES: The Coward is one who fails to institute a serious attempt to protect society due to fear or a mindset that equates personal safety over the moral and legal obligation to protect others. Any officer failing to place him/herself in harm's way because of such an attitude is guilty of non-feasance at best or malfeasance at worst. A coward is also one who flat-out ignores suspicious activity in order to avoid dangerous confrontations. One of the duties of a Field Training Officer is to weed cowards out of the ranks. Of course, if the FTO is a coward ....

In response to an article on this subject, one police chief wrote: "Most officers are just like everyone else. Their main goal is to get home safely at the end of each shift." Wrong! Police officers are not "just like everyone else" they are the only ones with a sworn duty to protect "everyone else". "[T]o get home safely" might be a great concept for sanitation workers or lawyers, but contrary to what this public official espouses, the "main goal" of a police officer should be to serve and protect the public.

There is no mandate that any officer should be expected to sacrifice his or her life, but it does mean there are certain inherent risks that come with the badge and take precedent over the desire "to get home safely". U.S. Secret Service agents' main goal, as we have seen in notorious film clips, is to protect the protectee even if it means using their own bodies as a shield. Should they not do so to insure that they can go home at night? Where would we be, if for the same self-serving reasons, American soldiers had forsaken their duty to engage the enemy during past wars? To put it on a more personal level; suppose you're caught in a firefight—what main goal would you expect of your backup?

A police officer who doesn't believe that cowardice

is a fate worse than death, is in the wrong business.

The standard that one may use deadly force if one believes he is about to be the victim of a lethal force assault is well established in law. This doctrine of self defense applies to cops as well as civilians. Of course, this belief must be based upon something other than pure fear, such as the perp has a gun or a knife. Even then, being afraid the perp might use the weapon is not sufficient. There must be some overt action or non-action such as refusing to drop the weapon that can only be interpreted as life threatening and immediate. Unleashing a hail of hollow-points without those qualifying conditions is the mark of a coward.

HERO TYPES: Ordinarily, in the presence of danger, most citizens become excited as their blood pressure rises and fear registers. Contrarily, the heroic type, when facing confrontational perils, tends to experience a stabilization of vital signs and a calming effect as discipline, training and faith in themselves takes hold.

The Hero is one who realizes an officer's primary duty is to protect and serve the public. This American idol firmly believes he would rather be a dead hero than a live coward and would shun another officer who acted in a cowardly manner. However, this officer is not the fool inasmuch as he/she learns and practices safe tactics and procedures. American policing is the standard of the world, the epitome to which all others aspire. We didn't get that way by unilaterally changing the rules of engagement for egocentric rationality.

Except to those who like to make excuses, there is not a fine line between when prudence becomes cowardice or bravado. An officer advised of a man brandishing a gun in a school should request immediate backup and then, without hesitation, proceed into the building. His goal is to find and end the risk. Anything less is cowardice, non-feasance and against all of what America stands for. On the other hand, if the officer is advised of a bank robbery in-progress, rushing in might be a foolish move. But, not placing oneself in a position to engage the suspects upon their exiting the bank— even before backup arrives—would certainly be deemed cowardice. Likewise, if a crazed gunman opens fire in a shopping mall, public square or school duty demands drawing fire away from the unarmed civilians

The prudent-heroic persona should be the ultimate goal for officers. One can teach prudence to the heroic type person, but not the reverse. Heroism, like cowardice, is intrinsic and not readily learned—a 7th sense. Self-preservation is inherent in all humans, though, unlike cowardice, it is not over-riding to the heroic type. Teaching self-preservation as a primary function goes against the grain of the heroic type.

THE MAIN ISSUE—TRAINING: Training, be it class room or on the street, begets predictable behavioral results. All officers must prove to their fellow officers that they are not cowards—that they can be counted on to help a fellow officer under any and all circumstances. Civilians, for the most part, are thankful for this machismo as this is what compels cops to risk their lives to protect civilians.

However, there have been far too many well-documented (some on video tape) Rodney King type beatings. These modern day "blanket parties" are acts of cowardice—actions of police officers who are in reality, cowards, trying to prove their manhood by acting aggressively when there is no chance they will be hurt. Beating the

147

stuffing out of some murderous scumbag might be the only punishment the perp will receive, but it is not, under any standard, an act of bravery. Besides, as justifiable as it might seem, police are only empowered to apprehend criminals — not inflict retribution.

MENTAL BRAVERY: This text book ethics stuff is all well and good, but what happens in real life when a sworn police officer witnesses a fellow officer violate the law. Does he/she arrest the offender? Tattle-tale to the supervisor? Adhere to the "code of blue silence?" Used to be the answer was: "It depends on the infraction." If the violation wasn't something major, like a class A felony, and the public hadn't witnessed it, then it was kept quiet or it was left up to a ranking officer. Problem was, just where do you draw the line? What infractions are reportable? Petty theft? Perjury? DUI? Violating a citizen's civil rights because he spit on you? Turning your back, averting your eyes, not volunteering information are all acts of cowardice.

When it comes to police deviance there are two factors that determine the level of compliance: Peer pressure and trust. Peer pressure dates to grade school and is reprehensible when practiced by trained, sworn police officers who, by their very job description, are individuals. A person who is so mentally weak — cowardly — that he is compelled to go along with the illegal activities of others of his/her group, is not qualified to wear a badge. It's one thing for a bunch of civilians to sneak off the work detail for a beer and an entirely different matter for professional — armed — officers to do the same.

No lying, no cheating, no stealing. No exceptions, no excuses.

Trust in the form of reliance is sometimes difficult to differentiate from trust in the sense of confidentiality. Confidentiality belongs to the "you ain't dirt if you're not a cop," "good ol' boy," "blue code of silence" schools. Not conducive to professional stature, this type of trust falsely conveys a belief that if an officer "covers-up" or keeps quiet about improper activity he can be trusted as backup when things get really scary. Any professional who stakes his or her reputation on keeping their mouth shut when they are under a sworn oath not to, is not worthy of the honor of being one of "America's finest." Second, any officer staking his/her back-up support on a partner who supports the confidentiality mind-set may wind up dead.

Trust in the form of reliance, on the other hand, is of extreme importance to the functioning of any police agency. Cops, being individualists, sometimes need unquestioning reliance from their fellow officers. When an officer's back is exposed during a lethal force or other dangerous situation, this officer needs to know that his/her partner—backup—can be counted on to defend him/her to the death. Being the kind of officer who has mastered the "code of blue silence" is not any indication of how that officer will respond under conditions of extreme stress. The only sure method of determining trust by reliance is the oldest application of trial by fire. On the other hand, an officer who is known for his/her unquestioning honesty would be the type of officer who couldn't honestly not take risks to cover your backside.

> *The American Police Officer: A balance of benevolence*
>
> *to the community with enforcement of the law, in concert*
>
> *to the Constitution, all the while adhering to*
>
> *highest moral and ethical ideals.*

A few years ago when cops were underpaid, undereducated and selected more for brawn than mental capacity, a certain amount of "discretion" was expected. Not today. Patrol officers routinely earn a decent living wage, have excellent health care packages and retirement plans that customarily exceeds the general population. The substantial amount of on-going training, education and certification police officers receive has elevated their status from that of tradesmen to the level of professional. All professionals have a code of ethics. A doctor will not treat the patient of another physician unless referred and an attorney won't have direct contact with clients of other lawyers. The cop's stock-in-trade is honesty and integrity—he/she must, above all, not compromise these.

Police officers are in the business of honesty. This is their stock-in-trade, forte', signature, persona, identification and what differentiates them from other professions. When one police officer violates this trust, this code of honesty, all are tarnished. Adherence to or practice of any form of "blue code of silence" is counter to the code of honesty that is part of each officer's sworn duty—his/her existence for being.

The trust each officer places in their fellow officer must be based on the proposition that truth, not cover-up or silence, will save his/her career. For a police officer or anyone with sworn obligations, justice is more important than friendship.

An LEO who acts as a coward by adhering to the code of blue silence to cover-up the illegal, unethical and/or immoral behavior of a fellow officer must be removed from office.

SUMMARY: The terroristic assaults of 9-11-01 evidenced true acts of heroism. In a feature article in Smithsonian Magazine (September 2002), two naval officers, "... turned against the flow of people fleeing to safety and headed toward what appeared to be the point of greatest destruction." At risk to their own personal safety and though severely injured, these officers were responsible for saving lives. This is what America is all about—duty and honor in the face of death.

Police officers, who possess the 7th sense will never stray from the protect the public first standard and accept the reality that placing oneself in harm's way and sticking to the truth regardless of the consequences is part of the job. As the entire country prepares for the certainness of future terroristic attacks we must be secure in our persons and places that America's Finest will not ignore their heroic duties and always act in the most ethical of ways. If America's first line of defense fails this simple edict, America and the American police profession are lost.

Police Misconduct

O.J. Simpson has been in the news again due to it being another anniversary of his acquittal of criminal charges for the murder of two innocent persons. Though he was found not guilty of the crimes against his former wife and a delivery person, he WAS found responsible, in civil court, for slashing these two to death. Note that the significant event hyped is his acquittal—not the heinous crime itself. Ain't that America.

The media and the Jesse Jackson's of the world have always insisted that the police doctored the evidence because The Juice was black and his victims were white. There is little doubt that the cops did taint the crime scene, but the real reason why they did it—has nothing to do with race.

My experience in the police world, coupled with observations and correspondence with police officers, is that the LADP was trying to avoid the embarrassment of a not guilty verdict. They were worried—even though they had a good case against him—that he would obtain powerful attorneys who might be successful in having some of the evidence tossed out. Therefore, they desired to make this good case better by "enhancing" the evidence. Also, knowing that their main suspect was a high profile figure and the trial would draw a lot of media attention, a loss in court would not only cause the police to lose face, but they might be suspected of racial motives in charging O.J. in the first place. These weren't beat cops. These were detectives and ranking officers that conspired to make sure the guilty person was punished. This, of course, is not the function of the LAPD or any other police agency. The larger the agency and the higher up the police hierarchy you go, the less demographics becomes a factor and the more politics, covering your backside and saving face become the driving force for criminal investigations.

Though there will always be crooked cops, there are far too many American police departments that condone and/or practice unethical tactics on a regular basis. One example: Statistics kept by police agencies sometimes are "adjusted" to yield targeted results. Suppose

151

the cops want to demonstrate that their policing efforts are reducing robberies. One way is to change the reports (or method of reporting) of a Robbery to the crime of Theft (when no shots were fired). Or, of course, if the police wish to show that robbery is increasing, they do the reverse and then whine to the politicians that they now need more officers/guns/radios/whatever to combat the "statistically proven" increase in crime.

SOLUTION: Require police officers, including ranking officers, to submit to periodic polygraph tests — conducted by a non-police affiliated agency and under the control of elected officials.

Stay Ethical

The term "Be Safe" or "Stay Safe," as a closing comment or sign-off, has become ubiquitous. Officers use it among themselves, trainers finalize sessions with it and police columnists end their writings with this same line. Not that this is wrong or not good. To the contrary, looking out for the well being of fellow officers is one of the requisites of being a police officer.

Wishing one to be safe can also apply to other professions as well. We surely hope all firefighters, truck drivers and pilots conduct their details in a safe manner. There are very few livelihoods where "safe" is secondary to the profession. Law enforcement is one of those where ethical being trumps safety. Police officers, by their every nature, are charged with not only putting themselves in harms way for the physical protection of society, but must be the stalwart, the guiding beacon of honesty and integrity—the last line of defense against violence as well and moral decay. Should an officer lose his or her moral compass, all who witness—or learn—of this lack of ethics, will begin the breakdown of society.

We have often heard the line, when relating to American police officers, "our country's last line of defense." This has usually been in reference to physically standing guard against enemies' intent on committing violence. A truer meaning has not been tendered. But, seldom espoused is the underlying definition of the American police officer—he and she stand for the epitome of civilized society. America's very existence depends upon the rigid blue line never wavering in the face of outrageous criminal conduct, civil riots or political trickery run amok.

However, when it comes to wishing the best for our guardians of the future, there might be a better term we can use: "Stay Ethical." Here, the speaker is not only acknowledging the audience is already ethical, but is encouraging/reminding them to continue to place ethics in the forefront of their world. USA police officers are the envy of the world and it's not because they are safe. It is due to their professionalism, a qualification that generates, exudes and is based on a high ethical and moral standard.

It is surely every LEO's daily practice to live safely, to protect and serve, to stand beside and back-up fellow officers and … to always do the right thing. Safety is mostly a matter of practicing rules of common sense. There is little temptation to violate safety procedures. Not so, ethical matters.

> *Temptations abound to subvert those of power*
>
> *to commit lapses in discretion for the gains of favor.*

Law enforcement trainers find it most difficult to teach common sense, likewise ethical behavior. All LEO instructors can and should set the moral example while always being on the lookout for those badge wearers who might be subject to temptations.

Next time you sign-off with a fellow officer, consider acknowledging the exclusivity that this LEO is an honest, trustworthy person and that you wish him/her to remain so—just say Stay Ethical.

Extrapolation & Projectors:

History, in and of itself, is just memories.
Memories, coupled with extrapolation,
are the lessons of history.

If there is one word that should be understood and practiced by anyone studying ethics and morals it is *extrapolation*. To extrapolate is to make estimates or inferences in order to arrive at a result or scenario by hypothesizing from known facts or observations. Being able to project intentions, ours and those of others, is prerequisite to distinguishing between right and wrong. Having the ability to predict what is in store from published words or actions yields the advantage of being able to decide, in a timely manner, whether the statements or actions lead toward ethical goals. This may be too abstract to have much meaning at first reading, but the illustrations given below should provide some substance to focus on.

Most people see what is projected for them, be it a visual, verbal or written scene. Some can see what the projector, the one presenting the scene, sees—his view or his motive, ulterior or otherwise. Rare is the one who can read the intent of the projector's projector. What is meant by the Projector and Projector's Projector will become clear from what follows.

Let's say the instructor (Projector) enters a classroom and says to the students: "Today we are going to learn self-defense." Most will interpret this to mean they are going to learn how to fight. For those who can read the Projector's purpose, he is saying, "I will teach survival skills of which physical fighting might only be a part thereof. For those few reaching the next level it will be apparent that the Projector's Projector (the one who taught the Projector) might have different goals from those of the Projector, such as:

a) The students will be taught to believe they have all of the necessary skills to pragmatically defend themselves, whereas in reality they have only the skills that I (the Projector's Projector) want them to have. Thus what skills that were not taught to them are their weaknesses — known only to me (the Projector's Projector).

b) The students trained in self-defense are now better able to protect themselves thus act as a deterrent to the criminal element, which in turn reduces the need for additional police.

From this relatively simple, localized, not altogether nefarious scenario one can extrapolate to more grandiose schemes that can have far reaching consequences for our country. Substitute "Government Spokesperson" for Projector and "Powers that form Political Correctness" for the Projector's Projector. Further, replace "self-defense" with "solutions to societies social problems" and a glimmer of how things work on this scale may be visible. Just who the Projector's Projector is varies through time and conditions. Anyone who uses their power to change conditions by tendering agendas that are false and misleading is a Projector's Projector.

At the highest level, the Projector's Projector can be the President of the United States — or — the political party behind him. Not all presidents, however, have indulged in the use of power to such ends and those who have, did not do so during all of their tenure. FDR, while he was a master of political manipulation, was open about what he wanted to achieve through his programs. Everybody knew where he stood on these undertakings. JFK might have used power for undisclosed purposes if he'd live longer. Nixon, Ford and Carter didn't, and Reagan, maybe for very short periods did.

Any opportunity George H. W. Bush had to do so was lost with his reversals of "no new taxes" and gun control. Clinton commanded an astounding ability to utilize power. He demonstrated his latent intents (Projector's Projector) with such stratagem as telling the Israelis that he will always support them while Hillary talked of a Palestinian State.

George W. Bush was very up-front though it appeared (and still does to some) that the reason for invading Iraq was to eliminate the "weapons of mass destruction." The real reason for the war IN Iraq was stated only a few times — publically. But it was stated clearly. GW said: "We can fight them over there, or we can fight them over here." His clear intention was to keep the terrorists so busy fighting on their soil, that they wouldn't have the resources to continue

156

conducting assaults on Americans in America (this was in response to the 9/11 plane attacks on the World Towers in NYC). It is difficult to argue with success — there have been no terrorist attacks in the USA since.

As of this writing, it seems obvious that Barak Obama will use his executive powers to usurp congressional resistance to his programs, such as gun controls. He gave no hint of this underlying conspiracy while running for his first or second term. If he will abuse his executive powers for this reason, we can extrapolate that he will not hesitate to force additional personal goals upon Americans. We can take comfort that many LE agencies and individual officers (our 4th Branch of Government) have gone on record to say they will not act as his enforcement arm for any unconstitutional edicts.

Probably the clearest historical example of a projected view of government power, as presented by the Projector on the one hand and orchestrated by the Projector's Projector on the other is afforded by the interpretation some persons give to Lyndon Johnson's Great Society programs of the 1960s. The Johnson era saw an awakening of discontent with racial disparity. Race riots threatened the heretofore basic way of American life. To counter this threat, the Projector (voice of the government) introduced massive welfare programs, including payment of child support to fatherless families. During this period it also became painfully clear that blacks and most other minorities, in addition to being financially disadvantaged, had a lower educational level than members of white society. Therefore, the Projector (indirectly on the federal level and directly on the local level) lowered educational standards to increase the number of black high school graduates. It wasn't difficult to read the Projector's message: We will spend money and make cultural sacrifices to keep blacks from burning our white cities and towns.

The quid-pro-quo arrangement even seemed to be working quite well for a while. The whites got security, the blacks got a, albeit, pseudo leg up and America became a better place for everybody. There is nothing wrong with such a quid pro quo as long as there weren't latent agendas or ulterior motives. But, according to this interpretation, behind the Great Society measures lay the hidden agenda of the Projector's Projector (the President) that reveals a not so benign aspect of all this:

a) Those receiving this gratuity, with constant platitudes from the Projector, will feel obligated to repay their benefactors by voting the Democrat ticket in future elections;

b) By throwing small amounts of money to fatherless families within this class of people, we will encourage the breakdown of their collective family structure, thus enslaving them to the government dole;

c) In a generation, the children of fatherless families will tend to become social misfits thus requiring greater government action to control them (imprisonment), thus keeping control of society with the whites;

d) Lowering the standards of education will produce a class of artificially educated citizens beholden to the Democratic party.

Again, it is difficult to argue with success. LBJ might have been the all-time greatest vote getter for the Democrats. He might not, however, had visions of 40+ years into future (today, 2013) where his latent agendas produced an America where whites are now a minority and uneducated black gangs are rampant. Gangs that are comprised of 1st and 2nd generation fatherless familes.

This patently cynical interpretation has been cited not as a necessarily factual description of government/presidential intent during the Johnson years, but as an illustration of the Projector/Projector's Projector relationship and how it works on a national scale. Only the reader can decide the truth for him/herself.

Taking a lesson in history—the Hungarian revolution of 1956—we can extrapolate to a future scenario. While it may seem somewhat improbable, it is perhaps not entirely implausible. Suppose the Projector, in the form of the official voice of the current administration in Washington, announces belief in a "New World Order." A world where the United Nations becomes a global peace keeper and has the only military force (guns) allowed. That would perhaps not be so hard for some persons to accept as presented to us by the Projector. There would be only one army; a detachment of world cops. If there is trouble anywhere the UN forces will be sent to control the situation. This, of course, will relieve us from having to risk American troops (other than those committed to UN use) as we have been doing since the end of World War Two. It should also lessen our defense spending inasmuch as the burden will be shared by other nations.

Continuing with the extrapolation, the Projector's Projector's vantage point allows for a slightly different picture. Trouble anywhere in the world includes hot spots right here in the USA. A few years ago an unofficial poll was taken by a lower echelon member of the U.S. military forces. The poll asked enlisted men and women if they were deployed to quell a stateside civil disturbance would they shoot American citizens if ordered to do so. Overwhelmingly they replied in the negative. In response to this eye-opening revelation, the Projector's Projector began looking for countermeasures, i.e., methods of retaining control, and found one.

In the New World Order if blacks, whites, Hispanics, Jews, Protestants, militias or whatever groups take to the streets to demonstrate or protest their treatment it won't be the National Guard or Federal troops that are called in to "restore order" … but rather UN troops who won't have any qualms about shooting Americans. This is a lesson learned from the Russians. In 1956, their satellite country, the once sovereign Hungary, staged a major revolution. Russian troops who had been living among the Hungarians were found to be reluctant to shooting civilians—the very people they had become friends with and were now their neighbors. The USSR, always with an ace up its sleeve, immediately brought in Mongols from the Central Asian Republics. These disaffected foreign troops had no qualms about following shoot-to-kill orders. An added benefit to this style of keeping control is that the decisions will be United Nations military and therefore no American politician can be blamed if things go wrong.

As a domestic police officer, you should understand that when the UN troops arrive at a trouble spot they won't be asking, "Where do you want us, Chief?" It will be more like, "We are relieving you and your men. Go home."

Repression As Repression Is Inconvenience
Repression As Hypocrisy Is Oppression.

On a level of more immediate relevance, consider the multiple shots theory where you are the Projector. With guns drawn, you and two other officers are facing a deranged man armed with a weapon. The man suddenly makes an overt move. The officer next to you opens fire. You and the third officer also shoot. The man falls dead with a total of 12 bullet wounds. The official line, the Projector's (your) view, is each officer felt threatened and fired to stop the perpetrator's unwarranted, unlawful and lethal assault.

The Projector's Projector's reasoning might be slightly different. You and the third officer fired to protect the first officer from the man's attack *and* from the possibility of law suits. If the first officer was the only one to shoot, then some sharp attorney can probably persuade a jury that if two other officers didn't shoot, they obviously didn't feel threatened. Therefore, the first officer might have acted in haste. Is this reflexive shooting right? Is it ethical? Is it legal? In today's litigious society, is it prudent? These are not easy questions nor are there simple "covers-all" answers. You're a human being with fears, hang-ups and fallacies, not a machine that never makes a mistake or decides matters clinically.

The first officer, in the preceding scenario, trusted that his fellow officers, i.e., you and the third officer, would back him up. And woe be an officer that fails to act courageously under fire. Cowardice, in any police department, is the only attribute that cannot be overlooked or condoned. But, does this trust extend to improper or illegal conduct?

Suppose the first officer, for whatever reason—bad hair day, quick tempered—fired before you saw the perp move? If you shot because of your training, maybe the training needs critiquing. If you shot out of fear of being labeled a coward, that's a human fault which is not excusable. In the real world, these scenarios do happen, but Grand Juries are most reluctant to indict a LEO for a human fault.

To be an ethical police officer it is not just making the distinction between right and wrong, it also involves knowing where your peers, teachers, supervisors and elected officials are leading. And if extrapolation reveals their path to be headed toward unconstitutional or other ethical violations, you must be a very strong right-knowing person indeed to remain ethical.

The Greatest Protection We Have Against Oppression,
In Any Form, Is The Rule Of Law.
And The Best Protection The Rule Of Law Has
Is The Police Officer.

The Creed

In his famous speech given at West Point, 12 May 1962, World War Two hero, General Douglas MacArthur, explained the obligation of soldiers with three words: "Duty, Honor, Country." Nothing could be closer to the American ideals of our fighting forces. To law enforcement officers those three words also apply, but so too, do: **"Integrity, Courage, Allegiance."**

It is surely every law enforcement officer's daily practice to live safely, to protect and serve, to stand beside and to back-up fellow officers and … to always do the right thing. Safety is mostly a matter of practicing rules of common sense. There is little temptation to violate safety procedures. Not so, ethical matters.

To a LEO ethics means, no lying, no cheating, no stealing—no exceptions, no excuses. Ethical behavior is also defined as a set, or system of, moral values and principles that are based on honesty and truthfulness and have been accepted as professional standards. To police officers the ethical mind-set additionally includes: Integrity, Courage and Allegiance.

Integrity: A strong unyielding adherence to a code of moral uprightness. Non-police personnel transactions might be honest and moral within their vocation while straying from their ethics in private life. Professionals, such as lawyers and doctors, may hold to high standards of ethics while dealing within their trade, but involve themselves in questionable behavior in their private lives and still be acceptable to their colleagues. Not so, police officers. LEOs must have Integrity and embrace ethical and moral conduct in all their private as well as public comings and goings. Conduct unbecoming an officer applies to on-duty as well as off-duty comportment.

Courage: It may take a lot of courage for a lawyer to face a jury or for an iron worker to scale buildings. But to act when other lives are in sudden and immediate life-threatening danger is an obligation that only applies to police officers. Not only must the man or woman with the badge be courageous, but they must also remain ethical while facing duty-bound lethal risks. Engaging in a firefight where the bad guy is shooting at you takes courage. But, racing to the scene where the shooting is occurring involves a much higher level of valor. An immense amount of courage is also required to stand your ground when reporting the illegal conduct of persons who, with their political or financial powers, can get you fired—or worse. What's worse? Public smear campaigns that drive your family apart and destroy your reputation because you exposed the wrong-doing of some scumbag who happens to have power.

Allegiance: Sworn to act with ethical integrity and courage; add now the requisite of loyalty to their profession, their fellow officers, all of the laws, court rulings and constitutional mandates. This does not in any sense mean a devotion to any form of "code of blue silence". "The good ol' boy," "blue code of silence," "blue-flu" schools are not conducive to professional stature. This type of trust falsely conveys a belief that if an officer covers-up, shirks his or her duty or keeps quiet about improper activity he or she can be trusted as backup when things get really hairy. Professionals who stake their reputation on keeping their mouth shut when they are under a sworn oath not to, are not worthy of the honor of being one of "America's finest."

Cops, being individualists, sometimes need unquestioning steadfastness from their fellow officers. When a LEO's back is exposed during a lethal force or other dangerous situation, this officer needs to know that his or her partner/backup, can be counted on to defend him or her to the death. Being the kind of officer who has mastered the "code of blue silence" is not any indication of how that officer will respond under conditions of extreme stress. An officer who is known for unquestioning honesty, however, would be the type of officer who couldn't in good conscience—not take risks to cover your backside.

Police officers are in the business of honesty. This is their stock-in-trade, forte', signature, persona, identification and what differentiates them from other professions. The addendums—**Integrity, Courage, Allegiance**—to the simple definition of ethics is what separates police officers from everyone else. To serve in this capacity marks a citizen as the epitome of what America is and what every decent, law-abiding, citizen aspires to be.

All this yea-team, feels-good rhetoric most certainly instills confidence and champions the great American spirit. But when events start to get out-of-hand — insurrection, riots, foreign invasion, martial law — the significant issue is; who are you really obligated to serve: The public (per se)? Individual citizens? The agency that signs your paycheck? Your state Constitution? The Constitution of the United States? Yourself and your family? A military officer? All of the above? None of the above? To a non-LEO their remedy might be found in the lyrics of the 1960s Bob Dylan song: "The answer, my friend, is blowin' in the wind." To the American police officer the reaction will always be faith in the law officer's creed: **Integrity, Courage, Allegiance.**

The Last Line Of Defense

Four score and 140+ years of The Rise of the American Empire, and it is clear that the world has taken "LITTLE NOTE" nor "HAS LONG REMEMBERED" what has become of "…GOVERNMENT OF THE PEOPLE, BY THE PEOPLE.…"

Four score and 140+ years has produced "THE BRAVE MEN [and women], LIVING AND DEAD, WHO STRUGGLED HERE," and in the Caribbean, Korea, Vietnam, Iraq, Afghanistan and over there twice who might have died in vain.

Four score and 140+ years finds an obese and incestuous government so entrenched its elected and bureaucratic officials, can twist, spin, violate and ignore, with impunity, the mandate "SHALL BE BOUND BY OATH OR AFFIRMATION, TO SUPPORT THIS CONSTITUTION."

Four score and 140+ years and tyrannical provisions, never intended by those who wrote about "UNALIENABLE RIGHTS," have become common place.

Four score and 140+ years and self reliance has evolved into protect-us-from-our-self laws and political correctness has expunged constitutional righteous offending all who have ever pledged, "…ONE NATION…WITH LIBERTY AND JUSTICE FOR ALL."

Four score and 140+ years finds us falling back upon our Last line of Defense and if they fail us, "…THIS NATION, SHALL…PERISH FROM THE EARTH."

~~~

165

IV FIREARMS, SURVIVAL and THE RIGHT TO KEEP & BEAR ARMS

Prudent Man Rule

"PRUDENT adj. 1 capable of exercising sound judgment in practical matters, esp. as concerns one's own interest 2 cautious or discreet in conduct; circumspect; not rash 3 managing carefully and with economy." (Webster's New World Dictionary, Third College Edition).

The courts have long used the prudent man rule to rationalize behavior of those who have come before it. Basically, it is the measure by which you will be judged should your actions in a LETHAL FORCE INCIDENT come before a court. The court will try to determine if your actions and reactions are what a prudent person would have done under the same circumstance.

The second to last thing a morally responsible, prudent person

wants to do is kill another human being regardless of how

reprehensible, villainous or dangerous that person might be.

The last thing this morally responsible, prudent person.

wants to do is be killed by that reprehensible, villainous and.

dangerous person.

A person exercising prudence would not be rash and would use sound judgment and act with caution. For example: suppose, while legally carrying your favorite concealed sidearm, you walk into a retail store during what appears to be an armed robbery. A man holding a gun shouts at you, "Get out of here man, right now." To do anything other than comply with this demand might not be the prudent thing to do. Unless the gun is pointed at you, the threat of imminent death might not be present, the prudent person would make use of an opportunity to escape—besides the man with the gun could be an undercover cop involved in a legal arrest detail!

BECOMING A PRUDENT PERSON:

a) KEEP A DIARY OF YOUR DAILY EXPEDITIONS AND CONTACTS. Such a document will help establish your routines, patterns and alibis;

b) AVOID TRAVELING INTO HIGH CRIME AREAS; Staying away from trouble spots will support the fact that you are not the kind of person that goes looking for trouble;

c) BE COGNIZANT OF RESTRICTED AREAS. Stay away from places that preclude the possession of firearms when you are armed;

d) STUDY IMPORTANT WORKS ON THE USE OF LETHAL FORCE. Read some of the recognized writings by experts such as Massad Ayoob, Brad Steiner, Dave Spalding and other noted authors;

e) DEVELOP A PERSONA THAT EQUATES WITH A PRUDENT PERSON. Maintain memberships in organizations that project you as a responsible and professional person and in general, establish a lifestyle of exemplariness.

RAMIFICATIONS:

a) Carrying an instrument that can produce instant and irrevocable physical damage, i.e., death to another human, conveys latent as well as prime facie perils to the carrier as well as others. Just strapping on a mega-shot tool of destruction without proper mental, physical and ergonomic prerequisites could render the carrier more of a victim than one might wish

b) Packing a concealed firearm requires the carrier to not only be sufficiently trained in its use as well as be knowledgeable of the consequences of its exploitation and the impact its utilization will have on the user. State laws vary from state to state. Some either outright or in a de facto sense prohibit their citizens from carrying a weapon for self-defense. Whether these laws are in the best interest of the residents is problematic. Dissimilar to these rules are numerous recent and historical precedent setting legal rulings which also impact the carrier.

> *Knowing how to shoot*
>
> *is the easy part. Knowing when*
>
> *is the important part.*

DUTY TO RETREAT?

a) Though this country is founded on the basic principles of English law the right of standing one's ground is in contrast. Americans have long held that to turn and run is cowardice and "un-

American". The roots of the doctrine of self-defense, of standing one's ground — in lieu of capitulation — has deeply permeated our civilian dealings with other people as well as our military and foreign relations. President Eisenhower in a 1953 televised speech referring to his boyhood idol, Wild Bill Hickok, decreed: "Meet anyone face to face with whom you disagree…if you met him face to face and took the same risk he did, you could get away with almost anything as long as the bullet was in the front." George H. W. Bush's "line in the sand" during the Gulf War conflict is most assuredly a modern day refusal to retreat on the highest level. Here the Commander-in-Chief of our armed forces, in unambiguous language, told the world that Americans do not back down from armed confrontations.

b) From the earliest of court decisions such as the "true man" case (Erwin V. State) to the more recent matters such as the 1984 "subway vigilante" self-defense shooting by Bernard H. Goetz in New York City, the American right to self-defense is well entrenched. In Erwin, the Ohio Supreme Court wrote: "…a true man, who was without fault in a confrontation, was free to stand his ground against any menacing assailant, regardless of the consequences". Further, the US Supreme Court, under Chief Justice Oliver Wendell Holmes, upheld the doctrine of "no duty to retreat" (Brown v. United States). Justice Holmes summarized: "…that if the defendant, Brown, had reasonable grounds of apprehension that he was in danger of losing his life or of suffering serious bodily harm from Hermes [the assailant] he was not bound to retreat". In other words, a private citizen otherwise engaged in any legal pursuit is not obliged to turn tail and run when faced with actual threats of great bodily harm.

c) However, just because one doesn't have a duty to retreat, per se, does not stand in place of good old common sense. Not exercising an option to retreat might not be fatal to the defense of self-defense, but the burden of proving an act was in fact necessary to defend yourself might preclude success. Placing yourself in harms way when the prudent move is to just walk away could make it appear, to a jury of your peers, that you were the aggressor. Remaining in harm's way when there is a safe escape, might be construed by jury as looking for an excuse to blow someone away.

All the rules, statutes, 911calls,
hand to hand combat technique,
aerosol spray Mace or other pseudo
protective measures will never equal the
effectiveness of a firearm when faced
with an unwarranted and deadly
criminal attack.

Firearm Related Problems & Suggested Solutions

PREFACE: Notwithstanding the tragedies of Sandy Hook, Norway, West Virginia, Columbine, et. al.; think about the equally innocent and young fatalities of the Holocaust—victims from a country with the strictest of gun laws. We have never lived in a perfect world, we don't now and, until the return/arrival of the Messiah we will never experience a utopian society.

While you're grieving for the above noted losses, try empathizing with the thousands of Americans who are spared rape, robbery, or murder. Spared because they, or someone else, did have a gun. Many of these incidents, usually ignored by the main stream media, are recorded by the NRA (http://www.nraila.org/gun-laws/armed-citizen.aspx).

When solutions are raised the usual suspects include banning various types and kinds of weapons and/or their components in addition to the cry of, "more cops." I am convinced we—all Americans—can agree that intentional, horrendous, homicidal acts (and the media coverage/portrayal thereof), are a complex situation. Hopefully, we can also agree that the current GUN FREE ZONES (read: self-defense free zones) don't work. America, since its inception, is a gun-culture society—that's not going to change. Not only do a huge number of citizens use guns for hunting, collecting, target shooting and self-protection, but employment and taxes generated by the firearm industry is intertwined with our economic status. Thus, if the culture can't be changed, it might be in American's best interest to learn ways to live with it.

PROBLEM: Defensive Protection. The knee-jerk reaction has been to place uniformed police officers in each school. Certainly that would be a powerful method of protecting our children. However, the numbers don't work. There are about 650K sworn law enforcement officers in the USA and over 300K schools. Placing one officer plus the need to cover his/her off/sick days would increase

172

the number of total LEOs by at least 50%. Most communities today are struggling to meet current payrolls where police departments consume up to half of city and county budgets. The NRA's mantra of placing paid police officer in every school might just be a political ploy (http://home.nra.org/pdf/Transcript_PDF.pdf). They know of the economic fall-out, but by taking this stand anyone who opposes it could be ostracized for being against protecting our children. In addition, it is a high level starting point where they can negotiate down to ... (see following SOLUTION).

SOLUTION: Encourage the placement of volunteer armed personnel in each school. Retired LEOs and civilians/parents who have undergone background checks and specialized training would be an economical and viable option. Butler County, Ohio is considering creating substitute teachers out of retired LEOs. This might work IF they can get enough retired LEOs to volunteer. Also, a police officer's divided attention between teaching a class and staying in condition orange (high level of awareness) might be problematic.

PROBLEM: Restrictions on firearms. Today's anti-gun protagonist's wish du jour is to limit the number of rounds a magazine can hold. They miss the obvious: a practiced shooter can change standard-capacity magazines very quickly—especially when no one is shooting back. In other words, in a "shooting gallery" the shooter has time to change low capacity magazines at his/her leisure. In still other words, there is little difference between a killer with a 30-round magazine, or one with five 6-round magazines. Well, maybe the shooter is at a disadvantage should the 30 rounder fail, whereas the killer with back-up mags could just insert a fresh mag— one reason cops carry multiple magazines.

SOLUTION: Repeal burdensome and un-American anti-gun laws.

PROBLEM: Human Nature. Many American citizens are afraid of guns, per se. They tend to believe a person with a gun will resort to its use if ever provoked—such as over a parking dispute, family argument or to resolve matters of a personal nature. This reasoning is most likely due to the fear that that is what they would do if they had a gun. In other words, a hoplophobic reasons everyone thinks as they do—that if in possession of a firearm they don't trust themselves not to use it to settle non-life threatening matters. There are tens of millions of gun owners who have and do engage in various quarrels and never resort to lethal force.

SOLUTION: Institute mandatory classroom and range training. Beginning at an early age children should be taught the importance of self-defense, the inherent dangers of mishandling firearms, the power/life-ending use of such weapons and the legal consequences of the use of deadly force. The NRA's Eddie Eagle Program (http://eddieeagle.nra.org/) is a great beginning in championing this endeavor.

PROBLEM: Posting of Signs. Signs saying "No Guns Allowed" obviously are an encouragement to the criminal bent on violence. Entering these "Gun Free Zones" they tend to feel secure that there will be no resistance to their evil deeds (and they're usually correct).

SOLUTION: Perhaps, and in conjunction with allowing armed persons on campus or in other "self-defense-free-zones" signs were posted saying: "CRIMINALS BEWARE, PATRONS AND/OR EMPLOYEES MAY BE ARMED."

(http://chuckkleinauthor.com/Page.aspx/163/guns-in-the-workplace.html) the potential for criminal behavior will be significantly reduced. It would surely give robbers/killers pause to rethink their plan A.

PROBLEM: Recidivism Rates of Prisons. Our prisons have become a haven—a goal—for the uninitiated. There are a significant number of persons who *want to* be in prison. Here is the only place they enjoy free medical care, housing, food, clothing and—most important—status for their criminal conduct. In other words, it is not a punishment to be sent to prison, but a reward. In still other words, some of us have to be a victim so they can receive their reward.

SOLUTION: Restructure the prison system to inflict real punishment. Make the criminal dread being sent-up.

PROBLEM: Vicious and Gratuitous Media Violence. TV, movie productions and computer games glorify not only killing, but multiple and mass deaths, sans consequences to the victims and aggressors.

SOLUTIONS: Electronic blocks such as parental controls are easily voided by today's computer savvy kids and are no longer an effective means of protecting our children. We need to stop the depiction of violence before it's distributed. While the brain-tweakers continue to debate the effects of violent visual media, censorship should be deployed over the industry. Yeah, I know the 1st Amendment says there is a right to freedom of speech. That "right," like the 2nd Amendment right to bear arms, is NOT an absolute.

FINAL THOUGHTS: Of course it's tragic when innocent children are killed, but also disparaging when the ill-informed and cowards among us blame the inanimate gun for their loss. There are over 300M Americans and of those a tiny portion are killed by firearms — mostly black on black drug deals gone bad.

(http://online.wsj.com/article/SB100014240527023048307045774 96501048197464.html). What we, the law-abiding and legally armed civilian members know is that there are more persons saved by the use or even the mere presence of a firearm than those illegally harmed by one.

This I know! I wouldn't be writing this now had I not had a gun with me on more than one occasion — not only as a police officer or licensed private detective, but as a civilian also. These accounts are documented in court records and in my books: (http://chuckkleinauthor.com/Page.aspx/135/books.html — http://chuckkleinauthor.com/Page.aspx/187/ohio-ccw-case-klein-vs-leis.html).

I'll end this with questions I have previously put to anti-gunners — none of which have yet to provide an answer:

Would You Feel Uncomfortable:

- * In the presence of an armed uniformed LEO? How 'bout a plain-clothes cop? An armed soldier? Someone like me, a former LEO, licensed and trained by the state to CCW?

- * Would it make a difference where you were — in a mall, on a street, in a school? In an unsecure building with "no guns allowed signs"? In an unsecure building with signs posted saying: "Criminals Beware, Patrons And/Or Employees May Be Armed?"

- * Where do you draw the line?

Personal Survival—Unarmed?

"SURVIVE!" is a self-defense class making the rounds that defines threats based on four types of perpetrators. The instructor is a woman whose only apparent qualification is, she is the wife of a police officer. Her premise is, if you choose to be unarmed you can survive lethal force assaults. These classes have been conducted in many cities and have been shown on PBS stations. The four threats, according to her theory, are: Money, Frustration, Psychotic, Assassin.

The ASSASSIN threat was dismissed as there was nothing one could do if targeted by a person randomly, or purposely shooting people. She said the Assassin is the most dangerous of the four. No argument there. But, there are acts and procedures that can make a difference should some sniper open fire. Your best move might be to keep moving, as in move quickly to cover. A moving target is most difficult to hit and while on the move you will be able to determine where the fire is coming from. Of course, solid concrete walls are best, but any cover is better than being in the open inasmuch as once out of the gunman's sights he will, hopefully, lose interest in you.

According to the instructor the person who is only after your MONEY will not harm you. She fails to enlighten her students in how one can tell the perpetrator is only after your money. Maybe she can tell, but my investigation turned up, "only the Shadow knows what evil lurks in the heart of man." As further proof, please recall Michael Baney, the musician who was shot dead AFTER giving up all his money in a Cincinnati parking-lot robbery a few years ago.

The cop's wife defines the FRUSTRATION person as one who can hurt you. Someone who has a political agenda, a guy mad at traffic, a spouse, government or…. The instructor's shtik—and this is the heart of her program—is to use verbal commands to intimidate your assailant and to keep him from getting within elbow distance. Once a perp is that close (she uses a hula hoop to demonstrate one's personal space), she champions a strike for the Adam's Apple.

The PSYCHOTIC, she admits, is a dangerous person, but he and all others can be dealt with if one does not allow them to get closer than elbow distance. Again, this is assuming the attack is by an unarmed person.

Unarmed self-defense tactics against an unarmed assailant are very effective — if you are sufficiently practiced and have the physical strength to incorporate them. However, most deadly attacks come from armed thugs where screaming, hiding, cowering probably won't make much difference. There are only two reasons a massacre-bent killer stops massacring; he runs out of ammunition or some brave soul disables him.

Strong verbal commands, when time permits, do have a controlling effect on some types of criminals — those who have become institutionalized — used to capitulating to the orders of a jailer. Others, especially those with authority figure problems, might respond with violence to anyone who attracts attention to themselves by shouting. The greatest fallacy of relying on the physical defense tactics of striking for the Adam's Apple is, if you miss this tiny spot or your thrust is weak your attacker is going to be really angry! Only those who continually train at this practiced tactic and are physically capable can, with any reliability, effectively strike the Adam's apple of another person — especially if the perp is significantly larger in height and/or stature. BTW, women don't have Adam's apples and they can be just as violent.

Other alternatives might be: always remain in Code Yellow, mentally prepare yourself to resist assault and if ever under attack, go for the eyes, the groin and the throat — over and over again until the threat has past. Oh yeah, and always carry a gun.

> *If you're ever in a situation where another person*
> *is about to murder you,*
> *at that moment, you'd trade all your worldly possessions*
> *for a firearm*
> *And, if that threat was to kill your child or your grandchild,*
> *you'd sell your soul for a gun.*

Glock: There's A Reason They're So Popular

Note: As Firearms Editor for P.I. Magazine for twelve years and writer for multiple police and gun magazines, I've tested and reviewed many firearms—from the tiny NAA mini revolvers to the H&K MP5 sub-machinegun with sound suppressor.

In my capacities as a Licensed Private Investigator and former police officer, I have carried a concealed firearm—on or off the job—where ever I've gone for over 40 years. Though I've never shot anyone, I, like most of us in these professions, have had to "use" a handgun to save my own hide—on more than one occasion.

CARRY CRITERIA: There are a lot of "cute" or heavy-on-the-bells-and-whistles guns out there, but when you carry for survival—all day, every day—there are only three things that matter: Weight, Reliability and Fit. Aside from being uncomfortable, a carry-gun too heavy for your frame will cause a loss of concentration when having to shift the gun's position or compensate for the discomfort in other ways. Losing focus during a critical time could jeopardize your life. Reliability goes without saying. Most (not all) modern guns from any of the major manufacturers are very reliable. Reliability, also includes stopping power inasmuch as a self-defense gun, even if it functioned with every pull of the trigger, would be of little use if it were of such a lesser caliber that it couldn't be counted on for stopping a lethal force assault.

Fit takes in proper holster to body compatibility as well as fit to the eye/hand. The goal of a defensive arm is one that will go from concealed carry to placing center body hits—BEFORE being incapacitated by your assailant. Any firearm relied upon for self-defense must come into battery pointing at the target without readjusting the grip or lining up the sights. If your eyes are looking at the target that is where the gun should be pointing after the draw. You should be able to draw your gun and hit a 12" square at seven yards without using your sights or changing your grip regardless of whether the target is in front, behind, or to your side.

I've known for a long time that the Glock series of pistols were very popular—especially with the police. But, I've resisted securing one for testing and evaluation because, well, I hate to be a follower, it might be just a fad and...I'm a wheel-gun-man at heart.

Fate intervened. During a training session at Tactical Defense Institute, (West Union, Ohio, www.tdiohio.com) where I was teaching my specialty, Instinct Combat Shooting, I was offered a chance to shoot a fellow instructor's Glock. It was love at first shot!

Most of the instructors carried Glocks and I was always a standout with my Dan Wesson .357, Model 15. This revolver never put me to a disadvantage as I could, even at my advanced age (60+), match the other instructors, to wit: The 3- shot/3-target timed fire exercise. Here, a timer is held to the hearing protector of the shooter. Upon hearing the starting tone, the shooter must, from the chest ready position, react and then shoot three times at three different targets (all 21 feet distance). The goal is to do it in under one second. Very few can—most of the instructors being in the 1.5 second range. My best—with the revolver—was 1.08. Most students, by the time they complete level 5 of the TDI course, shoot in less than 2 seconds.

Though I haven't had the opportunity to test my skill and reaction time on the 3-shot trial with the Glock, there is no doubt, after some 600 rounds of practice, plinking and analyzing, I will be most competitive. For test ammunition, I used Hornady .45 ACP 185gr JHP/XTP because of my past experience with their uniformity and accuracy. There were no miss-feeds, jams or malfunctions of any kind throughout the testing.

Most manufacturers allow writers to purchase the supplied test weapon (a used gun—after the testing) at a significant discount. I can't keep all the guns I test due to space and money constraints, but this one's a keeper and has become my main carry piece.

HISTORICAL NOTES: The Glock system was developed by Gaston Glock, circa 1980, for the Austrian Army. Being in a country that is short of steel mills, they were looking for a firearm that could be produced with non-strategic materials—such as polymer. The Glock Model 17, in 9mm Luger, was the result. In 1984 the pistol surpassed all NATO durability and strength standards and has now been accepted as the issue sidearm of many other nations.

Glock, Inc. USA, was formed in 1990 to service the huge demand of American police and sport shooters. Today, Glock offers 15 basic models in three sizes (full, compact, sub-compact) in calibers of 9x19, .40, .357 Sig, 10mm, .45 ACP. Options include: compensated barrels, adjustable sights, Trijicom night sights and Meprolight night sights.

WHAT IS A GLOCK? Aside from its polymer frame, which is fitted with treated steel slide rails, it is the safe-action firing system that makes it mechanically unique. This double-action-only trigger system offers the distinct benefits of optional trigger pulls. Most DAO pistols have only one setup: long and hard. My factory sample came with a 5.5 pound trigger pull of only 3/8" distance. By way of comparison, my SIG Sauer P230 has an 8 pound pull of 1.2" and my AMT Backup is at 9 pounds and 3/4" distance. The AMT and the SIG, like most other semi-autos, do not have adjustable triggers.

Light short trigger pulls are nothing new — on single action pistols where manual safeties are incorporated into the design. Manual safeties combined with a single action function can be a detriment inasmuch as deploying the safety takes time/thought/dexterity. A weapon with less than a 3 pound trigger pull (common for SA pistols) might be subject to accidental discharge. However, the Glock utilizes three independent and automatic safeties; one to control the trigger, one to secure the firing pin and an enertial safety to guard against a dropped (or severely jarred) weapon. There are no manual safeties — levers, switches or buttons to manipulate — just pull the trigger.

WHY IS IT SO POPULAR: Three words: Simplicity, Ergonomics, Reliability. Simplicity of design and function. Here the designers used only 34 parts. With fewer parts to malfunction or break, the reliability factor is enhanced. GLOCKs work — period. On the range at TDI, and aside from occasional ammunition (reloads) failure, there were virtually no malfunctions of GLOCK pistols — mine, other instructors or students. The pistol (and, as an aforementioned wheel-gun-man, I hate saying this) is as reliable as a revolver. Ergonomically the gun just plain fits. With its ambidextrous finger grooves, thumb lock and trigger-finger indent to its 108 degree grip angle this gun shoots where it points and points where you look.

Additionally, and probably the most important feature is the combination frame/grip. Being made of polymer it is very easy to file and sand slight changes to the finger placement. My fingers are on the short side of normal, but I had no problem mating the Model 36 to my hand by removing about a 1/16" from the backstrap and elongating the trigger finger groove on the right side. I chose the Model 36 (single stack, .45 ACP) over other models because double stacks are too wide for my hand and .45 ACP is a proven assault stopper.

Plan B

We joke about having a "plan B" when things don't go right the first time, but when it comes to personal security, many don't even have a plan A. Everyone should have a Plan A, even if it is to only observe, stay calm or run like hell.

Recently, there have been a series of survival guides such as the Worst-Case Scenario Survival Handbook that, in a humorous way, tries to describe honest solutions to real, but impossible situations. The book begat a TV series. Though entertaining, cluttering your mind with tactics for dealing with sharks, killer bees, jumping from a moving car or other matters you may never need to know might be questionable. The greatest benefit from these books/shows, however, might be in that they stimulate thinking and discussions on how to survive.

Police and firefighters play a game of "what would you do if" where one officer describes a scenario and the other officer then expounds upon what he would do under the tendered circumstances. It's an important learning/training experience and a great way to kill a little time when things start to drag around 4:00 a.m. Try it with friends and/or family members next time the conversation lags during a meal or car trip.

Let's play now: What would you do if you and your young daughter are in a convenience store when an armed, masked man suddenly announces a holdup? Though you are unarmed and standing within five feet of him should you jump him? Probably not. What if, while waving his gun around, he points it at you? Your child? Again, probably not. What if, while pointing the gun at you, he says words to the effect that he is going to shoot you or take your daughter with him? Or, he orders everyone to lie on the floor — face down. Now we're getting into the Plan B time.

There's lots worse things than being killed by some thug — one is: watching a family member die at the hands of this thug because of your inability to act.

Plan B is the line-in-the-sand, the point-of-no-return, the pull-all-stops position where blend-in, prayer or compliance is forsaken for active and drastic action. It is the point where you have pre-decided that if you don't act, not only will the present danger increase, but your window of opportunity or the advantage of surprise will be lost. Read that again.

For each person this line-in-the-sand is different, but usually only incrementally. Plan B is more than re-acting, it is acting based on a mind-set worked out in advance. A person without a Plan B, in the convenience store matter, would most likely try to physically hold on to their daughter and/or become hysterical. Either reaction draws attention and might further aggravate the robber, who, in an attempt to eliminate the source of aggravation, could begin shooting. Whereas, someone with a Plan B and the grit to put it into play might distract the robber, which will allow the daughter time to escape.

What could be done? Aside from grabbing the robber's gun, one might look and walk away, waving and shouting "POLICE, OVER HERE." Or, while knocking things from the shelves and shouting, "DIRTY #@$%&*, THEY'VE BEEN RIPPING ME OFF FOR YEARS—ROB 'EM ALL." Of course, if you haven't played the game your daughter might not know this is her cue to run....

The brave passengers of the hi-jacked airliner that crashed in the Pennsylvania country side, September 11, obviously and communally determined they had reached their point-of-no-return. It was at this "let's roll" point they decided things would get worse if they didn't act. Surely they believed their death was certain if they failed to take any action. Once that conclusion, consciously or subconsciously, was reached they were sure that they would improve their situation from certain death to survival if they attacked the terrorists. Of course there are no guarantees in life and though their actions were not successful, inasmuch as they themselves died, their heroic deaths saved many other lives.

Some criminals only want money, others enjoy terrorizing but don't intend to kill while a few kill for kicks, gang initiation rites, political agendas or…. How can you tell? Sometimes you can't—for certain—but key words or tell-tale body language, to those who think survival have the best chance of surviving or, at least, of saving others.

Reasons Behind Common Sense Actions

From early childhood we're told: Don't run across streets, lock your doors and never argue with a traffic cop. It is never explained why (at least to me it wasn't).

Here are some of the REASONS:

WALKING (approaching any potentially dangerous situation): When an emergency, such as a car suddenly changes lanes and is presenting a threat, you are able to increase your speed at least three fold (by beginning to run). This safety factor is akin to having a Plan B. In other words, if you were running in the first place — operating at full speed — there is no backup or auxiliary plan to counter an unforeseen danger.

The mind is a unique computer inasmuch as you approach a street you can, without much conscious thought, compute the time and distance of traffic in relation to where you will be. This tabulating of factors begins about 10 − 20 feet before you step off the curb — time-wise, about 2-3 seconds (given a normal walking speed of 3 MPH). If you are running at 9 MPH, you have now reduced your mental computing time to one second or less.

Of course, if you fall while running across a street (a greater chance than while walking) your computation of approaching vehicles is significantly altered because your speed and direction will be impacted.

LOCKING DOORS: On its face, keeping doors locked seems the prudent thing to do to keep bad guys out. In reality, it doesn't, but it does give great weight to criminal intent. Meer locks, especially those that only secure glassed enclosures, such as automobiles or a front door, are of no deterrent to a thug bent on entry. If the perpetrator is able to gain access to your car, home, boat, etc., without producing any evidence of force, he can, if caught, say that it was you who invited him in and then attacked him. To an investigating police officer, everyone is treated the same — all are presumed to be telling the truth until the evidence proves otherwise. Just because you appear to be an upstanding, clean-cut citizen doesn't mean the police (and the courts) are required, absent evidence to the contrary, to accept your story over that of some dirtbag (who will be the picture of wholesomeness when attending court).

DISPUTING A TRAFFIC STOP is akin to expectorating into the wind. In grammar school we learned all Americans are presumed innocent until proven guilty. That's still true, except in the matter of traffic tickets.

Traffic violators, per se, are de facto guilty until they prove themselves innocent in court. That's not exactly the way the law is written, but that's the effect. When you are stopped for a traffic violation you are, in reality, having your trial right there on the street. If you can't convince the cop that you don't deserve a ticket the chances of convincing a judge are almost non-existent. There is a reason for this.

In the court room, where all are sworn to tell the truth, it usually comes down to your word against that of the arresting officer. If, for instance, you claim that the light was not red and the cop swears it was, the judge is going to have to decide who is telling the truth and who isn't. To find you not guilty he would, for all intents and purposes, have to call the arresting officer a liar. This is not to say that one of you is lying. It could be that due to the different observation points of the parties, it appeared to the officer the light was red and to you the light was not. The point is; the burden of proving the color of the light is with you.

Without uncontroverted evidence that the officer is not telling the truth, judges are most reluctant to rule against them for two reasons. First, to take the word of an ordinary citizen against that of a trained (and presumably unbiased) officer would tear at the very roots of the system. Second, and maybe more on the pragmatic level, a finding of not guilty is tantamount to leaving the arresting officer and his employer (usually the same one who pays the wages of the judge) open to a law suit for false arrest.

Cops, just like the rest of us, are human and make mistakes. Usually, if they realize they may have ticketed you in error or there were mitigating circumstances they will agree, with the consent of the prosecutor, to drop the charges. Sometimes, if the cop is embarrassed by his mistake he might not show up for court which means that the judge can dismiss the charge for lack of evidence. Dismissed charges are not the same as a finding of not guilty—law suit wise. Of course, if you acted like a jerk during the stop, you can bet he won't cut you any slack!

Carrying Concealed Firearms

PREREQUISITES:

a) Regardless of all the rights to carry a concealed firearm, if you can't, in all honesty, kill another person then you have no business packing a weapon. Brandishing lethal armament and being unable, for any reason, to use it could result in that weapon being taken away and used to kill you or another innocent person. This worst case scenario, if you survive, could later be judged your direct or indirect fault thus costing not only the mental anguish of your foolhardy bravado, but may ensue civil as well as criminal action against you;

> *If you believe that*
>
> *carrying a gun will somehow enable you*
>
> *to bluff your way out of dangerous*
>
> *situations, you might be "dead" wrong.*
>
> *Lethal force confrontations are not*
>
> *poker games. Losers with nothing to*
>
> *lose can't be bluffed!*

b) It's easy to imagine some dirty, murderous scum, in full view of dozens of witnesses, brutally attacks a little kid with a knife. Disabling him with gunfire would be expected, if not, heroic. But would you really be able to pull the trigger on another human being?

Could you handle the mental torment that will work at your mind—possibly forever, as it has in most other recorded civilian versus civilian mortal warfare? Even police officers, quasi-military practitioners of killing methods, have been known to have hung up the shield after being involved in the finality of a firefight. It might be macho, self-assuring and even advisable to pack a weapon. But, this tool of instant life-changes—for all—could be of greater danger to you if you are not the kind of person who not only knows how and when to use lethal force, but has the mental make-up to actually use a firearm. To some there are worse things than their own death.

Killing an innocent person, failing to kill to prevent the death of an innocent person or maybe just killing anyone, innocent or not are a few "I'd rather be dead than" scenarios for some people;

c) We are living in very dangerous times with ever increasing drug dealing shootouts, gang warfare battles, disgruntled murderous employees, psychotic killers, stalkers and robbers with no feelings for human life. In addition, add the terrorist and politically motivated fanatics venting their rage with lethal force on a daily basis. Increasing this escalating violence is the multiplicity of super-predators or just plain bad guys that are now carrying guns. The proliferation of firearms in our social makeup has made being proficient at hand-to-hand defensive techniques academic.

BASIC RULES:

When I attended the police academy, a fellow recruit asked the OIC if we should carry off-duty. Norwood, Ohio Lieutenant Umbaugh's answer was so profound that not only have I taught it and written about it, but I've lived it. He said: "One either never carries a firearm, or one always carries, but one never sometimes carries."

a) A follower of the Lt's simple rule will always know where he/she stands, i.e., his/her mind set will be acclimated to appropriate response when confronted with a dangerous situation. Sometime carriers might be caught reaching for a hard thing that is not there when needed. Or the weapon might be there when it is not wise to be armed—like when entering an airport or other restricted area. Never-carriers can allow themselves to go about their business in condition white;

Those who always carry must, by reason of common sense, conduct all goings and comings in at least condition yellow. The person in condition yellow will be cognizant of the fact that a loaded firearm is ready at hand and must remain concealed at all times. Thus he or she can't indulge in consumption of alcoholic drink, enter restricted areas and above all must observe people and actions with an eye toward the unusual. This is not to say that an unarmed person can not be observant, only that a carrier must never allow him/herself to be lax, lest he/she get caught unawares;

b) If you do carry, then by all means, use a secure, concealable and quality retainment device. A gun loose in your pocket can, at the most inopportune time, snag on the lining, fall out or transmit its presence by outline thus giving away the element of surprise;

c) So as not to cause alarm of other citizens firearms must remain concealed. Walking into a retail store or bank with a gun in hand, in an exposed holster or "telegraphing" its presence via a conspicuous bulge under your shirt would surely cause many people alarm. In most states this is the crime of Inducing Panic;

An openly carried firearm or even a "tell-tale" bulge under a shirt could be deemed an attractive nuisance whereas the temptation to a snatch-and-grab thief would be very powerful. Should a fight ensue for the control of the exposed weapon—in an exposed holster or bulging under a shirt—the carrier or a member of the public at large, especially in a crowded area, could be injured in the ensuing fight for control of the firearm. In addition, conspicuous carry also telegraphs "shoot-me-first" to a crazy bent on a rampage. The element of surprise is lost when the perp is able to learn that you are armed;

d) If you're going to spend all day with a rig that is constantly chaffing at your arm pit or its weight requires hitching your pants every so often you'll most likely be made by the criminal element or worried citizens. Covert or surreptitious operations are dependent upon blending in. A carry arm that is uncomfortable or causes periodic readjustment is a distinct disadvantage and possible threat to your, as well as the public's, safety;

e) Make sure you are practiced, not only with the use of your chosen arm, but also with the ability to withdraw it from under its cover.

A PERSONAL DECISION:

a) Carrying instant death on one's person is a responsibility of the highest order and the decision to go armed is not to be taken lightly. Knowledge, personal persona and expertise are required lest innocent people become victim to the improper and possibly illegal use of a good guy carried firearm. The decision to carry a concealed weapon is, and should be, left to the individual who must decide whom the prudent person really is;

b) The act of causing the injection of the lead portion of a cartridge into the body of another is something each person must decide at the "point of no return". However, certain standards can be pre-established on an individual basis. These criteria, about which you will risk your life, cover, or life of another to engage in mortal battle requires careful thought and study.

All consequences must be addressed before pre-deciding a do-or-die scenario. Some conditions that usually indicate action is demanded include the belief that death or great bodily harm is imminent. This certainty might be based on what the perpetrator has verbally, or by gesture, indicated. In other words if a gun-toting robber says that he is going to kill you, your only recourse might be, and at a very early opportunity, to draw-on-the-drop. Most situations might be more subtle such as when the bad guy orders you to lie down, surrender your weapon (assuming he knows you're armed), has fired his weapon or menacingly points his firearm at you mouthing words to the effect of "You're dead" or "Bang."

Instinct Combat Shooting—The Tricks

Note: This is one of a series of articles on this subject. Klein's book, INSTINCT COMBAT SHOOTING, Defensive Handgunning for Police, is in its 3ʳᵈ edition and has been in continuous print since 1985.

Warning: For these "Tricks" to be successful, the shooter must be practiced in the subject field and is thus advised to read Klein's book or other publications of similar expertise.

Causing a bullet to impact the target where you intend is akin to throwing a baseball, dart, bean bag or other similar eye/hand/mind events. These challenges can be overcome when instinct and practice are combined. The technique, the trick, is to not only look at the target, but to look at the smallest part of the target while devoting full concentration just before and during release of the shot/throw. This focus on the target is more than a visual knowledge of the target, it is total attention to the target-within-a-target. You don't have to stare at the target, only see it and focus on a small portion of it while the body/hand is moving to point of fire.

INSTINCT COMBAT SHOOTING: The act of operating a HANDGUN by focusing on the target and instinctively coordinating the hand and mind to cause the HANDGUN to discharge at a time and point that ensures interception of the target with the projectile.

In the stay-alive world, if you see the perp (target) advance toward you with deadly intent, you will most likely be looking at him with your undivided attention. That is not enough. Having decided to engage in a close-quarter firefight, you should—while in the process of going from that point of decision to battery –– focus on a small point (button, stain, shirt pattern). This intensity of vision and concentration—at the instant just before firing—will allow your natural mental powers to coordinate the hand and trigger finger to cause the firearm to discharge at the most opportune moment.

192

All of this needs to happen in a very small time frame, e.g., just short of simultaneous.

1) See the target;

2) Decide to shoot;

3) Start the gun moving toward battery (the point where the gun is at its shooting position—usually when the support hand contacts the shooting hand);

4) Focus on a small target-within-the-target;

5) Pull the trigger at the instant the firearm reaches battery.

Some might call this intense focus tunnel-vision. It is. Though tunnel-vision has been projected as a no-no, it is mandatory during the brief moment when you transition from deciding to shoot to the completion of that shot(s). Of course, you have to be aware of additional threats and the background (innocents), but only before the decision to shoot. Once the time frame of decide-to-shoot to completion-of-the-shot(s) has begun, full concentration—oblivious to all else—is required. This time frame during which you are engaged in tunnel-vision is only a matter of milliseconds. Perhaps, World Champion race car driver, Phil Hill said it best: "True concentration is not aware of itself." (Car and Driver, November 1962).

Many articles, columns and books have espoused the virtues of "watching the front sight" while engaged in combat shooting. If these reports are studied closely, it is evident that the writers are, in almost all cases, relating to shooting contests at inanimate targets. During real life-death scenarios survivors seldom have the luxury of taking their eyes off of the threat to focus (adjust point of aim) on the front sight much less seek a perfect sight picture.

Shooting for score/time during a close-quarter combat match is a recreation where the danger lies in forming negative survival skills/habits. Shooting to survive should be a self-mandate. Practice what you need to survive and save the fun stuff for your retirement years. It is my suggestion that during close-quarter police style matches the sights be taped (covered) on all competitors handguns. In addition, aerial targets (using paintball, Simunition or pellet/BB gun) should be included in the contests.

Timing, as they say, is everything. And in instinct shooting nothing could be more critical. This is the hard part. You can have all the basics down pat, be an expert at mechanical exercises, stare intently at a pin point on the target, but ignore the body/mind instinctive reflexes. Having the timing as second-nature will allow hits on non-prearranged targets from non–standard body positions. It's not only about staring at the target or even the target-within-the-target. It's also about timing, e.g., a series of motions and actions where the mind's computer—from visual input—instructs the arm and trigger finger when and how to act. The mind computes much faster than the body can react. Thus, it is not necessary to stare or spend more than an instant focusing on the target-within-the-target. This is especially important if the target is moving. To be successful during a close-quarter firefight, you must be conditioned to instinctively override your pre-set want to look at the sights.

The human brain has an uncanny ability to adjust trigger pull, arm motion/angle and other related tactics—all without consciously thinking about it. That's why it is possible to hit a moving target—even with a handgun. As the eyes follow the target, the mind almost instantly computes and directs the course and speed of the firearm as it moves toward the focal point giving the trigger finger the command to act at the instant of battery. From another perspective, if the mind is forced (ingrained teaching) to focus and adjust for a sight picture it takes more time and throws the timing off.

Another part of timing is firing the shot at the instant the gun comes to battery. If you've identified the target, decided to fire, focused on a pin point, but wait even an instant longer, you will have a greater chance of a miss. This is due to the body's inability to react to the mind's change of plan in a timely manner. If the brain is instinctively conditioned to shoot when the gun reaches battery, but you consciously over-ride this function you will not be able to readjust to the added conditions. This is because the gun is always moving, Skeet and bird hunters, who shoot instinctively, practice this technique. On the clay bird or hunting field, a shot-gunner shoots the instant his gun contacts his shoulder and cheek—his body moving with the target and eyes having locked on to the bottom edge of the target or head of the bird while the gun comes to battery.

Flash sight picture, front sight only or aimed fire defeats real-time instinct shooting. Body parts can't react to the mind's ability to make changes at the same speed. Trying to focus on a mechanical sight, look at the target, and then make a decision to adjust or not adjust the alignment takes time. In other words, in that nanosecond where:

1) Your eyes have picked the target-within-the-target;

2) Your firearm is moving toward battery;

3) Your mind is coordinating the exact instant to send the message to pull the trigger;

… if the eyes send an additional message to realign/confirm the sight picture the timing will be off and though it might only take a split second to do so, that split second could cause a miss.

Everyday as part of my exercise routine, I practice instinct combat shooting, albeit, sans a gun. With my hands in the chest ready defensive position, I begin by scanning the room. When I locate a target, I start my simulated draw while focusing on a target-within-the-target and pull-the-trigger as my hands come together at battery. On the range (I live on a 125 acre farm), I toss wood blocks out in front of me and, using a handgun, try to hit them while they're airborne. Great challenge! If you have room to try this, but be sure your misses and deflected hits don't go over/around the backstop.

Just like making a pitch or basket, shooting-to-survive requires conditioned reflexes that are best accomplished by practice, commitment and familiarity with the task. However, to successfully and instinctively place your strikes/baskets/shots, the player must be conditioned to trust his or her instincts. Instinct combat shooting is not trick shooting, it's practicing the "tricks."

The Fallacy Of "Reasonable" Gun Control Laws

The Second Amendment clause, "The right of the people," indicates that the framers were acknowledging a right rather than granting a right. Therefore, this right "to keep and bear arms" is an inherent and intrinsic right that predates the Constitution. A preexisting right cannot ever be malum prohibitum — wrong because legislatures, courts or political correctness says it's wrong.

Regardless of recent Supreme Court of the United States (SCOTUS) decisions supporting this legal fact, our detractors have continued to work to disparage our right. Their next assault might be to the effect that, though the Right to Keep and Bear Arms (RKBA) is an individual right, it is not absolute. They will contend that even a SCOTUS mandate is not absolute and thus is subject to restrictions.

Contrary to what some over zealous pro-gunners want to believe, the antis are correct inasmuch as the RKBA is not an absolute. If it was, we would have to allow little children and prison inmates to keep and bear arms. Therefore, some limits must be acceptable. But limits do not mean anything the legislature/courts want it to be. Bearing arms is not an absolute right under all conditions anymore than free speech allows one to yell fire in a crowded building when there is no fire. The constitutional right to bear arms does have limits, but these confines are only limited to two factors: Citizenship and Other's Rights.

> *"The greatest dangers to liberty lurk in insidious encroachment by men of zeal, well-meaning but without understanding."* Justice Louis Brandeis, 1927."

CITIZENSHIP: At the time of the Constitution's inception the framers, "all men in a man's world," clearly gave little thought to anyone other than the man as the defender of family, property or country. Whereas, in Eighteenth-Century England, only the landed rich were empowered to defend honor and country. This concept of all men being full citizens and having the right, empowerment and obligation to self preservation was unique to America.

A citizen, circa 1785, was considered to be any white, American, male over the age of 21 and not a felon. The idea of civilian gun controls was unconscionable. It is was also inconceivable that a Thomas Jefferson or a James Madison would refuse to take a musket away from a drunk, a child or someone conspicuously deranged. Had one been able to ask these learned, most-sacred-document framers of the conflict of such a restrictive action; they most likely would have replied with words to the effect that the drunk or mental incompetent were, at least temporarily, not citizens. A child was, of course, not a man and a felon had forsaken his citizenship.

The controversy of the 2nd Amendment exists because, erroneously, some have insisted that the right to keep and bear arms is a state (as in Ohio, Texas, Florida) right and not an individual right. However, it is clear that the first clause: A well regulated militia being necessary to the security of a free state, means a free America. The word "state" also means nation/country, such as "the State of Israel" or "the Arab States" or "Secretary of State". In other words, the nation can best form a well regulated militia (army/navy) if its militia (originally, men between the ages of 18 and 45) are free to keep and bear arms.

With the ratification of the 13th, 14th and 19th Amendments all of-age Americans were recognized as full, ruling-class citizens. Arms possession was, AND STILL IS, the signature of being a citizen—not a subject to some monarchy and most assuredly not mentally inept, a child, a felon, or a substance abuser.

OTHER'S RIGHTS: Violating the rights of others is cause to restrict gun rights. Allowing certain persons, such as children, felons, drunks, etc., to possess firearms most assuredly creates a substantial risk of loss of someone's life or liberty. However, restricting the RIGHT of a law-abiding, bona fide citizen from carrying a firearm that is concealed from public view where it can not induce panic or be available to a snatch-and-grab thief, does not present a substantial risk of damage to anyone. Likewise, machine guns, assault rifles, or short-barreled shotguns, while in the possession of law-abiding citizens, are of no danger to others.

Constitutional rights are only such when they don't infringe on the constitutional rights of others. One's right to swing his fist ends where the other person's nose begins. Of course, if one keeps his fist concealed in his pocket he is violating no ones rights. On the same token, if a law-abiding citizen goes about his legal business with a firearm concealed in his pocket he is no more infringing the rights of any other person than the theater-goer who keeps the word "fire" concealed in his mouth.

Some citizens might wish to exercise their right to the "pursuit of happiness" by not wanting to be in the presence of guns. On their own property, not accessible to the public, they can do as they please. However, where public property is involved such as court houses, police stations and legislatures guns can be restricted by instituting the use of metal detectors and storage boxes that the carrier can store his/her gun until he/she leaves that secure area.

But, what about the reasonableness factor? Other "rights" such as those found in the Third, Fourth and Eight Amendments are subject to this doctrine of reasonableness—why not the Second? Our enemies might argue, that, under the reasonableness doctrine, it is reasonable to ban certain types of arms or exclude bearing of arms into specified locations without incorporating metal detectors/lock boxes.

Unlike other Articles and Amendments there is no such provision for "reasonableness" in the Second Amendment. Discretion is not part of the right to bear arms. In other portions of our Constitution we see the following discretionary wording:

> *Article I, Section 4: "Each house may determine the rules...."*
>
> *Amendment III: "...but in a manner prescribed by law."*
>
> *Amendment IV: "...against unreasonable searches...upon probable cause."*
>
> *Amendment VIII: "Excessive bail....nor excessive fines...nor unusual punishments."*

If the framers of the Constitution had intended for the bearing of arms to be anything other than what it says, they would have included in the Second Amendment subjective words or terms such as "reasonable," "excessive," "prescribed-by-law," "upon-probable cause," "unusual," or "may."

Reading discretionary or reasonableness provisions into the Second Amendment of our Bill of Rights, is no different than reading the First Amendment to say: "Congress shall make no UNREASONABLE law respecting an establishment of religion..." If the legislature or the courts are permitted to insert reasonableness into the Second Amendment, what's to prevent them from saying a national church or attending church only on Tuesdays is not unreasonable. Not in America, not yet anyway!

SUMMARY: The Second Amendment RKBA is a conditional absolute right. Conditional, insomuch as restrictive conveyances can only be based on citizenship and the rule of other's rights. In other words, if you are not precluded from owning a gun and your exercising of this right does not infringe on anyone else's right, you can bear any type of arm anywhere you wish. Until such time as the Constitution is amended, keeping and bearing any type of arms is an intrinsic and absolute right for all citizens. While on the other hand, non-citizens do not have an absolute right to a firearm. However temporary that condition might be; The "American ruling class" (aka voters), if they so desire, can change the definition of citizen or establish some restrictions—but ONLY by amending the Constitution. Though voters may change the Constitution and are empowered to repeal portions or amendments thereof, they may not abolish intrinsic and fundamental rights such as the right to self-protection and the means to maintain that right.

Use Of Lethal Force

RULES OF ENGAGEMENT:

a) To justify the use of lethal force and establish the defense of self-defense the discharge of a firearm at another person may be instituted only when ALL of the following apply;

b) Pay close attention to KEY WORDS, such as: Imminent, Great Bodily Harm, Lethal Force. Refer to a recognized dictionary or the Police & Firearms Nomenclature portion of Part III of this book for definitions used herein:

1) YOU WERE NOT AT FAULT OR DID NOT CREATE THE SITUATION THAT GAVE RISE TO THE USE OF LETHAL FORCE. You can't set someone up or cause them to attack you so you can then kill them. If you find yourself in a confrontational incident, such as a traffic accident, you must remain cool at all times. Should the other party start name calling or issuing threats it is imperative that you back off, apologize if that's what the other party is demanding, or just leave the area. Lest you later be deemed the aggressor it is always better to save your explanations for the police. If you find yourself in an altercation that seems headed for violence — withdraw and say words to the effect that you are capitulating. This restores your right to self defense. If an affray grows violent and your adversary becomes disabled, walks away or indicates that he has had enough and the threat is no longer real — the right of self defense loses its necessity. Because you're carrying the ace-in-the-hole you must never be the aggressor.

2) YOU BELIEVED YOU WERE IN IMMINENT DANGER OF DEATH OR GREAT BODILY HARM. The threat of death or great bodily harm must be immediate — at the time you pulled the trigger. Killing a man who is two blocks away and brandishing a machete while saying he is going to kill anyone who gets in his way most likely wouldn't be justifiable. The threat does not have to be real — only that you had reasonable grounds to believe, and did believe, that you were in immediate danger of death or great bodily harm.

Mere threats alone are not sufficient to permit the use of deadly force. Your attacker must have the means and capability of carrying out these threats at the time you introduce deadly force as a means of protecting yourself.

You may exercise your right of self defense to defend another person such as a family member. However, you stand in no better position than the family member if your family member had been the aggressor and had not withdrawn. Only under unusually unique circumstance can you take the life of another in defense of a total stranger. If, for instance, while you were a customer/employee in a retail store a perpetrator points a gun at a patron saying he is going to kill him. You might be absolved of killing the bad guy on the premise that by defending the stranger you were defending yourself from the same fate, i.e., you believed that you would be next and took the opportunity to dispatch the robber while you had the chance.

Situations involving strangers might not always be what they appear, e.g., the young girl screaming, "Help, I'm being kidnapped," as a man is trying to force her into an automobile might just be his overly dramatic daughter.

The fact that your attacker does not have a weapon does not necessarily rule out the use of deadly force. If, for instance, your attacker is much bigger and stronger than you and you believe he is about to commit acts of great bodily harm to you, you might be justified in using a lethal force weapon to stop his unwarranted attack.

3) YOU MUST NOT HAVE VIOLATED ANY OPPORTUNITY TO RETREAT OR AVOID THE DANGER. If you waited for the man with the machete (see 2 above) to get close enough to establish an imminent threat when the simplest thing to do was just walk away you might not be successful in presenting a defense of self defense. On the other hand, if you're standing in a doorway and a man pulls a knife saying he is going to kill you, you do not have the obligation to turn your back on him in order to make a retreat—he might be a faster runner than you. Note: This is not in conflict with the "No Duty to Retreat" rule. There is a difference between duty and opportunity.

4) YOU EXHAUSTED ALL OTHER MEANS TO AVOID THE USE OF DEADLY FORCE. There were no options open—the use of lethal force was necessary to save your life. If an aggressor, brandishing a knife, can be frustrated by just closing a door or driving away you must avail yourself to these options. Of course you must have a bona fide belief that your actions will succeed.

Suppose while walking down a street a man accosts you by showing you a gun in his waist band while demanding your wallet. On the pretext of producing your wallet you might be justified in producing your own weapon while backing away. But unless he makes a move for his gun you might not be in danger of imminent death.

5) THE USE OF DEADLY FORCE PRESENTS NO SUBSTANTIAL RISK OF INJURY TO INNOCENT PERSONS. If an assailant holds a hostage while advancing upon you, you might be guilty of murder if your shot kills the hostage. Just because your life might be in danger doesn't bestow the right to open fire in a crowd.

LETHAL FORCE IS FORBIDDEN:

a) To affect an arrest. Attempting to invoke a "citizen's arrest" could place you in the position of being the aggressor;

b) To protect property no matter what value. A man about to torch your unoccupied, brand new BMW is not reason to use lethal force against him. Of course, if you are in the vehicle, can't drive away and do not violate any of the rules of engagement, and he is about to torch the car—that's a different matter.

WARNING SHOTS NOT PERMITTED:

a) Warning shots shall not be fired for any reason. The danger of ricocheting bullets striking innocent persons exceeds any benefit of such action;

b) Shots fired as a warning may be misconstrued. The victim and/or police may later decide that the warning shot was an act of intimidation (assault) and criminal and/or civil charges may follow;

c) A warning shot may cause another person to believe he/she is being attacked and, in legal defense of him/herself, return fire;

d) Warning shots may cause innocent bystanders to panic and thus injure themselves by running into traffic or cause acute medical problems such as heart attacks;

e) Discharging firearms, except in legal defense of one's life, or at a legal target range is a crime in some jurisdictions.

SHOOTING TO WOUND IS FORBIDDEN:

a) It is nearly impossible, under stress of a lethal force incident, for even the best of marksman to stop a deadly attack by intentionally wounding;

b) A wounded person may not cease his life-threatening actions and can intentionally or unintentionally kill innocent bystanders;

c) The most effective means of immediately stopping a deadly attack is by causing your bullets to strike the largest area—center mass—of your assailant's body.

SHOOTING TO KILL:

a) The only reason—the sole purpose—for using lethal force against another person is to stop his illegal, unwarranted, life-threatening and aggressive action. You are allowed only the number of shots necessary to stop him. Your reason for use of lethal force is NOT to kill him—only to STOP him. If, however, he dies as a result of the wounds you inflict upon him it is his misfortune.

Suppose, after one shot, your attacker falls down dropping his weapon—out of reach. Now he is no longer a threat and if you shoot him again you become the aggressor.

It is well established in police training that the most effective means of stopping an assault with gun fire is to shoot two or three rapid shots to the center mass. If the attacker has not been stopped, it can now be assumed he is either wearing body armor or is so high on drugs that medical shock reaction has no effect on him. At this point additional shots to his center mass will only be wasting your rapidly depleting ammunition supply without reducing the risk of his continued assault. Therefore, your next shot might be for the head.

Reality Of Self Defense

ACTUAL ENGAGEMENT:

a) If it becomes obvious that a firefight is about to ensue — and you have the time — take cover. Nothing, absolutely nothing, enhances your chances of surviving a shootout than protective cover. Of course barricades and time are not always available. However, if your mental state has been in "condition yellow", like it should be every time you carry, then cover should have been one of the items mentally check-listed for every scene you enter;

b) Once the shooting starts set your mind not to capitulate until your assailant is stopped. Even if you are wounded — continue the engagement. Quitting just because you are injured will not ensure your survival, but it most assuredly will increase your opponent's opportunity to finish you off. Individuals involved in the serious level of the martial arts learn, as part of their vital survival mind-set, Koryo. This ancient Korean word translates in English to: "unyielding spirit and strong conviction". The spirit or will to survive — the ability to retaliate without reserve. This is a key to winning close encounters of the heart-stopping kind. Anything less, in life threatening situations, is merely an exercise of the fundamentals;

c) Firefights are not games with rules of fair play. You can't call "kings" or "times" when you stub your toe and expect the bad guy to give you an opportunity to regroup. Neither should you give any quarter. If the attacker verbally calls it quits don't relax only to be taken in by a cunning perp playing on the persona of American fair play. This person with whom you are engaged in mortal combat might have a hidden second or third weapon! Do like the police are trained to do — take cover and, using strong verbal commands, make him keep his hands weapons free and in plain view.

DOWNSIDE OF LETHAL FORCE USE:

a) All right, so you, a prudent person, studied the applicable law of your state, practiced until proficient with your favorite handgun, then found yourself in a situation that required you to execute the lethal force option. Now what?

b) First, and up on top of the list of things to do after you are sure your assailant is no longer a threat, BE COGNIZANT OF SECONDARY TARGETS. Just because you successfully engaged the main threat doesn't mean an accomplice isn't lurking nearby. The prudent person doesn't stand around patting himself on the back while allowing another perp to take careful aim at him. Do not point your weapon at spectators or others as you sweep the room for suspects—bring your firearm to the chest-ready position (up close and pointed up) before moving your body/arms;

c) Once the scene is safe, engage your firearm's safety and secure your weapon, lest you be mistaken for the assailant upon the arrival of the police. Aside from seeing that the police and life squads have been called, do your best to guard the shooting scene and the perp's weapon against tampering by non-police personnel. In addition, and if you have the presence of mind, eyeball and identify as many witnesses as possible. Ask someone to gather names and other identifying information such as age, employment and school;

d) Upon the arrival of law enforcement officers politely state—in most unambiguous language—that you are not the perp and were defending your life from imminent threat of great bodily harm or death. Whatever you do don't tell any lies—not even little white ones. Do not change events—the slightest detail must not be altered. Other than that, give only your name and vitals and a respectful request that no further questions be asked until you have had an opportunity to confer with your attorney. While waiting to consult with your lawyer make every effort to clear your mind and try to remember exactly what happened and what was said, in chronological order. Ask for paper and pen to record these fresh recollections of what each person at the scene was doing and what they said. Make diagrams of where people and objects were.

THE AFTERMATH:

a) Do not make any comments or statements to the press. Expect the press to examine your life and pick at any and all transgressions in your past. You will most likely be more infamous than famous and your picture and background could very well be splashed across the newspapers and local television;

b) Do not expect to be made out to be a hero regardless of the risk you took or the despicable act of the perpetrator. Almost without exception, the most despicable of perpetrators will have some redeeming characteristics. Assume that the person you were forced to dispatch, this scum ball who tried to kill you or another innocent being, is some mother's apple-eye, a son of great promise, father to an idolizing child, wonderful lover or husband, grandson, grandfather or maybe just a best friend of another dirtbag. The media, in many cases, will tend to ignore the perp's misdeeds and glorify his, in some cases, single saving trait. It is because of just one of these redeeming characteristics that the person who shoots him will most likely be sued and even judged evil by some;

c) If your assailant is of a different race, creed or religion, regardless of the fact that you were totally justified in a successful defense of an unwarranted and illegal assault, you still might be labeled a racist or worse. What's worse? Being accused of having gone "looking for a fight" or "looking for an excuse to practice what you've been practicing;"

d) There will always be a few that will condemn your actions, no matter how heroic. Some family members of the criminal who attacked you might bear a grudge thus prompting paranoia and other worries, both real and imagined. Follow the lead of the more progressive police agencies and get psychological counseling — and watch your backside!

e) Expect to experience all or many of the following post-shooting traumas: nightmares, depression, sleep disturbances, appetite disorders, aggression aversion, family and other forms of stress. Some of these conditions may last a lifetime.

UPSIDE OF LETHAL FORCE USE:

a) You're still alive and though you might be judged by twelve it's better than being carried by six.

V ESSAYS, EDITORIALS and Other Such Stuff

Semantics, Terms That Sometimes Cause Confusion

Too many times I find myself in discussions with another person where we both might be on the same page, but end up comparing apples to oranges. In most cases, the difficulty with verbal intercourse is due to either a misunderstanding or unfamiliarity of certain terms. Many words have more than one meaning, especially in the English language, lending more confusion to communication. Some organizations, such as our military, "coin" or write their own definitions of words to fit a particular situation. Used to be the goal of a soldier was to kill the enemy. Today, the military talks about "servicing the enemy." Does that mean kill? Injure? Wound? Change his oil?

COMMON LAW: Principles of law which are based on custom or judgments of courts rather than upon an enactment of written law. Though our nation is based on custom and historical decree, we are not a common-law nation—we are a statutory country whereas only conduct expressly forbidden by statute is punishable by law.

CONSERVATIVE: A person whose political thinking is to the right side of the political scale. Capitalistic. Conservatives lean toward viewing less government control as being better than more control. One who tends to believe in conserving or preserving established rules and traditions and one who believes that when change is needed, the proper procedures should be followed.

CONSTITUTION: Basic and underlying system of rules of which all other laws and behavior is judged. The supreme law. The rule of law.

CONSTITUTIONAL CORRECTNESS: Sometimes called Strict Constructionist. Persons who believe in a rigid adherence to the rule-of-law. These citizens believe that if the majority of the citizens wish to act in contravention to a constitution, the only legitimate method for doing so is by amending this Constitution.

CRIME: An act which has been determined (by enactment of a law) to be injurious to the public. We are a statutory nation inasmuch as unless there is a law against a certain act, the act is not a crime. If the subject law is in violation of any constitutional provision, it is not a crime to violate that law.

DEMOCRACY: A nation that is governed by the concept of majority rules. In a true democracy the people decide all issues by whatever the majority wishes. Without any guiding provision, such as a constitution, the rules of conduct change as the majority of the population changes. If the majority is comprised of X persons, they can repress or control Y persons. If there is a shift in population where Y persons suddenly become the majority, then they are free to discriminate (retaliate with their vote) against X persons. America is not a democracy, it is a republic (see REPUBLIC and RULE OF LAW) where this discriminating practice is negated. Some Americans erroneously believe they can enact and enforce any law (anti-gun, school prayer, etc.) merely by garnering the majority of votes to pass these statutes, regardless of constitutional mandates.

INALIENABLE: (aka unalienable) Something that cannot be taken away. An intrinsic right such as the right to life and with it the right to use what tools (firearms) necessary to protect that right.

LAW: Rules, customs and practices a society has established to regulate and control the actions of its constituents. The "pecking order" is: Ordinances (city/village laws) are subordinate to statutes (state laws) which are under federal acts and laws. All of which must be in compliance with the Constitution (see Rule-of-law).

LIBERAL: A person on the left side of political beliefs. Socialistic. Considers more government control to be better than less control. Persons who view our Constitution as a guideline inasmuch as they believe it can be circumvented and molded to fit the POLITICAL CORRECTNESS du jour—as opposed to amending the Constitution.

LIBERTARIAN: A person who believes in full individual freedom and a very limited size and role of government. It has been said that a REPUBLICAN is one who was robbed last night; a DEMOCRAT is one who was arrested last night and a LIBERTARIAN is one who shot the person robbing him.

MALA IN SE: (Latin) Acts that are wrong in and of themselves—morally wrong. American's don't need a law to tell us that murder is wrong. Championing (voting) to pass laws that violate one's constitutional or INALIENABLE RIGHTS is MALA IN SE.

MALA PROHIBITA: (Latin) Acts that are wrong only because society says it's wrong. Parking your car in a no parking zone is only wrong because society, via laws, has deemed it so.

POLITICAL CORRECTNESS: A rhetorician, with a virtuosity complex, who ignores the rule of law to further a political agenda. A slang catechism meaning the most expedient thing to do regardless of legalities. For example, those who desire to restrict or control firearms by passing unconstitutional laws, will justify their position with the pseudo belief that their actions are (in their opinion) in the best interest of society. (see RULE-OF-LAW).

REPUBLIC: A nation operating under a RULE-OF-LAW where its citizens have the sole power to elect representatives to enforce the rule-of-law and conduct the nation's business to the best interest of its citizens—in accordance with a constitution. The difference between a true democracy (see DEMOCRACY) and a republic is in a democracy the majority rules, i.e., there is no controlling factors (constitutions) to hinder the will of the majority of the citizens or their representatives. In a republic, the citizens/representatives can only act in accordance within the established RULES-OF-LAW. Of course if the majority wishes to act in opposition to their own rule-of-law (a constitution), they must first change this RULE-OF-LAW/Constitution.

RIGHTS: aka privileges or immunities. That which belongs to a person by law, nature or tradition. Some rights have been established by law, edict, court decrees and constitutions. Others are intrinsic (see: INALIENABLE).

RULE-OF-LAW: An organization (including a nation) that has agreed to live (operate) by a set of pre-established rules or laws and that these codes take precedent over all else. The U.S. Constitution is our rule-of-law inasmuch as it is the set of laws to which all other laws, statutes, ordinances, court orders and executive edicts must conform. It doesn't always work to perfection as witness the Judicial Branch's forced and uncontested opinion of the law upon juries in direct conflict with the 6th Amendment.

The Rule Of Law

It has often been said "We are a nation of laws." Nothing could be further from the truth. We are a nation of constitutions—laws, statutes, court orders, executive decrees, etc., are subservient to state and the Federal Constitution.

Henry Hyde, in his eloquent address to the House of Representatives, based his entire justification for impeaching the 42nd President of the United States on the rule of law (Clinton Impeachment Trial. Congressional Record, 105th Congress, 19 Dec. 1998):

> *"The phrase 'rule of law' is no pious aspiration from a civics textbook. The rule of law is what stands between all of us and the arbitrary exercise of power by the state. The rule of law is the safeguard of our liberties."*

What rule of law could he be referring to other than the mother of all made-in-the-USA laws, the Constitution? It is in this sacred document where we find the rules of all laws. Here is the foundation guaranteeing freedoms and requiring compliance. The law Mr. Hyde referred to in the impeachment matter is the obligation of the House of Representatives to bring articles of impeachment against a sitting president if there is probable cause to believe the accused is guilty of treason, bribery, or other high crimes and misdemeanors. Though some members of the House voted to ignore this constitutional mandate, the rule of law prevailed and Mr. Clinton was impeached (the Senate then acquitted him).

Throughout history there have been many tests on a commitment to a rule of law. Possibly the earliest comes from the Talmud, the Hebrew interpretation of the Torah (the first five books of the Bible). There is a story told by noted author, Herman Wouk, of a young Jewish boy who uses the "meat" dishtowel on the "milk" utensils. When chastised for this transgression, he questions a Rabbi about the seriousness of mixing the Kosher towels. The answer from the wizened student of the Talmud: "Once you compromise, the whole thing will break down. You have to stick to the rules." (Inside, Outside, Little, Brown and Company, 1985, ch 39). This simple answer is the reason the Jewish people have—for 5000 years— survived pestilence, war, famine, a Holocaust, The Inquisition and even assimilation. The United States, at only slightly over 200 years, regularly struggles with this lesson.

> *The number of voters impacted by government-originated funds is directly proportional to the proliferation and power of governmentand inversely proportional to the ideals of a republic.*

America's strongest modern test of the rule of law was probably when President Kennedy faced down Alabama Governor George Wallace over the admission of two black students to the University of Alabama. In June of 1963 the Governor defied a Federal Court order by claiming sovereignty of his state to conduct its business without the interference of the Federal Government. The President could have sent in Federal troops, but he chose, instead, to federalize the Alabama National Guard. Now the true test of the rule of law was laid on the Commander of these troops, Brigadier General Henry V. Graham. The General could have resisted the proclamation and we might have had to fight the Civil War all over again. He didn't and the rule of law was preserved. The Federalized General, on the steps to the Admissions Building, challenged his, under normal times, Commander-in-Chief and fellow southerner. It was at this point that Governor Wallace, saluted General Graham, and capitulated (The Schoolhouse Door, Segregation's Last Stand at the University of Alabama. E. Culpepper Clark, 1995, ISBN: 019509684).

Hot-Rodding, The Glory Years

HOT ROD: n. Performance enhancing a factory vehicle to increase its horsepower, acceleration and speed.

Though hot rodding began in the 1930s the effects of the Great Depression and World War II greatly suppressed its numbers. The glory years really didn't get started until the 1950s and carried on into the early sixties. Hot rodding, especially street racing, became more prevalent due to an improved economy that had hindered the cash-strapped/gasoline-rationed past generation. Sans sanctioned drag strips, racing on the streets and highways were the only option for this new generation of pioneer hot rodders.

In addition, lagging police technology fueled this open road mentality that made "getting caught" a remote probability. More powerful Detroit-built cars were often the result of hot rodder innovations such as multiple carburetors, hi-performance cams and machining techniques that pushed the limits of factory production. Most of these mechanical changes were discovered by trial and error, but when they worked the "Big Three" (Ford, Chrysler, GM) took notice. Many of these "trials" really improved performances. "Errors" occurred when, say for example, one hot rodder learned that someone had successfully shaved .100 in. off his flywheel to which this hot rodder would think: if .100 in. is good for more speed, then .125 in. would be better. Sometimes these innovations worked and sometimes they caused the modified part to come apart at high speed. Additionally, hopping-up an engine put increased strains on other parts of the car—strains not envisioned or engineered for by the factory.

One very enthusiastic rodder installed a full race Mercury Flathead engine into his, otherwise stock 1949 Ford. This engine included porting & polishing, oversize bored block, a new crankshaft to increase the stroke, a racing camshaft, six Stromberg 97 carburetors, hi-compression heads and a few other goodies. He had a lot of added horsepower, but he never made it to the end of the quarter-mile drag strip. Every time he ran some stock part, such as a universal joint, rear axle, clutch or transmission, would break from the strain of all this added power.

Drag racing, at first, was a hobby whereas the hot rodder needed his rod for everyday transportation and thus couldn't have a "full-race" engine or a show-quality finish. Fact was these modified and customized vehicles were usually never completely finished. Most exhibited primer paint and lacked upgraded interiors and spit-shined/chrome-plated engines—in direct contrast to hot rods of today. This was mostly due, not so much because the rodder didn't have the time or money to complete the car, but usually as a result of taking on a new responsibility…such as marriage and all that comes with it. Sure, Hot Rod Magazine displayed a finished rod on its cover every month, but those were more of the exception than the rule.

In the Glory Years, drag strips were little in number and fought against by local politicians. However, once city fathers were convinced that hot rod clubs were serious about legal racing and would punish club members who were caught racing on the streets, drag strips became more prevalent. In most communities, hot rod clubs would ban together to form an association and then seek a sympathetic police officer to help convince the political powers to authorize the building of a drag strip.

The "Big Three," learning from the hot rodders innovations and demands for more horsepower, began offering factory options such as hot cams, multi-carb set-ups and engineered drive trains to handle this increase in engine power. By the mid-sixties hot-rodding, as the innovators had lived it, was passé. No longer was it possible to win a race just because you could hop-up or do a better tune-up than the other guy. The advent of the "muscle car" era marked the beginning of the, who-ever-has-the-most-money wins the race. Sanctioned, produced and funded factory vehicles made drag racing an expensive and technologically intense venture.

Another factor, police technology, also contributed to fewer street races. At the same time that political subdivisions were considering allowing sanctioned drag strips, they were equipping their police departments with "interceptor" scout cars. These interceptors were mostly just unmarked, V8 powered sedans with heavy duty brakes and dash or grill mounted red-lights. In addition, better radio communication and radar improvements also put a serious damper on those who did their racing on the street.

By the 1980s many former hot-rodders were settled in their careers, had a spare garage bay and began building modern street rods, drag-racing-only vehicles and show-only customs. Though these "finished" cars are what the owner had dreamed of in his early years, it wasn't the same. Then, as today, most all innovations had been discovered and with a spare garage and money one can buy most any part or pay someone to make his wish come true.

For an example, listed below are some of the vehicles owned by members of the Knights of the 20th Century Hot Rod Club (Cincinnati, Ohio, circa 1957). These unrestored, used cars in most cases were daily drivers and in various stages of completion. With maybe a few exceptions, none were ever "completed."

Studebaker powered '36 Ford;

Cadillac powered '54 Studebaker (Stude-a-lac);

Cadillac powered '50 Mercury (Merc-a-lac)

Full race '52 Olds (the one who's flywheel disintegrated because he removed too much metal);

Flat-head Mercury powered '49 Ford (the one that never made it to the end of the drag strip);

V8 Chev powered '39 Ford;

Chrysler powered '57 Chev;

Chrysler powered '40 Ford;

Olds powered '40 Ford Pick-up

Partly customized '53 Plymouth;

Unfinished, radically customized '56 Chev;

H-modified, Fiberglas bodied, sports car;

One "B" Dragster and a number of 55-57 Chevies and Fords.

Preamble To The Constitution (Annotated)

The Constitution begins with a preamble – a statement of purpose. Those who wrote the Constitution wanted to make sure future generations understood and didn't lose sight of their intentions. Having just survived a hard fought war to free themselves from a dictatorial and uncompromising government, the framers of this guiding principle of a new way of life, set forth in the Constitution, were adamant in their resolve that their meaning would not be misinterpreted.

We the people of the United States,

This simple beginning signifies that this new government is an entity, not of states, but of people. This differentiates it from the earlier form of government (Articles of Confederation, 1781-1788) where the states, in and of themselves, retained independence, freedom and sovereignty. The new Constitution introduced a new Nation that derived its powers from the consent of the governed in states that had chosen to unite.

in order to form a more perfect union,

This is the first of the six important reasons for writing the Constitution. The "more perfect union" refers to the new government being more perfect than the previous government under the Articles of Confederation. The new union, its thirteen member states having united, would be stronger and better than thirteen individual countries.

establish justice,

Having suffered under the tyrannical control of the King of England, one of the colonists' first orders of business was the establishment of uniform, fair and equitable laws that would be applied equally to all citizens.

insure domestic tranquility,

To settle our own internal disputes (as opposed to relying upon a King or court located in a foreign land).

provide for the common defense,

Once we were free of the English ,it was obvious that an army and navy would be needed to protect the states from foreign attack.

promote the general welfare,

Now the people could focus on raising their standard of living without having to pay the King his excessive taxes.

and secure the blessings of liberty to ourselves and our posterity,

The sixth of the principle reasons for establishing a new nation; it clearly shows the intent for the people and their descendants to be free now and forever.

do ordain and establish this Constitution for the United States of America.

An unambiguous declaration that this Constitution, a supreme body of laws and the institutionalization of the rule of law, shall be the authority for the government of the USA.

Bill Of Rights (Annotated)

PRECURSOR TO THE AMENDMENTS

In one of the first acts of the new Congress a previous issue was addressed. During the writing of the Constitution many of the framers wanted a Bill of Rights to be included in the original draft. Mainly due to time constraints the convention did not get to these human rights. However, in order to secure the ratification of some of the states, promises were made to prepare and present for ratification a list of rights.

An ACT OF CONGRESS, New York City, the Fourth of March 1789:

The Conventions of a number of the states, having at the time of their adopting the Constitution, expressed a desire, in order to prevent misconstruction or abuse of its powers,

The framers feared not only misapplication of the governmental powers of the new government, but outright abuse upon the citizenry. The delegates to the convention, having had to deal with the abuse of power of the English Government, were very wary of even their own newly formed government when it came to individual rights.

that further declaratory and restrictive clauses should be added: And as extending the ground of public confidence in the Government, will best ensure the beneficent ends of its institution

The restrictive clauses and declarations are to be restrictions against the government to assure individual freedoms which, in turn, instills confidence in the government.

Resolved by the Senate and House of Representatives of the United States of America, in Congress assembled, two thirds of both housed concurring, that the following articles be proposed to the legislatures of the several states, as amendments to the Constitution of the United States, all or any of which articles, when ratified by three fourths of the said legislatures, to be valid to all intents and purposes, as part of the said Constitution;

The requisite two-thirds (2/3) of both houses of Congress have agreed to the content of the proposed amendments. There were twelve (12) of these, but two, dealing with Congressional representation and Congressional pay, were not approved by the various state legislatures. The remaining ten (10), the Bill of Rights, became effective December 15, 1791.

Articles in addition to, and amendment of the Constitution of the United States of America, proposed by Congress, and ratified by the Legislatures of the several states, pursuant to the Fifth Article of the original Constitution.

Here Congress acknowledges its duty to comply with the intent of the Constitution by following the procedure for amending the Constitution as found in Article 5. The Act goes on to list the first amendments (12) which when ratified became the Bill of Rights, though only 10 in total.

THE FIRST 10 AMENDMENTS

The first ten amendments to the Constitution, known as the Bill of Rights, are in contrast to the Constitution's Articles, which (with some exceptions) codify rights, protection and limits on federal and state powers. Rather, these original and first ten Amendments record and list freedoms and liberties of the individual citizen and install additional limits on governmental intrusions

It is important to note that many of the "rights" contained in this Bill of Rights are NOT granted (given to) the people by the Government or by the document itself. Rights, such as the right to freedom of religion or the right to keep and bear arms, are intrinsic (rights the people had before the Constitution was written). The Bill of Rights only forbids the Government from trespassing on, violating or taking these rights away by passing restricting laws. Thus, and contrary to what some people believe, if for example, the Second Amendment were repealed, it wouldn't change the fact that the people would still have inherent rights to use what means are available for self-protection

Also significant, especially in the first ten amendments, is the use of certain words such as: "reasonable," "excessive," "prescribed-by-law," "upon-probable cause," "unusual" and "shall." The latter is not discretionary whereas the other words allow for some leeway or judgment. The term "shall" is mandatory.[see The Fallacy of "Reasonable" Gun Control Laws in Part IV of this book]

AMENDMENT I. [Freedom of Religion, Speech, Press, Assembly and Petition. Ratified, 1791].

Congress shall make no law respecting an establishment of religion, or prohibiting the free exercise thereof;

This is an order on the Congress not to pass laws creating or acknowledging a religion or stopping people from enjoying their own form of religion or methods of practicing it. Until passage of the 14th Amendment (1868), states were not precluded from passing laws that would infringe on these rights. The 14th Amendment corrected this oversight by establishing that if one has a national right not to be subjected to government mandated controls on these freedoms, the state must also be restrained.

or abridging the freedom of speech, or of the press,

Every citizen is allowed to speak and write his or her thoughts freely and without fear of government reprisals or restrictions. These rights, of course, like all individual rights are not absolute. If the exercising of one's rights violates another's right, then some controls are required. The oldest example: yelling fire in a crowded theater when there is no fire, which goes against the rights of those attending the theater, who have the right to peaceably assemble.

of the right of the people peaceably to assemble,

Whether one is attending the theater, a sports event or a meeting to discuss governmental changes, the government is powerless to block, restrict or criminalize this important right. Those who assemble for the purpose of infringing on other's rights, such as rioters, are not assembling in a peaceable manner and thus are not in legal exercise of this right.

and to petition the government for a redress of grievances

Little good would come of being able to peaceably assemble to discuss corrections to (redress of) governmental actions if the right to present these complaints (grievances) was not allowed. [see Power to Ignore in part VII of this book]

AMENDMENT II. [Militia and Right to Keep and Bear Arms. Ratified, 1791] [see The Fallacy of "Reasonable" Gun Control Laws and 28th Amendment in Part IV of this book].

The Second Amendment to the U.S. Constitution serves FIVE functions:

a) It acknowledges that the individual right to keep and bear arms is a preexisting right (a right that was in effect before the Constitution was written). Because this right is contained in the Bill of Rights and not under Articles I or IV, this Amendment is not a states right but an individual right of the people (as noted in the Act of Congress, March 4, 1789).

b) The Amendment operates to forbid the government from "infringing" (tampering, usurping, violating) this intrinsic and inherent right.

c) It acts as a reminder – an obligation – that the militia (originally, men between the ages of 18 and 45) must be ever vigilant and prepared. It is obvious the framer's wish that it is DESIRABLE to have available a militia ready to heed the call of need. This was only a wish because under the Constitution (Article I, Section 8) the Government is powerless to maintain a standing army.

d) It acts as an implied warning to the people to rely upon themselves, rather than the government, for protection and security.

e) Without this Amendment, there would be no ability to enforce or secure the rights to Life, Liberty, and the Pursuit of Happiness.

A well regulated militia,

The instrument is saying that it is DESIRABLE to have available a militia (whole body of able bodied men subject to call into military service). And that this body of men be "well regulated" (trained and disciplined). This was only a wish because under the Constitution (Article I, Section 8) the Government is powerless to maintain a standing army. Therefore, and in order to be sure that the "militia" is available should it be necessary to raise an army, it would be better for everyone if the "militia" were not only armed, but carried their arms with them. In those early days the people feared attack from foreign powers, criminals or savages. Today, though we are not under threat of foreign invasion, per se, we are subject to assault by terrorists and criminals, savage or otherwise.

being necessary to the security of a free state,

Because the Constitution (Article I, Section 10) forbade the national government from maintaining a standing army, each state, if it believed it had the need, could have its own regulated militia on call, i.e., the National Guard.

the right of the people to keep and bear arms,

It doesn't say the right of the *state* to keep and bear.... It says, "the right of the people...." The Bill of Rights is about people's (individual) rights not about states' rights (which are outlined in Articles I, III, IV). If the framers had intended the right to arms to be a states right (either country or individual states such as Ohio, Texas, etc.) the Second Amendment would have read something like: "The right of the state to arm its militia shall not...."

"Keep" refers to possession. "Bear" means to transport—carry. Keeping arms without being able to carry them would completely destroy the purpose and utility of the arms. "Arms" denotes weapons. The types of weapons are not specified. Therefore, whatever arms the individual wishes to "keep" and "bear" is in accordance with the Constitution.

shall not be infringed

Shall is mandatory. It does not mean maybe or at someone's discretion. Infringe means to encroach upon or violate the rights of another. This clause is a mandate upon the Government not to violate the people's right to own and carry arms. Other than protection from invasion (foreign army), no where in the Constitution or its Amendments is it guaranteed, pledged or warranted that the individual has the right to expect the government to protect him or her. Self protection is left up to each citizen by maintaining what arms are deemed best for that purpose.

AMENDMENT III. [Quartering Troops. Ratified, 1791]

No soldier shall, in time of peace be quartered in any house, without the consent of the owner, nor in time of war, but in a manner to be prescribed by law.

The colonist had been forced to quarter (house and feed) the British troops for many years. Though the framers recognized the pragmatic need to quarter soldiers in time of war, they were adamant that this practice was not to be done during peace time. When war was at hand, and as long as the quartering was prescribed by law (laws having been passed according to the Constitution), the individuals' homes could be used.

With today's army being a self sufficient unit, it seems like an out of date amendment. But if fighting was to occur within the borders of this country, the quartering of soldiers and their weapons, supplies and vehicles would become a reality, especially for those in rural areas.

AMENDMENT IV. [Search & Seizure. Ratified, 1791]

The right of the people to be secure in their persons, houses, papers, and effects, against unreasonable searches and seizures, shall not be violated,

Each person, as an individual, has the constitutionally recognized right to be secure (free of fear of loss) in their persons (on their body, clothes) houses (living quarters) papers (personal records) and effects (anything else the person owns or controls) against unreasonable (not justified) searches (visual or physical inspection) and seizures (arresting a person or taking possession of items found in a search), and this right shall not (mandatory) be violated (by the government). In other words, each person is entitled to be free of the fear of arbitrary government arrest or inspection and confiscation of his or her personal effects except when there is bona fide reasons to conduct such searches and seizures.

and no warrants shall issue, but upon probable cause,

The only way a person or his or her property can be searched (without consent) and made subject to seizure is by having a warrant (written document issued by a court, i.e., signed by a judge) issued. In addition, this warrant must be based on probable cause (reasonable belief that criminal activity is involved).

supported by oath or affirmation, and particularly describing the place to be searched, and the person or things to be seized.

The "probable cause" must be based on a sworn or affirmed statement and the warrant (written document) must describe the location to be searched and the individual or the items to be seized/confiscated. Someone, usually a law enforcement officer, must swear (or affirm) to the judge that he believes the reasons for wanting the warrant are genuine.

Many judicial opinions and court cases have defined and refined this most basic of rights. To balance the right of LEOs to be "secure in their persons" (free to protect themselves from surprise assault) with the citizen's rights under this amendment, some types of searches and seizures are now permitted without warrants, i.e., "pat-downs" or a search incident to an arrest.

AMENDMENT V. [Due Process, Grand Jury, Double Jeopardy, Self-incrimination, Ratified 1791]

No person shall be held to answer for a capital, or otherwise infamous crime, unless on a presentment or indictment of a grand jury,

No one can be held to answer (forced to present a defense) for a capital crime (punishable by death) or otherwise infamous crime (grossly criminal, shocking or evil act—felony) unless on a presentment or indictment (formal written statement) of a grand jury (a jury for the sole purpose of examining criminal accusations against persons to determine if there is enough evidence to bring formal charges on which the person will be tried in court). No one can be made to defend himself or herself against a serious (felony level) crime unless a grand jury has first looked at the evidence and issued an indictment.

The importance of a jury is noted three times in the Amendments. The 5th Amendment covers criminal grand juries, the 6th safeguards criminal trials and the 7th preserves civil protection. Juries composed of laymen and women have been attacked for their inexperience in dealing with complex and emotional issues. There have been many attempts to alter our form of judicial proceedings from instituting professional jurors to relying on judges exclusively. Though federal judges, being appointed for life, are positioned to safeguard our rights, they are not immune to political pressure due to the hand that feeds them belongs to the government. Juries, however, are beholden to no one.

except in cases arising in the land or naval forces, or in the militia, when in actual service in time of war or public danger;

This clause excludes members of the Army, Navy and National Guard (when they are on active duty during a war or when protecting the public). Only the Congress has the power to establish military code of conduct and military discipline. (Article I, Section 8).

nor shall any person be subject for the same offense to be twice put in jeopardy of life or limb;

Fearful of the English practice of keeping persons in prison after acquittal "until more proof came in," our framers made certain no one could be tried for the same crime twice. In an effort to right some alleged wrongs in our imperfect system, Congress has passed a number of laws that might be in violation of this clause, such as charging a person in federal court with criminal civil-rights violations after a state court had found the person not guilty when tried on a different charge for the same act. Without the power of Jury Nullification, this possible usurpation of power might not be addressable [see Judicial Accountability and the Slippery Slope in Part VI of this book].

nor shall be compelled in any criminal case to be a witness against himself,

The prosecution in all criminal cases must prove guilt without requiring the defendant to testify. This doesn't mean the defendant cannot testify, only that he or she cannot be forced to testify. This protection extends to direct testimony (on the stand or other by other verbal means) and indirect testimony (by papers, books and other forms of evidence that can speak in the place of the defendant).

nor be deprived of life, liberty, or property, without due process of law;

A person cannot be deprived of his or her life (be executed), liberty (be jailed) or property (be fined, have it confiscated) except with due process of law (the law of the land, the established form of legal proceedings such as the court system or certain bureaucratic procedures). The 14th Amendment also contains the same due process wording.

nor shall private property be taken for public use, without just compensation.

If the public (the government) needs certain property it has the right to take it for the public use as long as the owner receives just compensation (a fair price). No one person has the right to stand in the way of progress of the community. The courts continue to struggle with the definition of "public use."

AMENDMENT VI. [Jury Trial, Rights of the Accused. Ratified, 1791]

In all criminal prosecutions, the accused shall enjoy the right to a speedy and public trial,

Once charged with a crime the accused is entitled to a speedy (without unreasonable delay—usually a set number of days as defined by statute) and public trial (no trial can be held in secret). Without these safeguards, one could be deprived of liberty while being held for extended periods of time and without ever going to trial. Though it might be embarrassing to be exposed to a public trial, the consequences of secret trials would be an invitation to wholesale violations of other rights. The right of a public trial is also consistent with the right of others to know who is on trial and for what.

by an impartial jury of the state and district wherein the crime shall have been committed, which district shall have been previously ascertained by law,

One of the complaints of the Colonists in the Declaration of Independence was "for transporting us beyond seas to be tried for pretended offenses." Therefore, the framers included not only in this Amendment but also in Article 2, Section 3, of the Constitution, the provision against trials removed from the location where the crime occurred. An impartial jury means one made up of open-minded and unbiased citizens [see Dirty Little Judicial Secret in part VI of this book].

and to be informed of the nature and cause of the accusation;

Every person accused (charged by the government) of a crime is entitled to know exactly what he is accused of (which law he is charged with violating and how he is alleged to have violated said law).

to be confronted with witnesses against him; to have compulsory process for obtaining witnesses in his favor,

Again, the early Americans had had enough of the English practices of presenting depositions in court where the accused was unable to face the witness, much less cross-examine him. Compulsory process for obtaining witnesses means the right and power to subpoena witnesses.

and to have the assistance of counsel for his defense

Anyone charged with a crime that could result in his or her being deprived of life, liberty or property has the right to be represented by an attorney (someone practiced in the law). This right has been interpreted by court decisions to include the right to a government-paid attorney if the accused cannot afford his or her own attorney.

AMENDMENT VII. [Civil Law. Ratified, 1791]

In suits at common law, where the value in controversy shall exceed twenty dollars, the right of trial by jury shall be preserved,

Common law: The system of jurisprudence, developed in England and which is the basis of law in the United States, whose rules rest upon custom and usage or upon court rulings rather than upon enacted laws.

Though the right to a jury trial for common law civil suits is guaranteed, suits at common law do not include suits in equity, divorce, trust enforcement, suits for injunction, accounting, contract enforcement and certain other matters.

and no fact tried by a jury, shall be otherwise reexamined by any court of the United States, than according to the rules of the common law.

Once a jury has determined the facts (deeds done, words said or observations made) of a case, no judge or court can change this determination. Only points of law, constitutionality issues and rights violations are open to appeal by other courts and judges.

AMENDMENT VIII. [Excessive Bail/Fines, Cruel/Unusual Punishment. Ratified, 1791]

Excessive bail shall not be required,

Bail is defined as money or property posted (placed in trust), after arrest or indictment and before trial, to ensure that the person returns to face the charges. A reasonable bail is one large enough to deter escape, but not so large as to be beyond the accused's means. Under the 6th Amendment the accused has a right to a speedy trial in order to prevent him being kept imprisoned without being given a trial—a chance to present his defense. The excessive bail clause performs the same function, i.e., prevents a person from being deprived of his liberty due to a bail that is so high as to preclude his ability to be free to prepare his defense.

However, in order to protect the population or ensure the presence of the accused at trial, bail has been denied persons deemed dangerous or whose flight seemed certain. Though this practice has been upheld by the courts it is in violation of this amendment. A better way to deal with securing extremely dangerous or flight-prone criminals might be through enacting a new amendment.

nor excessive fines imposed,

Fines, like bail, should fit the circumstance. A fine of $10,000 per day against a highway contractor for failing to complete the work on time might not be excessive when considering the totality of the situation. That amount of money levied against a mom & pop grocery store who refused to shovel the snow from their walk would most likely be considered excessive.

nor cruel and unusual punishments inflicted

These terms evolve as society civilizes and technology emerges. Being kept in a stone building without running water and sufficient heat was not cruel or unusual, circa 1800. Today, having to do without those amenities most assuredly would be considered cruel and unusual. Execution of those convicted of capitol crimes has never been ruled cruel or unusual, though someday it might.

AMENDMENT IX. [Unlisted rights]

The enumeration in the Constitution of certain rights shall not be construed to deny or disparage others retained by the people.

The 9th Amendment, is seldom quoted or referenced because at first glance it seems confusing and obscure. However, upon careful dissection it is clear it was written as a reminder that the government is not permitted to negate or even reduce in meaning any of the "people's" rights. Beginning with the Preamble to our Declaration of Independence and continuing through each article and amendment of the Constitution, the underlying uniform theme confirms our forefathers' design to protect individual rights.

With the assistance of common definitions from Webster's Ninth New Collegiate Dictionary, the simplicity of this Amendment is explained:

***Enumeration:** List of items, such as the rights listed in the Constitution, e.g., right to keep and bear arms, right to peaceable assembly, right to free speech, etc.

***Certain:** Fixed, settled or determined, previously established things, i.e. inalienable—rights that cannot be taken away.

228

*Rights: That which a person has a just claim to; a privilege or immunity. Something that belongs to a person by law, nature or tradition. Rights are either contractual inasmuch as they are established by statute, constitution, court order etc., or by nature, such as the inalienable right to life.

*Shall: Mandatory, must be done. Contrary to this explicit demand of the 9th Amendment, the courts, in many instances, have ignored their obligation.

*Construed: Interpret: infer, deduce, to construct. To understand or explain the sense or intention of—in a particular way—or with respect to a given set of circumstance. The very act of incorporating the 9th Amendment into the Bill of Rights is construed to guarantee that these listed rights were not the only rights reserved for the citizens.

*Deny: To refuse to accept the existence, truth, or validity thereof. Lawmakers and some courts, in violation of the mandatory "shall" of the 9th Amendment, have consistently refused not only to accept the existence, truth and validity of our inalienable rights to life, liberty and the pursuit of happiness, but also to secure (guarantee) these rights. To acknowledge a right, but deny a means to enforce or protect the right is not a right at all.

*Disparage: To lower in rank or reputation, degrade. To depreciate by indirect means. If our power to defend our unalienable rights is degraded, depreciated or reduced, then those rights, in violation of this amendment, have been *disparaged*. There is no greater degradation of a right than to restrict the enjoyment of the right for lack of a way to defend it.

*Retained: To keep in possession, to hold secure or intact. Rights, listed or unlisted in the Constitution, belong to us, the citizens of the United States, and are not subject to political correctness, disparagement, denial or removal.

"The very purpose of a Bill of Rights was to withdraw certain subjects from the vicissitudes of political controversy, to place them beyond the reach of majorities and officials…fundamental rights may not be submitted to vote; they depend on the outcome of no elections." (Justice Jackson for the U.S. Supreme Court in West Virginia State Board of Education v. Barnette, 319 U.S. 624 [1943])

*People: Human beings making up a group or assembly or linked by a common interest. The citizens of the United States of America.

*Others: Being the ones distinct from those first mentioned or implied. Refers to the rights that are not listed in the Constitution as opposed to the certain rights that are listed there. These other rights are the inalienable rights that include, but are not limited to, those self-evident Truths: "Life, Liberty and the Pursuit of Happiness."

Thus, the Ninth Amendment could be stated in these words:

The number of rights listed in the constitution shall not be the only rights kept by the people and these other rights shall not be degraded, or depreciated or negated by refusal to accept the truth or existence thereof.

Or, in still other words:

The rights listed in the constitution are not our only rights, and what other rights we have cannot be taken away or even reduced in power or stature.

Modern American Law, Volume 16, Constitutional Law, (Blackstone Institute, 1921) also defines this amendment in simple terms: " …a declaration intended to preclude [rule out in advance] the view which might possibly be put forward that the specific enumeration of certain rights was exhaustive [complete, thorough] and therefore no others could be claimed" [notations added]. Here, the authors of this noted text point out that the framers of the Constitution were so fearful of future usurpation of government power, they wrote this hands-off-all-of-our-rights into the Bill of Rights.

Of the few court cases that have examined the 9th amendment, the United States v. Cook [(1970, WD Pa) 311 F Supp 618] did define the objective of this least cited amendment: "The purpose of the Ninth Amendment is to guarantee to individuals those rights inherent to citizenship in democracy which are not specifically enumerated in the Bill of Rights."

We didn't create a government to define or tell us what happiness, liberty or life is. That's the kind of authority we had when the King of England, with his edicts, orders and laws, was telling our forebears what behavior was required to being a proper subject. When we had had enough of being told what made us happy, we created a government to protect our right to determine for ourselves, individually, what made us happy, secure and what life style we wanted. Two-hundred-plus years of evolution has brought us back to where we started. Regardless of many well-intentioned legislators, judges and bureaucrats, we have returned to a government that, in far too many instances, is forcing its definition of Life, Liberty and the Pursuit of Happiness on us:

It is obvious that the framers of our body of laws intended for the government to keep its hands off our inalienable rights enumerated rights (unlisted) as well as off our enumerated rights (listed). Not only does our sacred Constitution put certain of our rights into print, but it also creates the rule of law forbidding the government from denying or disparaging (taking away or lowering in value) any of our listed or unlisted rights.

There is no constitutional requirement placed on any governmental body to protect the individual—to protect his or her rights. Part of being an American is accepting the responsibility to secure individual rights such as the right to life or liberty and all the other unalienable rights. Therefore, in order to secure these rights each individual has the implied right to use the means available, which today include the personal weapons, the individual arms needed to protect each person's life and liberty and all other unalienable rights. The arms of choice include rifles, shotguns and handguns.

If one has the right to life but is denied the means (use of arms) to secure this right, then the right to life is disparaged (lessened) and is not a right to life at all.

Finally: What are some of these other rights—none of which you will find listed in the Constitution?

* The Right To Be Presumed Innocent Until Proven Guilty: That's not part of the 5th or 6th Amendment as many mistakenly believe.

* The Right To Protect Yourself, Your Property And Your Family: Next time some "rights challenged" person proposes or supports a gun control law, ask 'em if that isn't "disparaging" your right to self defense.

* The Right To Own Personal And Real Property: Can you imagine laws, or worse, some bureaucrat saying you must have their permission to own anything?

* The Right Of Inheritance And Bequeathment: You think inheritance taxes are unfair, suppose the Government took it all!

* The Right To Privacy—To Be Left Alone: *"The makers of our Constitution undertook to secure conditions favorable to the pursuit of happiness …. They conferred, as against the Government, the right to be let alone—the most comprehensive of rights and the right most valued by civilized man."* [Justice Brandeis, for the U.S. Supreme Court in Olmstead v. United States (227 US 438, 478)].

AMENDMENT X. [Limitations on Federal Powers. Ratified, 1791]

The powers not delegated to the United States by the Constitution, nor prohibited by it to the states,

The Federal Government cannot pass any laws or acts unless specifically permitted to by the Constitution. The Government, condoned by the courts, has violated many times over this final member of the Bill of Rights. Many federal laws and acts of Congress have been upheld by the courts where the logic and justification of acceptance cited is the doctrine of the three sub-powers: Implied, Resulting and Inherent powers. Some historical examples of use of these non-enumerated powers are: The purchase of Louisiana, Florida and Alaska, the construction of the Panama Canal and land grants to railroads and educational institutions.

The government's reading into the constitution powers that are not explicitly there (implied, resulting or inherent powers) poses a grave danger to society and to the republic. Just because the deals for the land purchases turned out for the best doesn't make the skirting of the Tenth Amendment any less illegal. Additional examples of actions undertaken on the strength of these assumed powers include the Vietnam War, the Gulf War, flood control projects, disaster relief acts and the withholding (or threatened withholding) of tax money from states for refusal to comply with questionable federal mandates such as vehicular safety, highway speed limits and domestic violence offenses.

are reserved to the states respectively,

232

Those powers not prohibited (by the Constitution) are reserved (set aside, retained) for each state. Examples of states rights include laws regulating marriage, divorce, contracts, state court organization and other matters pertaining to the public welfare.

or to the people.

"Or to the people" means: Left up to the voters to decide. Under the Republic form of government we the people elect agents (Senators, Representatives, Executives) to conduct the business of the country in accordance with the powers granted the government under the Constitution. On the national level there is no provision for holding a referendum (direct vote of the people) to decide anything. The states vary as to what can and cannot be put to a vote by the people. Some states allow more issues to be decided by popular vote than others.

America is not a democracy it is a republic. A democracy is where a nation is governed by the concept of majority rules. In a true democracy the people decide all issues by what ever the majority wishes. This is accomplished either by direct election or indirectly through elected representatives. Without any guiding provision, such as a constitution, the rules of conduct change as the majority of the population changes. If the majority is comprised of X persons, they can repress or control Y persons. If there is a shift in population where Y persons suddenly become the majority, then they are free to discriminate (retaliate with their vote) against X persons. The difference between a true democracy and a republic is in a democracy the majority rules, i.e., there is no controlling factors (constitutions) to hinder the will of the majority of the citizens or their representatives.

A republic is a nation operating under a RULE-OF-LAW where its citizens have the sole power to elect representatives to enforce the rule-of-law and conduct the nation's business to the best interest of its citizens. In a republic, the citizens/representatives can only act in accordance within the established rules-of-law.

Some things, especially on a national level such as foreign policy (war), could (and should) never be decided by popular vote. The cumbersome referendum method would negate parry and feint tactics and could expose soldiers and civilians to unnecessary losses while awaiting the voters decision on whether to attack or retreat. On the other hand, voting for matters of great national interest should not be left up to .000002 of the population (Congress). In spite of today's extraordinary means of communication (compared to 18th century technology) the people's representatives sometimes have no reliable means of determining what the voters really want.

Whose God?

Somewhat over 3000 years ago, God delivered the Ten Commandments to Moses. All versions of the Torah//Bible (Old Testament) reference one of the Commandments with statements to the effect: *"I am Hashem* (also referred to as Yahweh) *your God, who has taken you out of the land of Egypt and the house of slavery. You shall not recognize the gods of others in my presence."*

In other words, Our God is acknowledging there are other gods, but that He is Our God. "Our" meaning, the descendants of Abraham who kept the covenant. Conventional thinking is, God is indicating idols, statutes and other physical property. Maybe not. Consider the possibility that "other gods" might mean the gods of different peoples, such as the Asians, Indians, Arabs, Africans, et al..

Additional explanations include the time line of planet earth and the universe, per se. The Torah begins (Genesis) with a chronology of how the earth and its wherewithal was formed. According to this accounting, "god" did not make the sun until the fourth day. Thus, without a sun for the planet earth to rotate about, there was no way to tell how long the first three days were.

This observation is unambiguously brought forth in the movie version of the 1920s Tennessee, "Scopes Monkey Trial," Inherit the Wind. Here, Clarence Darrow (played by Spencer Tracy), gets the bible preaching prosecutor, William Jennings Bryan (played by Fredric March) to admit, under oath, that the "first day" might have been 24 hours and one second. The logical conclusion, Darrow/Tracy draws, is that if that first day might have been 24 hours plus one second, it also might have been 24 million or 24+ billion "days" long.

Therefore, if we allow the possibility that the planet earth is being formed over a longer time than just four days—perhaps that would explain "pre-historic" mammals and dating's of other minerals, plants, animals and fish. It also might clarify the existence of "other peoples." These other peoples could have been fashioned in the image of their god. Perhaps the gods of these other peoples created a sun to generate light and energy, but that sun burned out or was burning out when Our God made Our sun. As to Noah and the great flood: The earth was believed to be flat at that time and thus continents — and their peoples — not of Noah's knowledge or view might not have been flooded.

Supplementary evidence that Our God is not the only god comes when Our God tells Moses to command Joshua to enter Canaan (aka The land of Milk & Honey, aka modern day Israel) and kill all the Canaanites. If Our God was the god of all peoples, why would He urge the slaughter of His own making? He wouldn't. Maybe, He is ordering the killing of another god's "people." Perhaps, Our God and the god of other peoples are in competition — at war — with each other and we, the images of these gods, could merely be pawns in their game of trying to best the other.

Jews — and those who have strayed from the tribe, i.e. Christians, are about to be tested against the Muslim god. Though the Christians believe Our God has already sent the Messiah (Jesus) who was killed and will return, those still holding to their historical lineage to Abraham believe the Messiah is yet to come. It makes no difference. Jesus was a Hebrew (Jewish) and so were his followers. Followers of Jesus decided to call themselves Christians, but they continued to believe in one god — Our God. For all intents and purposes, any Christian with European roots and who has been circumcised — or whose father has kept the covenant — is a Jew.

When the Messiah comes (or returns) no one will know the difference because there is no photographic, fingerprint or DNA evidence of exactly what Jesus looks like or what the Messiah will look like when He arrives. All Jews and converts (Christians) will recognize the coming of the Messiah and all will obediently serve Him as He will be the agent of Our God.

Alright already, I know this is just one man's interpretation of hearsay ... but, the entire Torah/Bible is made up of verbal accounts. Stories told by word-of-mouth, of course, are subject to spin and then there's the matter of semantics — what exactly do the words of Our God mean when translated from ancient Hebrew to ____ to ___ ... and finally to modern-day English? For example: One publication of the Commandments says, "Thou Shall Not Kill." Another English printing by a different Judeo/Christian bible says, "Thou Shall Not

236

Murder." There is a significant difference. If there is this much variance in this line, what other words/lines have dissimilar meanings?

These ancient renderings may be coming to a head—Armageddon (the battle between good and evil)—when the peoples of the Arab god turn their threats of annihilation of the peoples Our God into action. How else can the hatred against the descendants of Abraham, Isaac and Jacob (Christians and Jews) be reconciled? Believe what you choose, I'm just tendering different possibilities.

Christmas

There Is No Other Day Like It.

Christmas is an American National Holiday. It also might be a religious holy day, or a holiday in other countries, but it is — in the United States of America — a de facto, official, certified and recognized National Holiday. Kwanzaa, Ramadan, Chanukah, etc. are not.

THE CHRISTMAS TREE:

This may or may not be a religious symbol, but it most assuredly is a representation of Santa Claus and our National Holiday. As such, it belongs on government property. Placing a decorated tree in the public domain, sans religious ornamentation, is expected, proper and an American tradition. Manger scenes, menorahs or KKK crosses are not national holiday decor and thus have no standing for placement on public property.

THE MEANING OF CHRISTMAS WISHES:

* To wish someone a Merry Christmas, doesn't necessarily mean that you wish them anything other than they have a happy 25th of December. Nor does it mean that you, if not a Christian, are accepting their beliefs or forsaking yours.

* For a Christian to wish a non-Christian a merry Christmas is the epitome of what this special day is all about. The Christian is saying, *"This is my special day and I wish that your day will be as wonderful as my day promises to be."*

* Likewise, for a non-Christian to receive such a wish is a great compliment as in; here is a God-fearing, decent, Judeo-Christian-valued, fellow American who is wishing me a good day. Thank you.

* When a non-Christian wishes a Christian a merry Christmas, he or she is saying, "I applaud and honor your right to celebrate this day that stands for the good in mankind and our common values that make this country what it is."

MY PERSONAL CHRISTMAS WISHES:

238

* To my Christian friends: I truly and sincerely wish that you have and enjoy a very merry Christmas.

* To my non-Christian friends: Please join me in honoring this day by reflecting on how fortunate we are to live in a country that not only allows us to choose and practice our own religion, but protects these rights.

* To religious fundamentalists, be they Christian, Jewish, atheist, Muslim, etc.: Please recognize that when you try to force your beliefs on others with law suits, bombs, government sanctification or "majority rule" you're not exhibiting American values, merely, your own insecurities.

* Finally, to the little kids (of all religions) who are able to grasp Santa Claus and really don't understand religious matter: Enjoy. It's the only time in your life you will be happily conned and guilt free.

Christians and Jews are the epitome of decent,
law-abiding, productive citizens;
and as such, have raised the moral,
ethical and living standards of all peoples.

The Race Issue

The root of the race issue can be boiled down to one word: assimilation. Those who fail to assimilate, to meld into the melting pot, are doomed to being the outcast. Almost all minority groups that came to these shores learned to speak English clearly, shortened hard to pronounce family names, swore allegiance to the flag—Americanized themselves. They, with minimal help from the Government, cast off the "old country" ways, embraced their new home and become as much like a WASP—for their public interactions—as possible. Almost without exception each kept religion and heritage personal and private. The Jewish people even invented Reform Judaism to justify the forsaking of black clothing and hats, untrimmed beards and Saturday (Sabbath) activities. Each group, from the Asians to the Vietnamese, also faced discrimination based violence, name calling, employment rejection and ostracism.

The lone exception to this unwritten rule of Americanization is the Negro race. Though this class of immigrants arrived as slaves, they were set free at the cost of many non-slave citizen's lives. At least since the 1950s the remaining barriers to equality have fallen, yet these descendants have resisted joining the club. Instead of embracing Americanized names, attitudes and work ethics too many of the children of the slaves try to force their ethnicity on the rest of populace.

Yeah, I know what you're thinking: "What does he know, he hasn't walked a mile in my Reeboks." Maybe so, but my Florsheims have covered a fair distance. I can't personally relate to any of the six million of my people that were exterminated—in my life time—just because they were Jews. But, I can recount personal experiences such as: upon approaching the end of my probationary period as a police officer, the Lieutenant wrote to the Chief, "Patrolman Klein would be better off with his own kind of people." To say the Lieutenant made life difficult and tried to set me up for failure, would be an understatement. Or, the roofing nails in my driveway and the threatening phone calls after I, and a Black friend, stood up to the KKK.

I won't discount the fact that the American Black, per se, has been duped by its own government—more exactly by the Democratic party as far back as the 1960s. Lyndon Johnson, while he was President, set this country, and especially the Blacks, back one hundred years. His "Great Society" program was designed to enslave the Negro—to obligate all African-Americans to the government and make them beholden to the Democrats. Johnson's anti-assimilation plan of giving educational degrees and welfare funds has destroyed at least two generations. The Democrats' placate-to-stop-the-riots (circa 1965), coupled with the break-up of the family unit by rewarding women for having babies out of wedlock and encouraging such anti-assimilation practices as African haircuts and ebonics was a master stroke of genius. Brilliance, inasmuch as the over-whelming majority of African-Americans still vote the Democratic ticket. Recent proof is found in Cincinnati's Democrat Mayor Charlie Luken's handling of the April 2001 riots. The Mayor, following party lines of old, tendered money for meaningless summer jobs, promised street cleanings (placating) and ignored criminal conduct by Black "leaders" during council meetings (anti-assimilation). The city is still controlled by the Democrat Party.

America and Americans are not perfect and there will always be some level of discrimination. Governments can pass all the laws they want, but they can never force people to mix with those with whom they don't wish to associate. I don't believe it makes anyone a racist if they don't want to live next to or go to school with or frequent a business where certain persons flaunt an attitude, dress in prison garb, use foul language, trash the neighborhood, commit crimes or force their music on them, none of which have anything to do with skin color.

The overwhelming majority of African-Americans are law abiding, hard working citizens—just like other melting-potters. However, being law-abiding and hard working is not enough in and of itself. Being a "good" American not only entails conduct that doesn't offend your fellow man, but a willingness to help your brothers and sisters assimilate—to become Americanized.

The Evolution Of Rights And Wrongs In America

RIGHTS:

At first both the concept and practice were very simple. Right was right and wrong was wrong and the government's role, via the Constitution, was to make sure our rights were protected and wrong-doers were dealt accordingly. Our founding fathers feared more than anything else, government intrusion into their lives. In the early days there were few laws, almost nonexistent law enforcement, no bureaucracies and the ratio of government employees to civilians was minimal.

Prior to the Revolutionary War human rights were determined by the whim of the King or his designee. After the formation of The United States of America two distinct classes of rights were soon recognized and granted to all citizens: *Unalienable/Inalienable* and *Constitutional*.

Unalienable Rights were those rights that could not be traded, sold, bartered, negotiated or otherwise disposed of. All Americans were automatically free to engage in any activity as long as it didn't adversely affect another human—keep him from enjoying his unalienable rights. In other words Americans were entitled to live free and pursue whatever made them happy. Each person also had the unalienable right to use what means were available to him, including, but not limited to, military arms to protect and insure his life and property against any criminal assault; be the criminal another human being, corporation or...rogue government agency

Because our forefathers felt so strongly about some of our unalienable rights they included the most sacred in a Bill of Rights and attached this register of liberties to The Constitution—"the supreme law of the land." These constitutional guarantees are what distinguished America and Americans from all others. Violation of these rights is what causes the rage that seethes in almost any conscientious and constitutionally educated citizen. Not unlike

242

previous revolutionaries, this fury is the essence of militias and other groups that long for a return to a society where everyone abides by the same rules and regulations. These patriotic groups are not anti-American or bent on destroying America. Their members are livid at the government for the systemic disregard of our constitutional guarantees as well as contempt for our inalienable rights.

The Second Amendment, taken at face value, means that anyone may literally own and carry any type of "arms" anywhere sans licenses, permits or special taxes. Of course, reasonable citizens recognize that certain persons, such as mental incompetents or children, should be excepted. But, federal, state, local ordinances, and judicial rulings are NOT the legal and correct method of enacting these exceptions. It is not within the rights of the Legislative, Executive or Judicial branches to make these exceptions.

> *If "we the people" do not want ordinary citizens to have a .303 Vickers Machine Gun mounted on their SUV – then changing the constitution is the only way to incorporate the exception.*

Despite what detractors of the 2nd Amendment believe, the constitutional guarantee, our unalienable right, to do anything we want with regard to weapons is set in stone. Yet, arrest, confiscation, conviction and prison are in store for anyone who violates laws that prohibit certain arms activities, no matter that these laws are unconstitutional.

It should be understood that because something is set in stone doesn't mean that it can't be changed. But, only a replacement stone will work. Statutes, executive orders or judicial decrees will not, *legally,* change the stone's mandate. In plain and simple words: The only way to change a constitutional amendment is to make a new amendment.

However, HOWEVER, rights that are inalienable/intrinsic cannot be voided. Thus, it might be possible to re-write the Second Amendment to limit certain weapons, the basic right to keep and bear arms is assured.

Changing the Constitution is a lengthy process that sometimes yields unintended consequences, e.g., the Prohibition Amendment (18th) and the Income Tax Amendment (16th). This, coupled with a desire for control, is why judges, Senators, and Representatives often resist constitutional changes. Historically, it's been expedient for law makers and judges to deal with troublesome constitutional matters in their own bailiwick or simply ignore matters they deem politically incorrect. It is easier to unilaterally declare the 2nd Amendment does not apply to machine guns, sawed-off shotguns and concealed weapons, etc., than to risk rejection of a new constitutional amendment.

Today, a citizen's rights have become either negotiable or subject to judicial rulings. A negotiated right is somewhat like a plea bargain—you accept a penalty or loss of a right to avoid alternatives that may yield a more severe outcome. One example is to pay a fine rather than dispute a charge in court (which is monetarily costly) and the verdict is uncertain—even if you're not guilty. Another example of a negotiated right is one where the government says, if you want to carry a concealed weapon for your own protection, you must surrender your 2nd Amendment rights in exchange for the privilege of a state issued permit. Of course, if you desire to exercise your constitutional rights to "keep and bear arms" the government, with its unlimited funds, will force you into a very expensive and long trial. The outcome of such a trial has been predetermined by the many previous and precedent setting (unconstitutional) laws and *judicial rulings*.

A judicial ruling is a decision or holding of a court on a particular matter. When the constitutionality of a 2nd Amendment issue is raised, judicial rulings themselves have been shown to be in violation of the Constitution. Judges, when ruling in favor of restricting "arms", are violating their Article VI oath to "support this constitution...." A Judge's fear of going against political correctness is far greater than complying with The Constitution's Article VI. The reason for this is simple: There is no penalty—**it is not a punishable crime**—for violating Article VI, whereas, going against public opinion risks ostracism (see Dirty Little Judicial Secret in part VI of this book).

WRONGS:

Today where bureaucracies beget bureaucracies, government intrudes into almost every facet of daily living. Government employees, counting those from all levels of government, now makes up the largest voting block in history.

In western civilization, from the beginning of time, there have been only two kinds of wrongs: *malum in se*, from Latin, for a wrong in and of itself and *malum prohibitum*, also from Latin, for a wrong because society says it's wrong. We don't need laws to tell us that it is wrong to murder, steal or repudiate a sworn oath to God (although we need such laws in order to be able to prosecute those who so transgress).

> *Theft, murder and violating a sworn oath to God are MALUM IN SE, whether we have laws against those offenses or not.*

All other wrongs, from failure to acquire a building permit to bribery, are wrong because we, society, via our law-makers, have labeled certain acts to be against public policy. The United States is a codified republic inasmuch as nothing is against the law unless there is a law specifically saying so. Just like our rights, the basis for all malum prohibitum laws is found in the Constitution. The prohibited conduct and the conditions for declaring acts to be against-the-law are spelled out in a constitution, be it federal or state. All provisions governing both rights and wrongs mentioned in a constitution, must be adhered to as a constitution is the supreme law and can only be changed by procedures outlined in its own text.

When this country was established, there were procedures made for writing additional rules, orders and laws. These included statutes written by federal and state governments and ordinances enacted by lesser government entities. All rules, orders and laws must conform to every — not violate any — portion of the U.S. Constitution. There was no provision then, and there is no provision now, to permit the President, the Senate, the House of Representatives or any judge to change — **violate** — any portion of the Constitution of The United States of America.

> *This nation of Constitutions — as the supreme law — has evolved through an era of legal precedence into a nation of judicial decree.*

Beyond those wrongs listed in statutes and ordinances, we find today's wrongs addressed by edicts, penalties, and mandates that judges, elected officials and bureaucrats have unilaterally enacted. Acts that heretofore were malum in se, such as attacking and killing men, women and children, as in Waco or Ruby Ridge, are no longer held to be wrong if our government says so. Conversely, rights privileges and immunities, such as "the right to keep and bear arms," except under very narrow conditions, is no longer deemed legitimate.

There was no change to the Constitution; we the people never sanctioned a legitimate new set of rules. Rather, some elected officials, sworn to uphold our rights and support the Constitution, have slowly eroded many of our time-honored rights while closing their eyes to our supreme law.

Our system of ordinances and statutes, based originally on the Constitution, has given way to a pattern of judicial rulings, skirted by executive orders and bureaucratic decrees, of which the Constitution is treated as a mere guideline.

~~~

It's A Man's World?

PREFACE: As evidenced by the number of men in high positions who fail, embarrass themselves or otherwise screw up, there should be no question that the fairer sex are the more intelligent. However, there is one classification in which we are superior: The con.

PERPETUATING THE CON: Because women are basically honest they sincerely believe everyone else is. Using this to our advantage we have been able to convince them of some of the most outlandish scenarios, "facts" and schemes. Due to this self-claimed, inherent, mechanical abilities we have convinced them that we know how cars work, where electricity, steel and bricks come from (as if this is important). Thus, if we wanted to, we could fix the washer/car/screen door.

Men are always promoting this faux superiority — not necessarily for immediate gains, but for future times when we are backed into a corner or seemingly caught in a lie. For instance, if a wife were to complain about her washing machine's automatic "cool down" feature not working, requiring that she manually move the control to "cool down," a man's typical response might be:

1) "Sure, I can fix it, but it will have to wait until I can afford to purchase a micrometer [or some other tool he needs for his work shop that also might be totally unrelated to repairing of a washer]. Of course, if you really need it fixed, perhaps you could forgo your next hair coloring/cut/fluff-up [or other such non-essential and money wasting procedure] and I'll go right out and buy the tool and fix it — tomorrow."

2) "It can't be fixed and we can't afford a new one." [notice, I said 'it' can't be fixed. A man never admits 'he' can't fix it]. "I looked at it the other day while you were bathing/shopping/primping and could see that the cam-follower [or any other technically sounding term] is worn out."

If these simple explanations have failed to convince her, the guilt trip, in and of itself, or mixed with the above would surely follow:

"Please! I have provided you with a washing machine that only requires that you twist a small knob in order for it to function. You don't have to pound the clothes on a rock in the river or scrub the clothes on a board like my mother did."

When these maneuvers have become shop-worn, the stall tactic is best employed:

1) "Sugar, I've already ordered the parts, so please be a little more patient." This line can be followed up monthly with: "There's a strike/fire/vacation at the parts plant...."

2) "I'm not fixing it because—and I really wanted this to be a surprise—I am expecting this major contract/sale/order/invention any day and I was going to buy you a new house with all new appliances in it."

WOMEN NEED: Women have been convinced (conned) they need a man in their life if for no other reason than to protect them from the "bogeyman." This protection seems so important they have accepted beer-swilling, cartoon/sports-watching bozos as their protector. They've been led to believe that this couch potato will, when the chips are down, rise up and protect them from robbers in the night. The chances of a burglar/rapist (other than their own husband) breaking into an occupied home is less than being struck by lightning.

> *Any man who admits to his wife*
>
> *that he can sometimes be dumb,*
>
> *can get away with a lot of dumb stuff.*

The fact that we have been able to perpetuate this scam—as well as convincing them guns are too dangerous for them to use—is conclusive proof of our superiority (in lying, cheating and conning). The fact that we can lie, cheat and perpetuate confidence schemes better than our gender counterpart is shown conclusively by the number of men outnumbering women in our prisons...no wait, scratch that, let me work on this a little more.

> *Author's note: Yeah, I know this is a little dated, but it wasn't when I wrote it.*

The Political "F" Word

Liberals, a.k.a. Democrats, tend to say they are only concerned with what's fair. However, I have never heard or read exactly how they define fair. Is it something like what U.S. Supreme Court Justice Potter Stewart said when he stumbled with the definition of pornography: "I know it when I see it." (*Jacobellis v. Ohio* 1964)?

This begs the question: are liberals claiming elitism by saying they might not be able to articulate what's fair, but they know what's best for all of us? And because they possess that undefined, secret knowledge of fairness, we should blindly trust that their choices of politicians and bureaucrats will be fair in enforcing fairness?

Webster's definition of fair/fairness uses such words as equitable, impartial, unbiased, et al. Sure, the liberal could use these words when referring to helping those less-fortunate. But, the conservative could also argue "less-fortunate" is subjective and forcing (taxing) others to support such "help" is inequitable, partial, biased, et. al.

Okay, Klein, you say, what's your definition of "fair"? Fair-enough. Fair is: You may do whatever you want as long as it doesn't adversely impact me; and I'll do as I please as long as it doesn't negatively affect you. In other words, if you want to contribute all of your money to provide "fair" education, health care, employment, etc., to those who haven't earned these benefits, that's fine with me. Just don't try to force me to donate to your doctrine of fairness. Fairness is not fair if it forces someone else to give up what's fairly theirs.

I exercise my right to carry a concealed firearm for protection, but I wouldn't dream of making you do so. Say … maybe we should use tax money to fight FOR our 2nd Amendment rights rather than against them as the government has been doing? Finally, I believe "fair" is a government that works to reduce its power and size, encourages its citizens to stand by themselves, and supports charitable organizations to tend to the needs of those who are struggling.

I realize I might have offended Democrats by calling them elitists and liberals, but they have portrayed Republicans as beer swilling, NRA card-carrying, bible thumping, red-neck heathens. Well, I'm honored to carry my NRA Life-Membership card and I surely enjoy a cold beer on a hot day. I'm not certain what a bible-thumper is, but I believe in God, the Ten Commandants and that I am descended from Abraham, Isaac and Jacob—not monkeys. As to being a redneck: the dictionary defines a redneck as a member of the rural, southern, working class. I'm not from the South, but my farm is in rural Brown County, Ohio and up until I retired six years ago at age 64, I always worked. Heathen? I might have mud on my boots and stains on my bibbers, but I take regular showers and have my hair trimmed neatly at a local shop—where they don't make me smell all prissy.

Anti-Semitism—Again

In the late 1970s I moved my family to Switzerland County, Indiana where, over the years, I encountered a number of incidences of anti-Semitism. Although this was a full generation after the start of the American civil rights movement and well past 40 years since the onset of the Holocaust it wasn't shocking or new. A few persons, including the publisher of the local newspaper, told me they had never met someone who they knew was Jewish.

Today, you'd think that with all the government education, civil rights suits and media coverage on narrow-mindedness, racism and intolerance only a caveman would be so ignorant of discriminatory indiscretion—especially news editors and lawyers. Unfortunately, not so.

I now live in Brown County, Ohio and subscribe to the local paper, The News Democrat (http://www.newsdemocrat.com/). The 13 June 2010 issue of this bi-weekly published a guest editorial by a local attorney and president of the U.S. Grant Association. In writing about our Constitution he claimed that Thomas Jefferson (of Declaration of Independence fame) noted that "Ancient Principles" (unalienable rights) included equality, life, liberty and the pursuit of happiness. The attorney went on to say: "He [Thomas Jefferson] recognized that when the Israelites enjoyed and pursued those 'Ancient Principles' they thrived, but when they drifted away from those principles, their culture declined."

Though the Grant Association president is entitled to his opinion; saying the Israelites (Jews, per se) have forsaken unalienable rights and our culture has declined is not only inaccurate, but insulting. Of course, we not only are still thriving, but have thrived for almost six thousand years—longer than any others.

I wrote a letter-to-the-editor which was published in the next edition. The editor also personally responded to me via e-mail: "*My duty is to make sure it* [Guest Editorial] *is labeled opinion and that people know it is opinion.*" I replied to this with the question: "So, in other words, if your only duty is to make sure opinions are labeled as such, you would allow an editorial saying to the effect that blacks were no-good, shiftless, lying nig**rs—as long as it *was just 'opinion'? That doesn't seem any different to me than what Mr.[lawyer] wrote about Israelis/Jews."* The editor did not respond to this last query nor did he or the lawyer offer a retraction/apology in the following issue of <u>The News Democrat</u>.

There might be a fine line between slander, liable, civil rights violations and legitimate opinion, but for an attorney and news editor to tout "Ancient Principles" while dissing an entire society is the pinnacle of arrogance and stupidity. But, that's just my opinion.

We Jews can argue and disagree over which politician is best for us, the U.S. and/or Israel, but on the matter of assaults upon our heritage there is always unity. Whether intentional or due to ignorance, whether blatant or subtle we must be ever vigilant and never (as in Never Again) allow untruths, lies, insults and other such attacks against us to go unchallenged. To do otherwise implies to our enemies that we agree or are cowards and/or are too unintelligent to know we've been slighted.

Paranoia: At What Point Does Paranoia Become Prudence?

Most minorities have some form of "family voice," be it a radio station or published periodical. The purpose of these minority media, aside from social news, is to inform group members of concerns, dangers, and threats. At times, these closed media operations, for fear of offending their readership, falter when it comes to dealing with hard issues.

The Jewish people are heading down a historically familiar path— the path of entrusting their safety and lives exclusively to non-Jews. This is especially poignant since the 2001, September 11th attack on the World Trade Center (WTC) in New York City.

Rhetoric accusing the Jews of being the underlying cause of the WTC catastrophe started early and continues in some quarters to this day—and not merely in typically anti-Semitic circles. Brit Hume, a Fox News Anchor, said on national Television immediately following the WTC assault, "The attack [on the WTC] is because we [the USA] support Israel. Maybe it's time we stop supporting them [Israel]." Since then, many other commentators have explored the same premise—that the root of the world's problems is the Jews. This is the same logic Hitler wielded when garnering support for his "final solution" and American General (and later president) Ulysses S. Grant used in issuing his infamous Order No. 11.

IT ALREADY HAPPENED HERE:

During the American Civil War the North fell victim to profiteering by unscrupulous cotton traders. Although the two sides were at war they continued to trade in cotton—the South needing an outlet for its crop, and the North needing cotton to clothe its troops.

Though a small number of these traders were Jewish, the terms "Jew," "profiteer," "speculator," and "trader" became synonyms. When General Ulysses S. Grant was informed that "traitors and Jew peddlers" were gouging the Union Army, he didn't hesitate to issue orders saying, "No Jews are to be permitted to travel on the railroad southward into the Department of Tennessee...."

When this edict failed to halt illegal trading (an obvious indication that non-Jews were also deeply involved in the price-gouging) Grant issued General Order No. 11: "The Jews, as a class violating every regulation of trade established by the Treasury Department ... are hereby expelled from Kentucky, Tennessee and Mississippi within 24 hours."

Only heroic and tenacious efforts by a few Jewish leaders, who appealed directly to President Lincoln, rapidly got General Order No. 11 rescinded. Had it not been for the kindness of a Gentile.

This is not to say that non-Jews, per se, are our danger. Rather, the danger is that we Jews fail to put sufficient trust in our own resources in a world that, once again, is becoming increasingly hostile to us.

AMERICAN POLICE AGENDAS:

Prior to a recent High Holy days service, I had the opportunity to discuss security measures with management and officials of one of the local synagogues. To say there were significant holes in their plans and practices would be a gross understatement. Of course, since no attacks occurred they're confident that their preventative measures worked. That's like the guy who walks around constantly snapping his fingers believing that it keeps lions and tigers away. The fact that the natural habitat of lions or tigers precludes any being within 3000 miles is lost on him; the lack of attacks isn't due to his preparations.

In my book, *Lines of Defense: Police Ideology and the Constitution*, I devote a chapter to agendas. It is important to realize that individuals, agencies, and governments might have different goals and aspirations. A local police officer's definition of "best interest" might not be the same as a Jewish congregation's, the general public's, or even that of other police agencies.

Nothing sums this up more poignantly than the 1999 Columbine High School tragedy in Colorado. Infamously, the responding officers waited 40 minutes for the SWAT team to arrive before entering the school building—while children were being killed inside. The basis for this shameful inaction can be found in a public

254

statement by the county sheriff: "I didn't order the officers in, because I didn't want any of them to get hurt."

As a result of the Columbine disaster and similar incidents with other police agencies, I wrote a series of articles for law-enforcement journals contending that modern police training is producing a mind-set of cowardice. Naturally, these columns generated a lot of mail, both pro and con. One of the scariest statements was from a Midwest police chief who wrote, "Most officers … are just like everyone else. Their main goal is to get home safely at the end of each shift, and I agree with that philosophy 100 percent." In other words, and in contrast to past times, the police today are more interested in saving their own hide than yours or your congregation's.

Those smartly uniformed police officers look impressive in the foyer of your temple. But when push comes to shove, whom do you really want protecting you and your children—an experienced, armed, fellow Jew with his own family's safety at stake or a "40 minute" cop whose main goal is to get home safely at the end of his shift?

What's even more disturbing is that during September's High Holy Days, we had almost exclusively Gentile police and guards protecting us, our synagogues, and our clubs. As long as we allow our security to depend upon the resolve of Gentiles we will remain under their control and continue the victim mentality that equates "being a good Jew" with hiding and submission. I'm not saying we should establish our own police force or army, but we might stand a better chance if we took a lesson from the Israelis and looked within our own ranks for our first line of defense. After all, who has Jewish interests and security more at heart than we Jews ourselves?

PERSONAL EXPERIENCE:

Anti-Semitism is evident in American cities, suburbs and especially in the rural areas. The writer spent 17 years in a sparsely populated county of a Midwestern state and experienced numerous acts of discrimination. One incident of blatant bigotry involved the county newspaper. This weekly publication (the only newspaper in the county) published a letters to the editor column in which the writers were identified only by name and city. Writers were not allowed to include pitches or contact information for business. Unfortunately, the paper made a single exception to this rule.

The paper's editor regularly published letters from the local Imperial Wizard of the Ku Klux Klan. These very anti-Semitic and anti-Black "letters" were complete with a post office box and request for donations. In other words, they were a de facto, and free, advertisement not offered to anyone else. When none of the Christian readers wrote to complain (a la Martin Niemoller), this writer and an African-American friend called on the editor.

We pointed out that we had to pay to advertise our businesses in her paper while the Klansman got a free ad. It was obviously unequal treatment. Our position was that if the paper wanted to run articles promoting the KKK, then label them as such, and if the paper wanted to sell advertising space to the KKK to raise funds, then so be it. But keep letters, ads, and editorial content separate and treat us all the same. The editor stood firm on her First Amendment rights to publish as she saw fit and refused to label the KKK "letters" as an advertisement.

We called the paper's out-of-town owner who admitted he had never met a Jew, at least one he knew was Jewish, but was going to stand behind his editor. Besides, he said, the Imperial Wizard couldn't afford to pay for advertising. Calls from the Anti-Defamation League of the B'nai B'rith' and a Black judge only provoked an editorial by the editor gloating that even behind the scenes pressure couldn't obstruct the freedom of the American press.

As it turned out, the editor's husband, a prominent attorney in an adjacent and more cosmopolitan county, was running for circuit judge. The editor was told that unless she published a retraction the voters of this neighboring county would be informed that the wife of the candidate for judge was a Klan sympathizer, perhaps even a closet KKK member, and a demonstrable bigot. Soon thereafter the editor resigned and the paper's owner had a clarified "letters" policy published. My African-American friend received a few anonymous threats and I experienced the same, plus roofing nails on the driveway and a damaged mailbox. It could have been much worse, but everyone knew that we were licensed to carry concealed weapons—and did.

"Come on, Klein," you say. "You're just paranoid!" Maybe. But to survivors, paranoia becomes prudence long before pogroms and flying bullets strike.

TREACHEROUS DETAILS:

Steven Spielberg's Academy Award-winning motion picture, *Schindler's List*, was a compelling and moving depiction of 20th Century Jewish persecution. Thanks to the Ford Motor Company and NBC, the movie has had even greater exposure on prime time television than it did during its run in theaters. Now available on video and DVD, the film will forever be touted as a true depiction of the plight of Holocaust victims. Yet this movie is fatally flawed.

Viewed through the eyes of a Jew, or anyone with a working knowledge of history, the story is well told. There was a Holocaust and many were killed. However, if viewed with the paranoia of a Jew who takes the neo-Nazis/Aryan-nations/Fundamentalist-Muslim or anti-Semite groups du jour seriously, then this deluded horror film might fuel the fires of the next holocaust.

In one of the film's concentration camp's barracks scene, a prisoner relates how she heard from someone, who heard from someone who "was there," that all inmates of Auschwitz were gassed to death—gassed in a room these inmates were told was only a shower. Others in the barracks doubted her story. How could she know this if all had been killed? It's a good point. If all were killed then no one could have escaped to tell the story, therefore the story must be false.

Later in the movie, the women on Schindler's list are sent to Auschwitz. Here they are stripped naked and herded into what appears to be a shower. The background music becomes ominous while the camera pans the terrified faces. This darkened room must be the rumored gas chamber. Then the questions, rumors, and doubts are answered conclusively when the shower heads spew only water, not poison gas. This corroborates the earlier assumption that rumors of mass killings were merely wild tales.

Scenes in this movie depict hundreds, maybe thousands, of deaths by gunshot. But Shindler's List depicts not one single killing, let alone millions of killings, by mass mechanical methods. Nowhere in the entire movie is anyone shown dying in a gas chamber. If this feature film is to live as a true accounting of the Holocaust then our credibility, as victims and historians, is seriously tarnished. The irony of the televised showing of this production is that it was sponsored by Ford. Henry Ford was a hard line anti-Semite.

Sometime in the future there will be another push to claim that the Holocaust never happened. And what better "proof" than an award-winning film, made by a Jew, that not only fails to exhibit scenes of the most horrendous killing machine that ever existed, but that claims that the now-alleged killing machine was only a shower, after all. Of course, the real death camps remain for anyone who cares to see. But a good propagandist can make it appear that the gas chambers were something else or were built after the fact as a Jewish distortion.

If there is one tragic attribute we Jews seem to have, it's the apparent inability to learn from history. Centuries of persecution and victimization have failed to dampen the spirit of a basically trusting and idealistic people—Israelis excepted. Many Jews, when confronted with the correlation of past to present, invariably counter with the familiar lines: "It can't happen here"; "We have elected officials"; "Our Constitution protects us"; "I'm an American first and a Jew second; therefore, my country would never allow this to happen."

HISTORY SHOULD HAVE TAUGHT US:

1) Adolf Hitler was an elected official. Our potential problem here in America is not so much that we might elect an evil person like Hitler, but that domestic or international catastrophic events could force American Jews, under an unsympathetic president, into untenable positions. When persecution arrives it is not how we define a Jew—Orthodox, Conservative, Reform, and/or parentage—that matters. What will matter is how the persecutor or the propagandists define a Jew. To them a Jew is a Jew. And "all Jews are alike." If future leaders of this country are similar to Brit Hume or Internet ranters who scream about "ZOG—the Zionist Occupation Government" or like a million more polite, everyday anti-Semites, that won't bode well for us.

2) Civilian control by elected officials (of which many are Jewish), is only in effect during peaceful times. If civil insurrection (gang

258

wars, plagues, terrorist assaults) force the president to declare martial law all civil rights protection will be at the discretion of the heavily armed military. The first step the Nazis took, long before the war started, was to disarm the people. Today, in the USA, there are many citizens, some even well-intentioned, who are working to remove all guns from civilian hands. Do we want to trust our safety to soldiers who may not have our best interests at heart—soldiers whose top priority might be something other than protecting a minority group to which most of them don't belong?

3) In pre-war Germany, Jews proclaimed that their primary loyalties were to the Fatherland. Many were proud that they, or their fathers, had fought for Germany in the First World War. Even as the oppressive anti-gun laws were passed, as their property was seized, and as they were forced to wear a yellow star, the German Jews never stopped thinking of themselves as Germans first and Jews second. But again, what mattered was not how they defined themselves, but how their government, their neighbors, and a highly propagandized media defined them.

4) Today, like yesterday, we Jews live in towns, states, and a country manned by largely non-Jewish police agencies, fire departments and military forces. From the beginning up to the present time American and European Jews, for the most part, have aspired to be doctors, lawyers, merchants, statesman—but rarely military or police officials. By our own choices, we live in a de facto ghetto, in which armed agents surround us while we render ourselves helpless.

NOT TODAY!

Upon establishment of the State of Israel in 1948, Jewish settlers coined the slogan "Never again!" to warn the world that they would never turn the other cheek when threatened. In Israel, service in the military for men and women is mandatory. Though their tiny Jewish army has proven its might they would be of little help if we American Jews needed them to fight for us on our vast shores. Legal problems might also preclude American Jews from staffing their own military unit for Jewish defense, but we can and should be prepared by encouraging our youth to enter our American armed forces and police ranks. Thus will our own sons and daughters be armed and trained to defend us on some future day when anti-Semitism takes its ugliest forms.

Because we Jews cannot stop the slams at us and our history, and because there will always be unintentional errors in depictions of Jewish activities, we should emulate our brothers and sisters in Israel. That is, we should cease to rely on the kindness of non-Semites for our protection.

American Jews may not have the clout nor the motivation to proclaim, "Never again!" But if we are vigilant we can decree that "Not today" are we Jews going to set ourselves up for future persecution.

EVERY JEW SHOULD ASK HIM/HERSELF FIVE QUESTIONS:

1) What preparations have I made to protect myself, my children, and my parents should a terrorist enter my home, business, or synagogue?

2) Don't we Jews owe it to the world to be in a position to save ourselves—or another minority—when the next holocaust, insurrection, or war arrives?

3) What have I done to repeal restrictive local, state, and federal gun laws?—laws that have historically disarmed my people (and other minorities) and left them vulnerable both to crime and to persecution in hard times.

4) Am I writing letters to the editor of my local or national "family voice" publication encouraging my fellow Jews to own defensive weapons and become proficient in their use?

5) Do I belong to and support pro-rights organizations such as the National Rifle Association (http://www.nra.org), Jews for the Preservation of Firearms Ownership (http://www.jpfo.org), The Second Amendment Foundation (http://www.saf.org), and Gun Owners of America (http://gunowners.org/), et al.?

LEARN FROM HISTORY:

In wartime Germany, Martin Niemoller (1892-1984), issued a warning that most of us are familiar with. In it, Niemoller lamented that he failed to speak up when the Nazis came first for the trade unionists, then the Jews, Catholics, and others. And, finally when they came for him there was no one left to speak up. A modern day parallel might read:

> *When they came to Waco, Wounded Knee, Ruby Ridge,*
> *I didn't speak up because I wasn't one of them.*
> *Then they came for the gun owners, but I never spoke up*
> *because I don't own any Saturday-night specials*
> *or assault rifles.*
> *Now they come – self-empowered bureaucracies*
> *fronting for constitutionally blind judges –*
> *to persecute my own people and I can't speak up*
> *because I am unarmed and afraid.*

Bibliography

American Jewish Historical Society;

Bartlett's Familiar Quotations;

Fox News;

National Rifle Association;

Gun Control, Gateway to Tyranny by Aaron Zelman.

Advice To A Teen-Ager

Youth is fraught with the futility of convincing your parents you know what you're doing.

Parenthood is fraught with the futility of imparting your wisdom upon your children.

Grand parenting is fraught with futility of observing your children trying to impart wisdom on your grandchildren.

Yeah, I know what you're thinking ... how could a guy in his 70s possibly write anything relevant to a 21st Century teen? Perhaps, but I am confident that due to a high level of intelligence, you'll find something of interest. Though the subject is serious in nature, please try to keep in mind a [my] guiding principle (somewhat canonized by a 1960s TV commercial): "You only go through life one time—get all the gusto you can."

"Never being able to satiate aspirations is better

than not having any fantasies at all."

LIFE'S PATHS:

Each person, from the age of understanding to the day of their death, will follow many paths. Every trail has intersections where choices or options are available—where decisions must be made as to which direction—course—is to be taken. All paths have consequences—good, not so good, bad. As a child you learned mostly by experimenting, such as the consequence of touching a hot stove was pain. As you age and acquire education, you gain the ability to learn from the results of others—a classmate disrupts the school room and is punished—or studies very hard and earns a high grade. The fall-out of following some paths are reversible, some irrevocable. If, for instance, you make the choice to play with your friends instead of studying for an exam, you might not do as well come test time. But, by making up the work and studying for the next test you can, most likely, bring your grades up. A non-reversible consequence could mean death—such as making the choice to walk on thin ice that breaks and causes your drowning.

One's level of wisdom is measured more by the ability to learn from the successes and failures of others, than by one's own triumphs and mistakes.

Most paths lead to other paths where additional choices are required. Almost everyday each of us must make choices—decisions as to which path to take. Some of these choices are no-brainers such as getting dressed before leaving the house. Other options are more difficult and/or complex. A friend dares you to steal something from a store. To make the choice not to accept the challenge could result in your being labeled a chicken. Taking the dare might end in your being hailed a brave person in the eyes of your friends. On the downside, failing to successfully survive such a challenge will not endear you to anyone—especially the ones who dared you. The choice becomes less complex and complicated when you learn how to deal with temptations from others (see Handling Difficult Questions and Situations below). The challenge is to recognize the difference between a harmless dare and a hot stove. Of course, not associating with persons who would do such things—persons who surely do not have your best interest at heart—might be the prudent direction.

Nothing written here is to suggest that you take no chances at all as such a life would not only be counter-productive, but boring. Taking risks is part of life where the trick is choosing the difference between taking a chance of permanently harming yourself or one that yields a positive opportunity.

The consequences of some paths taken early in life may not become clear for years, maybe even decades. Smoking cigarettes is an example of a chosen path that most likely leads to serious irrevocable harm later in life. Another example is palling around with the wrong people—those who delight in choosing paths that flirt with serious danger.

That inner voice, the message you get inside your head when

you're about to do something dumb, might be

your guardian angel trying to help you — listen to him.

The old sports adage, "The next best thing to playing and winning, is playing and losing," applies to most everything you do in life. Anyone can be a spectator or wear track/tennis shoes. But only players get the attention and self satisfaction. The thrill of seeing your favorite rock star on TV is ho-hum compared to going to the concert—and nothing to being a member of the band. Not everyone can be a star, but just making the effort to play in the games of life beats sitting in the stands. Traveling through your time on earth as a tourist pales when contrasted to going out on your own.

During your teen years you will most likely endure heart break/ache, and feelings/thoughts of insecurity, worthlessness, maybe even suicide. Plus having "best friends" turn on you, being lied to, talked about, snubbed and beliefs that you are unattractive are all part of the growing up experience. Not only is this normal, and I really hate to tell you this, but all of the above were experienced by your parents, their parents and their parent's parents during their teen years. Those who used these negative forms of education learned and gained insight and abilities to deal with future downturns.

So, when you've totally blown an exam, your best friend (now your former best friend) ignores you, or the cute girl/boy—the one you'd die for—doesn't even want to be friends, keep this in mind: Time is your buddy. How do you survive life's traumas? What's the secret successful adults know? All you have to do is get through the next ten seconds, the next ten minutes, ten hours … one day at a time. Life does get better—I promise, but you have to hang in there, sometimes ten seconds at a time.

Besides, look at it this way: Each negative encounter, an assault on you, is what builds your character—what develops your persona, makes you who you are. Each battle, set-back, trash talk toughens you for the next one. In time, others will recognize your strength and come to respect you—even if they won't admit it to your face. Guaranteed!

The rewarding life, however, is just as much based on past decisions as it is in choosing future paths. You will never stop having to select paths. But deciding which way to go gets easier as you gain experience and knowledge from making your own decisions as well as observing the paths contemporaries have taken.

As you get older, a significant challenge will be sorting advice from others about which path to take—that's why selection of friends is so important. Good friends who have also demonstrated sound path choices are in a better position to council you and for you to follow their direction.

MY PATH:

I was still in my twenties, working as a white collar executive, when I first heard the one-liner TV commercial, "You only go through life one time — get all the gusto you can." It changed my life. With complete clarity it made me realize age had already closed off a lot of things I still hadn't done. Oh sure, I could always do the mountain climbing/sailing boats touristy stuff that the young adults were doing in the commercial, but everybody-does-it programmed activities was never my style.

> *Everyone should have at least one job in his or her lifetime*
>
> *where they start each day with the revelation,*
>
> *"You mean they pay me to do this?"*

At age twenty-eight and with my wife's apprehensive blessing, I walked away from a secure job that yielded a more than adequate income to follow the path of becoming a police officer. Not that police work is cutting edge, but for the first in our family to do so, it was not standard fare. This "gusto" seeking attitude also led to paths of moving to a farm, private detective license, state certification as a firefighter and published author. Again, nothing extraordinary but certainly not what my contemporaries expected. I did, however, experience more than one exciting career. If I had the opportunity to live my life over, I wouldn't change a thing. The secret, at least for me, was to choose paths that led to better life styles — while having fun (and getting paid) at the same time.

> *Living outside the lines tends to spawn euphoric frustrations*
>
> *which oft-times is the only route to deep personal satisfaction.*

THE LAW:

No not the police or the courts, but The Law to live by. The Law is very simple and easy to apply to yourself and to anyone with whom you have dealings:

"NO LYING, NO CHEATING, NO STEALING. NO EXCEPTIONS, NO EXCUSES."

If you choose to follow this path … you have the right to expect those around you to also conduct themselves in a like manner. The three sins; lying, cheating and stealing, are most harmful because once committed others tend to wonder what else you have lied, cheated or stolen in the past or will lie, cheat or steal in future interactions.

One thing is certain; you will become the sum of your experiences, education and paths you have traveled. This "you," this persona is what you are and how you will be viewed by others. This compilation drives your reactions to events that shape your life. If you race down paths of deceit you will become an untrustworthy and unhappy person. On the same level, if you engage in honorable conduct your station in life will be rewarding and pleasant. This is not to say life will be perfect if you follow an ideal path, as perfection does not exist — only the perception of perfection.

Throughout life the paths you choose might be fun, exciting, even seem prudent at the time, but poor choices may have far reaching consequences. Sure, you can get away with a lot of dumb stuff while you're "underage," but if you go through your teen years with that attitude, it will be a pattern that will be hard to break as you get older. Trying to visualize yourself as a 40-something lawyer, parent, business agent and/or politician is most difficult while still in your formative years. However, I can promise you — if you live to be 40-something and you honored The Law — you will be anything you want to be.

LAW & CRIME:

Try to keep these observations in mind whenever illegal temptations are tendered:

1) The amount of time spent engaging in illegal conduct is directly proportional to chances of incarceration. In other words, the more time or times you are doing something dumb the greater the chances of being caught (A good investigator/detective/principal never asks a question unless he or she already knows the answer).

2) Most wrong doers are caught because their "friends" ratted on them. Rest assured, that when it comes to accusations by authorities, your partners-in-crime will choose blaming you to save themselves every time.

3) Where do you want to be tomorrow?

- In time-out or having the time of your life?
- In rehab or in a habitat with friends?
- Laughing or being laughed at?
- Texting on your cell or in a cell?

Every now and then it might be beneficial to take a look at the life and lives of others—classmates, family members, people you see in the public news. The ones who are enjoying life are those who have worked hard at choosing paths that have brought them to the good life. In contrast, try to place yourself in the position of a captured criminal such as those shown nightly on TV. That sullen look, vacant stare and fearful eyes are not those of a happy person or one who has many paths open to them. Persons who abuse alcohol or drugs fool themselves that they are happy. They are not and because of the effect of these mind altering consumptions are usually unable to choose paths to stop the abuse.

AUTOMOBILES:

Automobile driving is multi-tasking for real. Yeah, I know you can text message, watch TV, read a magazine, and eat dinner all at the same time. But if you don't spell a word correctly, miss a TV scene or even miss your mouth, it's no big deal. However, changing lanes into an oncoming truck because you paid more attention to a cell phone is a little more serious.

> *A driver of a motor vehicle who claims to have a year's experience, might only have one day's experience 365 times.*

When you become a driver try to keep this legal concept in mind: If you choose a reckless path that injures someone it might not be deemed an "accident" and thus could result in criminal charges. In addition, insurance only covers unintentional acts. In other words, if you decided to follow a dangerous path that results in a loss to another person, your insurance company might not cover you and/or cancel your insurance. Without coverage, the state won't issue you a driver's permit or license plates.

HANDLING DIFFICULT QUESTIONS and SITUATIONS:

Surely the best path is to always have the right answer to any question. Though that's difficult to do, the advantage can be yours if you learn a few of the basics. First, pause, take a breath and try to understand why the question is being asked. Also, please keep in mind you must not trespass onto other's private jurisdictions lest they say these question-stoppers to you.

Questions that begin with, "I heard" or "I understand," or questions that are inappropriate, embarrassing to you and/or are none of the questioner's business can sometimes prove difficult to deal with. I've always found the best way to handle such inquisitions, after a short pause, is to answer the question with a question.

Inquiries that are based on rumor, innuendo or untruths might best be handled with the question: "Where did you hear this?" Or: "What prompted this question?" Once that information has been obtained or refused, your next response might be: "In this state (pause for effect, and then say) slander is punishable by law."

This reply not only puts the offender on notice that he or she could be sued for slander, but it stops the subject matter from being perpetuated without your having to admit or deny the veracity of the information. Slander is defined as: A false and spoken statement that is damaging to a person's character or reputation.

If you're unsure of the inquisitor's motive, simply say: "Why do you ask?" This allows you to gain information that you might not otherwise be privy to. If the answer to your question is to the effect, "Just curious," a reply of, "not a sufficient answer," again, puts the onus back on the inquisitor. If the question is one you don't wish to answer because it is none of the person's business, or could put you at a disadvantage, simply say: "I can't (or won't) comment at this time (stop, or pause, and say), but I will provide an answer when I believe you have a need to know."

To keep matters from escalating or generating hard feelings always speak with a smile on your face. If a questioner has the audacity to rephrase the question or demand an answer, your next comment could be a light and friendly response to the effect: "Tell you what. I'll make you a deal. You can ask me any question you want, as long as I have the right to refuse to answer any question I want." If this still doesn't register; wipe the smile off your face and look the person in the eye while saying: "The subject is closed."

268

An exception to these rules are personal questions (health, marital, family, etc.) asked by very close friends that you do not wish to answer. To them, simply reply: "It's too painful to talk about, now. Could we discuss something else?" And then ask them a question or bring up a new subject.

Finally, try to be aware of people who are baiting you—asking insipid questions or making provocative statements—for the purpose of forcing you to lose your cool. Inflammatory or accusatory comments can sometimes be quashed with your question to them: "Are you asking me or telling me?" If in doubt, it's best not to say anything as in the old saying: "It's better to remain silent and be thought a fool, than open one's mouth and remove all doubt." But you already knew this!!

> *When meeting and greeting people,*
> *always look them in the eye. Speak clearly.*

VI CONCEPTS and IDEAS

Yeah, I know, some of these "ideas" are off-the-wall and might be simplistic and/or unrealistic — but perhaps, just maybe, one or more will inspire someone else to take it to the next level.

Creating Ideas,
A Formula For Originating Ideas

ORIGINATING IDEAS:

Ideas are the backbone of America. American ingenuity, creativity and inventiveness are the threads of life that continue to weave new products, new concepts and better ways of doing almost everything. Ideas are what this country is all about. From the idea of an individual's freedom guaranteed by a constitution to the idea of a "better mouse trap," Americans propagate creativity. Problems arise, not from entertaining new concepts, but from not shedding of old ones.

Nothing is more frustrating to a writer, scientist, engineer, sales agent or anyone under threat of a deadline, than to have to create ideas. Everyday minute-by-minute ideas are seldom earth-shaking innovations. Most fall into the realm of attention-getting sales letters, inspirational messages to subordinates and other routine problem solving matters. Nonetheless, for those charged with bottom line responsibility (or those aspiring to be so charged) having to produce new concepts and unique tactics can be Twinkie-consuming pressure. Knowing how to enhance and stimulate idea production is indispensable to success and can go a long way in reducing stress.

> *Writers, sales agents, crafts/trades persons, business leaders must produce fresh ideas on an on-going basis. Understanding how those new concepts are formed — the actual creative process — is paramount to increasing idea production.*

Much has been written about people who are creative — those who produce ideas — but little about how they actually arrive at new concepts, theories or a different way of viewing old notions. The term, creativity, is easily defined, however, a technique for achieving this highly acclaimed attribute is not readily found.

Idea production, like any other manufacturing process, is subject to and dependent upon an identifiable pattern. It makes little difference whether the creator is writing a book, seeking a solution to

272

a production line problem or looking to increase sales, the process of idea production is the same.

DEFINITIONS:

IDEA: n A mental image, concept, or notion not previously envisioned.

CREATIVITY: n (1875) 1: the quality of being creative 2: the ability to create. Also: The ability to make or otherwise bring into existence something new, whether a new solution to a problem, a new method or device, or a new artistic object or form.

HISTORICAL NOTES:

"The creative process is the process of change, of development, of evolution, in the organization of subjective life." Studies have shown that elevated intelligence, IQ above 120, does not appear to have much affect upon creativity. In other words, being highly intelligent does not enhance creativity. There has never been a reliable test to determine one's creativeness anymore than an examination can measure intuition.

Noted writer and poet, Stephen Spender, observed that fellow writer, Walter de la Mare, "must smoke while he is writing" and another of his contemporaries "drinks endless cups of tea when he writes." Spender, himself, admits, "coffee is my addiction, besides smoking a great deal, which I hardly ever do except when writing." He believes these traits to be the cement for his, and his fellow writer's, concentration. Perhaps, but it is more likely a form of distraction—a temporary escape into the subconscious.

Among the first to recognize idea producing exercises was the learned Italian economist and sociologist, Vilfredo Pareto (1848-1923). As an aside to his work, Mind & Society, Pareto determined there were only two types of people: Speculator and the Rentier. Translating from French; Speculator is one who is speculative, as in pre-occupied with possibilities of new combinations. The English translation for Rentier is stockholder or one who is routine and conserving—those whom the Speculator manipulates. Though Pareto recognized creativeness, it was James Webb Young, an advertising executive with J. Walter Thompson Advertising Agency, who defined the idea-making process.

The basic formula is simple to grasp and most "speculator" type persons already, unwittingly, utilize most of the practices. However, because many idea producers do not understand the process or have never given much thought to their successes they sometimes have difficulty in consistently coming up with new ideas on demand.

THE LATENT PSYCHE CONCEPT

The formula for creativity production is comprised of five distinct and separate steps, the Latent Psyche Concept. Latent, because it deals with the ideas and thoughts hidden away in the back of the mind. Psyche, for the involvement of the entire mind including the memory section, the intellect and the subconscious. Concept, because this word best defines the goal of seeking an idea, abstract notion or new outlook.

1) IDENTIFICATION: Identifying the problem and establishing goals. What do I wish to accomplish? Is it a script I want to write or is the hero of the story in a situation I can't get him out of? Is the production line slow because of worker inefficiency? Or are the workers inefficient because of mechanical aberrations in the line? Maybe the problem is simpler, such as: why don't I like a particular sales slogan?

When identifying the predicament it is important not to try to pursue detailed solutions to complex problems, i.e., if the problem is complex, seek ideas to one portion of the obstacle at a time. It is not necessary to work each section all the way through the Latent Psyche Concept before beginning the next section. The subconscious can juggle many tasks at once. What is important is to define the goals by identifying each problem. If the task is complex a visual list—something that can be periodically reviewed—helps keep the goals in focus and acts as a stimulant for the mind.

2) INFORMATION: The collecting of raw materials. Whether it is new research or data found in your own storehouse of general wisdom, knowledge is essential. Care must be taken not to clutter the mind with useless data and trivia such as daily social obligations. Keeping a calendar and day sheet of things to do and to log all appointments and responsibilities will free the mind for creativity.

3) MELDING: Digesting, sorting and collating—working over—INFORMATION in the mind. In other words, actively trying to come

up with an idea. The solution might be readily available and on the forefront of conscious thoughts. Brainstorming or think-tank sessions are forms of Melding.

Oft-times, during this stage, the realization that not enough INFORMATION is available and a return to that phase is necessary. Trying to cross the river before the bridge is in place is convoluted and non-productive.

4) LATENT PSYCHE: This is the crux of the concept. Mountains of Information can be accumulated and Melded with any number of problems, but without this stage new ideas are hard to come-by. During this interval the subconscious portion of the mind forces Identification to consort, fraternize and — Meld — with Information. Uncomplicated by conscious thoughts, and all its taboos and negatives, the Latent Psyche "mixing-it-up" stage is a playground for creativity.

> *Call It Magic, Pavlovian Action, Supernatural,*
>
> *God's Intervention Or Whatever;*
>
> *The Latent Psyche Concept Works.*

The amount of time the subconscious requires to develop an idea or view the problem from a different perspective is indeterminate. Some problems can be solved in seconds, while others might take overnight or even weeks. Writers and advertising executives among others who work with words have the unique problem of creating new text and ideas with almost every word. With libraries stuffed full of Information and thirteen million (Webster's 9th New Collegiate Dictionary) words in the dictionary the Latent Psyche stage is quite complex. Old practitioners of this process used to say "sleep on it" as a way of allowing the subconscious to act. This could be good advice for some, but to those on deadline there might not be enough sleep-time to beat the press, a competitor or sales quota.

Therefore, a new method was needed to permit the subconscious — the Latent Psyche — to come up with a creation. The trick is to have a switch or instantly available gimmick that would turn on the Latent Psyche mode almost at will. It has to be something that creates a concentration level high enough to block out all conscious thought of the project at hand. Of course, it has to be simple enough that its involvement didn't disrupt the project.

Driving across town to the gym for a work-out would hardly be conducive to time well managed. Hours needed for "sleeping on it" or for delving into a hobby that forces a stoppage when things are just getting fun is also not favorable to creativity.

Some possibilities immediately come to mind: focused, yet mindless, subconscious-stroking activities might include playing simple video games, especially if they can be accessed without leaving your keyboard. However, complicated video games might require memory space and analogy time which will crowd the mind with useless Information.

Smoking or drinking endless cups of coffee, as noted by the aforementioned poet Stephen Spender, can surely produce results, but the cost in personal health terms might be self-defeating. Spender's diversions to light a cigarette, or fill his coffee cup is in reality a work stoppage which allows his subconscious to mull over the current problem, a la, Latent Psyche Concept.

The card game, solitaire, is an excellent method for luring the mind into relaxed mode. There is no commitment to finish the game, save it or move on to the next level such as what other contests or engineered distractions might demand.

> A Deck Of Cards Kept On The Production Desk
>
> Can Be Used Anytime A Block Appears
>
> Or A Fresh Approach Is Needed.

Solitaire is not retentive inasmuch as the memory portion of the mind isn't compromised. Other diversions, such as hobbies, require thought process and memory action that might interfere with the Latent Psyche process of the current problem. In addition, when things aren't going well with a hobby, the negative mind-set can become counter-productive. Another alternative is to leave a radio on — volume very low. Focusing on a favorite song during stage four can sometimes serve as a mental picnic.

5) CREATION: The birth of the idea. The "Eureka" moment. The discovery or solution to the problem can be a single word, the key to a character's dilemma or the resolution to a complex business proposal. It can also be a fleeting instant such as when the suddenly crystal clear answer, amid a mind spinning with Melded Information, just as suddenly re-Melds. The light bulb turned on to

276

shine upon the creation can be turned off in an instant. Therefore, it is imperative that the idea or solutions are written down or somehow saved immediately. Even saying the revelation out loud can, in a manner of speaking, save it to memory. This latter tactic is most useful should the idea come in the middle of the night or while occupied with other consuming tasks such as driving an automobile. The human mind, while it is juggling the Information, might fail to shut down upon the discovery. The idea producing machinery, once set in motion, will continue to collate thereby losing the "Eureka" innovation. This is why it is important to be at the keyboard when the Creation is born and not at the gym or hobby room. It is important to deal with (write-down or save to memory) all ideas as they emerge. The first new concept might not be the best, but it, in conjunction with later innovations, might foster the winning idea.

6) REVERBERATION: Though not a step, per se, Reverberation to confirm the pragmatic aspect of the Creation is necessary. Just because an idea was produced doesn't necessarily mean that it is the correct or best idea to solve the identified problem. An idea has been created and the urge to celebrate by making use of the Creation is very strong. However, good business practice mandates bouncing the new thought around. The creative process of the Latent Psyche Concept is capable of producing many ideas—some better than others. It is during this stage that the good ideas are sorted out from the not-so-good ones.

IDEAS BEGET IDEAS: Many times, an idea seeker will create a creation only to later have to acknowledge, if to no one other than himself, "I should have written/done it this way." Reverberating, or bouncing the creation off someone else or just off a mirror saves a lot of time and potential embarrassment. Saying the new work out loud acts as a check and balance by letting the brain hear the concept from a different perspective. Looking at the idea from this oblique angle gives time to make observations such as asking, "is this the best idea. What if…" which leads to confirmation or back to any of the other phases—Information, Melding, Latent Psyche.

THEORY & PRACTICE: Many creative people believe that ideas are the result of association—the connecting of one piece of information with another. Ideas formed by stringing together visual or mental stimuli still utilize the Latent Psyche Concept. These stimuli are the Information that Melds with Identification and though an idea might come quickly, it still is created in the mind—Latent Psyche.

TIME PROVEN PRACTICES AND OBSERVATIONS THAT STIMULATE IDEA PRODUCTION:

•Join organizations, groups or clubs (Kiwanis, Lions, other volunteer) that are not of your circle of friends and acquaintances. Interaction with people of diverse backgrounds inspires creativity;

•Attend political meetings counter to your beliefs—not to argue your views, but to try to understand theirs from their perspective;

•Ideas are gleaned by listening to others;

•Resist tradition—color outside the lines.

IF THE IDEA JUST WON'T COME: START OVER

• Acknowledge the goal by writing it down (Identification);

•Do more research or restudy the background material on hand (Information);

•Try looking at the problem from a different angle or brainstorming with others (Melding);

•Take a break or begin work on a different task—even one that is totally unrelated such as writing a letter to the newspaper or a friend—or pull out the deck of cards (Latent Psyche).

Practitioners of the Latent Psyche Concept sometimes experience a fast-forwarding or skipping steps. But, study will show that in reality the subconscious had automatically processed the supposedly missed steps. For many, getting started—putting down the first words, machining the first part or turning the initial screw—is sometimes the hardest part. Therefore, it might help to begin with familiar portions and let the Latent Psyche work on the beginning. Now, let's see, what's a good title for this treatise...red three on a black four.

> *Little people talk about people;*
> *regular people talk about things;*
> *creative people talk about ideas.*

Bibliography:

Webster's 9th New Collegiate Dictionary

The New Encyclopedia Britannica 1979 Vol III, Pg 227

The Creative Process, Brewster Ghiselin 1952, pg. 12

The Creative Process, Brewster Ghiselin 1952, pg. 113

The New Encyclopedia Britannica 1979 Vol. VII, pg 754

Newspapers: Staying Solvent

The print media, especially the daily or weekly newspapers are struggling to compete with the Internet's version of the free press. Perhaps these ideas might help keep us in print:

1) FREE PAPERS: Give the papers away. The impact might:

a) Allow for an ad rate increase due to a larger circulation;

b) An expanded readership will increase literacy, which augments quality of life and thus benefits the community as a whole (including the bottom line of the newspaper).

2) GOVERNMENT AGENCY SERIES: A regular column reporting on individual local, state and federal agencies, departments and bureaucracies to inform the readers:

a) Who they are;

b) What they do;

c) Under whose control they are;

d) Their powers and rights, and;

e) Their location and contact information.

A compilation, updated yearly and in booklet form, could be sold to advertisers for free distribution or sold, sans ads, to the public

3) POLL: A subscriber poll where the publication sends out a question or two with each invoice. It would be on a special form (so as not to be copied) and without voter identity.

4) SAFETY RELATED EDUCATION COLUMN: People, especially teen-agers, are curious and will experiment on their own to satisfy the need to know. Columns could explain:

a) Self defense and the use of lethal force;

b) Making a gun safe (checking it for loaded rounds);

c) Dangerous household products;

d) Motor vehicle operation;

280

e) Boating, swimming — water activities.

5) USELESS LAWS COLUMN: A regular column researching local, state and federal laws that have outlived their usefulness and should be repealed.

6) DEAR DUDE COLUMN: A regular column — aimed at men — to answer questions pertaining to manners, dating, clothes and other subjects of interest to men.

~~~

United Rural America Vs. United Cities Of America

The huge divisiveness 'tween democrats and republicans can be found in the difference 'tween city dwellers and those living in the small towns and unincorporated areas of the USA. Perhaps if we isolated the big cities from the rest of the country two new nations could be established. De facto borders could easily be drawn by making the outer interstate belts that typically surround the large metropolises, the lines-in-the-sand. Call these combined municipalities *United Cities of America*. Label the rest of the country *United Rural America*.

The *United Cities of America* can then enjoy the pleasures of giving their constituents all the free housing, cell phones, grants and unlimited touchy-feelie programs they want. This liberal camp will have the emancipated power to pass gun control, health care and entitlements upon entitlements. Of course, how they pay for any of this without the taxes from *United Rural America* (those who do most of the proportional paying now), is their problem.

United Rural America probably won't need to pass a lot of laws, but you can bet we'll secure our boundaries to keep the junkies, drug dealers, prostitutes, bureaucrats, bleeding heart liberals, Muslim terrorists and other non-productive *United Cities of America* inhabitants out of our country.

Okay, so this is off-the-wall, but to the Tories, so was the Declaration of Independence.

~~~

Punishment

I don't believe we will disagree that crime is rampant, criminals are coddled and we're all tired of being victims. Our liberal bent has brought us to a life style where criminals are rewarded instead of being punished. The rewards are:

1) Peer recognition: Being acknowledged by our peers is an important human desire and goal—even for felons. Fellow inmates show respect for criminals who commit serious crimes.

2) Health care: Criminals, not being the type of person who holds a regular job and has a health care network; they subconsciously want to be sent to prison where they know they will be treated for what ails them.

3) Basics of life: After a run of "bad luck" most criminals end up hungry and tired and in need of food and shelter. A nice clean, air-conditioned jail cell with TV, clean sheets and clothes is an enticement to one who is down and out.

The bleeding hearts among us will commiserate with these "unfortunates" and believe they are entitled to all the help society is able to tender. This entitlement mind-set obviously hasn't worked.

Unfortunately for us, someone has to be a victim so these "unfortunates" can receive their entitlements. In other words, if Fred Felon has a tooth ache, is hungry or needs stroking by fellow felons, one of the law-abiding citizens among us must suffer.

Solving the crime/criminal problem comes down to: Effective punishment. Before I tender my solution to this problem, I admit that the Eighth Amendment to the Constitution forbids "cruel and unusual punishment" and that my plan, under current PC standards, is cruel and unusual. However, HOWEVER, the same Constitution allows changes, via amendments. Therefore, a new amendment should be drafted to address persons convicted of a major crime, i.e., rape, robbery, burglary, theft over xxx$ or any crime that directly or indirectly causes death or great bodily harm to another. This new amendment shall specifically state: "Cruel and unusual punishment" does not mean any of the following:

1) Conviction of a major felony shall require the government to surgically castrate the criminal and incarcerate him for (to be determined time). After release and until he is able to gain gainful employment on his own, he will be made part of a work detail similar to the WPA of the 1930s.

> *Framer's Intent: Castration will not only impair a criminal's testosterone driven aggression in the outside world, but will reduce incidents of prison rape. In addition, castration destroys a man's manliness — a significant punishment and reason not to commit crimes in the first place. Yeah, I know this has been done before (eunuchs as harem guards), but not as punishment, per se.*

2) Upon the second conviction of a major felony, the convicted shall be imprisoned and voluntarily or involuntarily addicted to heroin for a period of (to be determined). After which, the convict/addict will be forced to undergo cold-turkey withdrawal. This punishment shall be repeated until the prisoner dies. From the onset of this 2nd incarceration the inmate shall have access to a length of rope, should he decide to hang himself.

> *Framer's Intent: This two-step solution will reduce the recidivism rate and save a significant number of decent law-abiding citizens from having to become a victim so the criminal can be "rewarded." In addition, no additional expense will incur as prison guards and probation officers can become monitors for the WPA type work details.*

Before you write me off as a wacko, consider this truth: Only boring people criticize others; regular people talk about things; Interesting people talk about ideas — what's your solution?

American Education System

Regardless of whether you believe the liberals are too lenient or the conservatives are too strict, we, undeniably, have produced far too many government dependent, criminal idolizing citizens who have failed to assimilate to the American way of life. Whether our education system is the cause or the result of this is not the point. We need a fresh approach.

1) TEACHERS: Selected instructors will stay with a class for twelve years. In other words, a first grade teacher will continue to teach the same group of students every year until graduation at grade twelve. This way each child will have at least one long term responsible adult to identify with and relate to during his/her formative years. A teacher, as a role model for twelve years, should have a very positive effect on any child. Parents, and this special teacher, will become de facto partners in the development of a competent citizen.

Probably the most beneficial attribute of this program is that the special instructor will also be in the unique position of being able to monitor his or her students for signs of parental abuse or other problems by observing year to year changes. A child who develops negative attributes would be easier to spot if observed over a long period of time. Likewise, year-to-year counseling (befriending) would have a greater and more positive impact when applied for the long term.

Two significant changes might be necessary to implement this plan: One, the school districts will have to return to neighborhood schools and, two, teachers selected for this special 12 year commitment should receive extra incentives such as one full year off — with pay — for each 12 year stint.

It is envisioned, that over a period of years, the bonding between students and teacher would evolve into a friendship based relationship. And, what could be more beneficial to our children than to be friends with one of the most respected members of society—a teacher?

2) CURRICULUM: Homeroom class time—everyday—should include discussions of ethics, morals, manners and anger management. Graduation from Junior High will require a written dissertation, presented orally, on the definition of Right & Wrong and what it means to the student. For graduation from Middle School, the subject shall be Manners, and for High School, Ethics.

3) COMMUNITY SERVICE: All high school students will be required to do some form of neighborhood aid after regular school hours and/or on weekends. Even those involved in sports and other sanctioned after school events will have to pay their dues in service to their community.

Parent/teacher approved community service could entail such duties such as litter patrol, reading to the sick and elderly or even assisting their own parents in home/church beautification projects. Some schools have already been involved in such a program—but it needs to be expanded.

4) DISCIPLINE: The right and power to discipline must be legislatively returned to line educators with the student's right of appeal limited only to the school principal, i.e., students/parents cannot sue the school or it's employees over matters of discipline.

5) CONSEQUENCES: If discipline problems involve violence, drugs, non-attendance, or disrespect of faculty; Junior, Middle and Senior High students will be sent to a special disciplinary school for up to six months, as determined by the Principal.

DISCIPLINARY SCHOOL, LEVEL I: Students sent here will wear issued uniforms and will not be allowed any personal property while in the school. The school day will be extended in order to include intramural sports and additional classes in morals, manners, anger management and ethics. After the sentence has been successfully served, the student will be returned to the school from which he or she came. If discipline problems re-occur the student will be sent to Level II.

DISCIPLINARY SCHOOL LEVEL II: Students ordered here by a school principal will have a hearing before a Juvenile Court Referee prior to admission. Level II students will wear an issued uniform,

286

will not be allowed any personal property, will participate in school functions 12 hours per day and all students shall reside on campus. Recreation and entertainment will be limited to mandatory intramural sports. Television will be limited to news and educational programs.

Daily student contact with parent/guardian will be required, but weekends at home will be optional. Any other off-campus activity must be supervised by a staff member. Permanent exit can only be accomplished by the student reaching the age of 18 or receiving a high school diploma. The student who reaches the age of 18 without earning a high school diploma will be restricted, for ten years, from owning firearms.

6) MILITARY SERVICE: All American citizens, within six months of graduating high school or exiting Level II Disciplinary School, shall begin service in the military for a period of not less than two years. Those who do not enlist will be drafted at the end of the six month exploratory term.

Requiring military service will not only strengthen our military presence, but will present a more mature class of work/college bound youths.

> *Framing the 10 Commandments in our schools*
> *might work for some,*
> *but posting the first 10 Amendments*
> *would work for all.*

A Dirty Little Judicial Secret

USURPATION OF JUDICIAL POWER:

A practice has grown among the judiciary to reserve, exclusively, to a trial judge, the power of judging the law. This is not to say that judges, per se, refuse all knowledge of the Jury's right to judge the law. Many courts have recognized this right. However, what the judicial branch fails to do is to tell a jury of their rights, while at the same time not allowing an attorney to do so either (Sparf & Hansen v. U.S. 1895, 156 U.S. 102). The only exception to this "judge's law" is for the defendant to take the stand, and acting as his own attorney (pro se), tell the jury how the law he is charged with violating is unconstitutional.

There are two primary reasons judges insist on being the only definer of the law.

1) Because they believe common jurors are just that — regular people that are not sophisticated enough to understand the law unless a judge explains it to them;

2) Judges do not want to surrender their self-granted power to attorneys.

Judges, officiate in criminal jury trials for the primary purpose of ensuring a fair trial. They are referees or umpires whose duties lie in making sure the playing field is level — not to pass judgment. Judgments are reserved to the jury. Juries decide facts, and when appropriate, judge the law as well.

When a jury judges the law it has been commonly called Jury Nullification. It could be better labeled, Jury Prerogative, recognition of the juror's right and duty to judge the law as well as the facts of a case. Judging the law means comparing a law in question against an accepted standard. In America, the only standard to which a law can be assessed is a constitution, either state or federal. Jurors do not have the license to judge a law to their personal standard or opinions. To allow one to whimsically decide whether a law is good or bad based upon a personal view would be inviting judicial lawlessness.

288

HISTORICAL BACKGROUND:

The 6th Amendment to the U.S. constitution states, "In all criminal prosecutions, the accused shall enjoy the right to a speedy and public trial, by an impartial jury...." It doesn't say by a judge; it specifies an IMPARTIAL jury. A government employee, using his or her powerful position to 'charge' or 'instruct' a jury, is violating the 6th, 9th and 10th Amendments of the U.S. Constitution. A jury that has been subjected to this usurpation of power is no longer impartial—it has been influenced to the judge's uncontested bias.

Our Constitution, our rule-of-law, was written by laymen for laymen. No where in its articles or amendments is the judicial branch empowered to *tell* a jury anything, much less how to apply a law. Some states, in open confrontation to the Constitution, have even gone so far as to require jurors to report fellow jurors who refuse to follow the law as directed by a judge!

Our forefather's realized that judges, being human, carry their own prejudices. Because of this, the framers of our Constitution did not require judges, during a jury trial, to swear to tell the whole truth and nothing but the truth. In all criminal proceedings witnesses who are going to testify before a jury must swear, under penalty of perjury, to tell the truth. This rule applies to everyone including lawyers, police officers and other government employees even though they have sworn an oath to their office and the Constitution. The judge is immune to this rule of law because he is not expected to testify. Unfortunately, a practice has evolved where judges do testify in the form of their 'instructions' or 'charges' to the jury. It is during this 'testimony'—this propagation of their own power—that the judge will NOT tell the whole truth. The whole truth being a jury's right and power to decide the constitutionality of a law.

Many precedent setting rulings, dating from the decade of this country's inception to as late as 1972, have confirmed that Jury Prerogative is a bono fide right and power of a jury:

COMPARATIVE EXAMPLE: Just for the sake of argument, let's say that Public Law X makes it a crime to speak or write anything derogatory about any federal employee. Soon thereafter, your car is struck by a vehicle negligently operated by an FBI agent. In the heat of the moment and outraged that your new BMW damaged, you call the agent an incompetent jerk whereas you are immediately arrested for violation of Public Law X.

You're an honest person and do not deny that you made those comments. You place your faith in the fact that Public Law X is obviously in direct violation of the 1st Amendment to the U. S. Constitution. At the conclusion of the trial the judge 'instructs' the jury that if they find that you did utter derogatory comments to a federal employee they, the jury, MUST find you guilty as charged. Of course, the jury has the right and power to determine that Public Law X is in violation of the First Amendment. However, if the judge refuses to tell the jury that they have this right and your attorney is not allowed (ibid, Sparf & Hansen) then that leaves you in the open in a shooting war—and without a gun.

JURY PREROGATIVE—WHAT IT IS/IS NOT:

Circa 1988, a group of citizens formed a grassroots organization, The Fully Informed Jury Association (www.fija.org). Their intention was to inform jurors of their right to judge laws. However the FIJA misinterpreted the meaning and definition of Jury Nullification/Prerogative and have skewered, twisted and misapplied this 200 year old concept. They promote the notion that juries have the right to decide if a law is good or bad as judged against their own (individual juror's own) standards of good and bad.

In a recent California case (People v. Williams, S066106, 2001), a juror told a trial judge: "I simply cannot see staining a man, a young man, for the rest of his life for what I believe to be the wrong reason." This juror raised no issue of constitutionality—he was applying the law to his own personal standards. The juror was replaced by an alternate in what has been called a "Jury Nullification" case. It was not. There was no issue of constitutionality at bar.

The California Supreme Court correctly upheld the dismissal of the juror for applying his own standard to what the law meant. To evoke Jury Prerogative, a juror must believe the law under which a defendant is charged is unconstitutional. For example: if a defendant is charged with violation a law "A" and a juror votes for acquittal because this juror believes that law "A" is unfair, defective, unjust, not a good law or the law is stupid, the juror is not doing his duty.

290

However, if the juror is convinced that law "A" is in violation of a state or a federal constitutional guarantee, then the juror is obligated to vote not-guilty.

Jury Prerogative (nullification) is the right and power of a jury to decide the facts of a case and determine the validity of a law by judging the subject law against a state or the federal constitution.

WHAT THEY DON'T TELL YOU:

During jury selection the prosecutor, or the judge, will always ask prospective jurors, "Will you swear to follow the judges instructions and apply the law as he gives it to you?" Those answering in the negative or with words to the effect: "I agree to follow all instructions, laws, rules and statutes if these instructions, *laws, rules, and statutes are not in conflict with this state or our Federal Constitution,*" will be summarily dismissed.

Most first day jurors are required to view a very professionally produced 18 minute video tape:

"CALLED TO SERVICE," a Federal Judicial Center Production. During which, the narrator says:

"The accused's right to trial by jury is protected by the U.S. Constitution's Article III and the 7th Amendment." [There is no mention of the 6th Amendment]

"Jurors decide facts. Facts are not opening or closing statements." [The video fails to mention that jurors also decide law.]

"Judges decide all questions of law." [This is an assumed power — in direct violation of the 6th, 9th and 10th Amendments. And when practiced is indicative of prime facie judicial misconduct.]

"The jury is a panel that is made up of impartial jurors." [It is not possible to expect jurors to be impartial if the judge forces them to accept his opinion of the law.]

"If anything is in conflict with what the judge says, jurors must follow the instructions of the Judge." [This is the scariest statement, i.e., if the facts of the case are clear to the jury that 'A' did it, but the judge instructs the jury to find that 'B' is the guilty party, are the jurors obligated to do so?]

"During the judge's charge or instructions to the jury, the judge will explain the law that you must follow." [That's because the judge doesn't think you're intelligent enough to figure out what the law says.]

"The judge will tell you what you can and cannot do." [In contravention to the 6th Amendment. No where was there any mention of a judge's right to decide the meaning or constitutionality of a law.]

POSSIBLE REMEDIES:

1) Demand a full legal representation. Forcing a defendant to become his own lawyer just for the sake of arguing the law's constitutionality, is a clear violation of the 6th Amendment right to counsel. In other words, it is well established in case law, that the accused is entitled to representation at ALL levels of trial including even pre-trial interrogation and post trial sentencing. Therefore, how can the courts continue to support Sparf (ibid) which clearly forbids representation at a most critical stage of a trial — the "instructions/charge" to the jury? This quirk of forbidding attorneys to argue the law before the jury, but permit pro se testimony seems to have escaped the logic of the judicial system.

2) Join the JUDICIAL ACCOUNTABILITY INITIATIVE LAW organization. J.A.I.L. is working to enact Special Grand Juries to sanction judges by levying fines, forfeitures and possible removal from the bench against judges who usurp their powers. (www.jail4judges.org)

3) Consider filing suit against your local Jury Commissioner to require the Jury Prerogative option be disseminated to prospective jurors.

4) If you are charged with a crime and you can show the law under which you are charged is in violation of your state's or the Federal Constitution, demand a jury trial and mount a challenge to Sparf & Hansen v. U.S..

5) If you are not successful with your challenge to Sparf & Hansen at the trial level, have Plan 'B' ready: Consider acting as co-counsel. Because the judge will not advise your jury of their right to judge the law and also refuses your attorney that power, your only option might be to tender the summation yourself. Acting pro se, you can

292

say almost anything to a jury as acknowledged by the 1972 case, U.S. vs Dougherty (473 F.2d, pg 1137): " Thus, a defendant's ability to present his demeanor and often even a kind of testimony, without exposure to impeachment or cross-examination, may be a tactical consequence of pro-se representation, and even a moving cause of its invocation...."

"The jury has a right to judge both the law as well as the fact in controversy." John Jay, 1st Chief Justice U.S.Supreme Court (1789)

The jury does and always has had, in the words of Justice Holmes, "the power to bring in a verdict in the teeth of both law and facts." (Horning v. District of Columbia, 254 U.S. 135, 138, 41 S.Ct. 53,54,65 L.Ed. 185 [1920]).

"The law itself is on trial quite as much as the cause which is to be decided." Harlan F. Stone, Chief Justice U.S. Supreme Court (1941).

"The pages of history shine on instances of the jury's exercise of its prerogative to disregard instructions of the judge...." (U.S. vs. Dougherty, 473 F.2d 1139 [1972])

Other Related Cases And Writings: Duncan V. Louisiana, 391 U.S. 145, 156, 88 S.Ct. 1444,1445,20 L.Ed.2d 491 (1968). Fear of Unchecked Power; Kalven & Zeisel, The American Jury pub. Little, Brown (1966). Scheflin. Jury Nullification: The Right To Say No, 45 So.Calif.L.Rev. 168, 182 (1972). Howe, Juries as Judges of Criminal Law, 52 Harv.L.Rev. 582 (1939). STATE v. Burpee, 65 Vt. 1, 34-35, 25 A. 964, 974 (1892). Judge Rifkind's comments in Follow-up/The Jury, Center Magazine, 64-65 (July 1970). 2001 Ohio App. LEXIS 589 STATE V. JACKSON, No. 00AP-183. 1987 Ohio App. LEXIS 9364 State V. Gribble, No. 87AP020016. 1984 Ohio App. LEXIS 11437 State V. Culmer No. 3604. 1981 Ohio App. LEXIS 11772 State V. Floyd, 81 CA 18.

Judicial Accountability Law

EXCUSES IN HISTORY:

Early in this century, when even the "politically correct" (PC) had a sense of right & wrong and fair play, it was believed to be in the best interest of this country to ban the sale and consumption of alcoholic beverages. Those in power, back then, were subscribed to doing what they wanted to do in the legal and proper way. First they discussed passing laws to ban booze. But, after a cursory study of the Constitution it was clear there was no provision in this great body of supreme laws to permit the "majority rule" or any government body to outlaw alcohol, sans a constitutional act. Thus, the 18th Amendment was born, passed and ratified all in due order. This formal and official constitutional decree forbid: "the manufacture, sale, or transportation of intoxicating liquors...." Political correctness or even majority rule is not the way this country was set up to run. We are a republic, a nation of constitutions — not a nation of laws.

Fourteen years later, with the onset of the Great Depression, it was clear prohibition was not a good plan. With this eye-opener came three revelations.

- It was then considered in the best interest of the country to encourage legitimate liquor producing businesses. This not only made for a taxable commodity, but in an era of economic downturn, a major fiscal impact came from employing men in transportation, bottle, label, and box manufacturing industries.

- Enacting amendments to the constitution are burdensome, unwieldy and time consuming. In addition, Federal politicians found it insulting and repugnant to submit to state legislators for ratification of their wise and guiding acts.

- The federal government felt it had to find some form of employment for the now out-of-work liquor agents. Up to that time it was well established that if one worked for the government, one could expect low pay, but a layoff-free job (today it's high pay, no lay-off, PLUS a virtual termination-free environment).

Just before the repeal of prohibition informal studies and polls were taken by the PC. The preordained results indicated that the greatest threat to America was the proliferation of machine guns and other dangerous ordnance. This was evidenced by sensational news stories about mass killing by the mobsters who controlled the illicit and illegal liquor industry. Never mind that these guys were out of business with the repeal of the 18th Amendment and thus the legalization of liquor making.

The government again faced the same dilemma it had in 1917; there were no provisions in the constitution that would allow for the banning or controlling of machine guns or any other weapons. In fact the Constitution's 2nd Amendment expressly forbade infringing the right to keep and bear arms. The correct and legal way, if "the people" so desired a change, was the enactment of a amendment to control or ban whatever guns they wanted. But, a new amendment takes time and then there's that humbling matter of having to beg the states to ratify it. Besides, the PC was convinced it needed to find jobs for those soon to be laid-off liquor agents. The quick fix, the feel good way, the start down the slippery slope way was to just pass a federal law. Hence the National Firearms act of 1934.

THINK IT CAN'T HAPPEN?

"They," the politically correct, our government, anti-(fill- in-the-blank) groups, and news media are setting us up just like "they" did to the tobacco makers. There is no provision in the Constitution to allow the federal or state governments to force exorbitant taxes or otherwise harass a legitimate business. What "they" did was, using government funding, establish pseudo health organizations such as the Center for Disease Control to declare and publish findings that cigarettes are not only harmful to the health of Americans, but as such, the health burden to treat these unhealthy citizens cost the government money. The truth of the health issue is not the point—it is the use of tax dollars to unconstitutionally disparage the assets of stockholders of legitimate private corporations (See Bill of Rights, Amendment IX in this book).

The fact that there is also no constitutional justification to allow, permit or require any state or federal government to treat its citizens (socialization of medicine) totally escapes the mentality of the politically correct—not to mention the judges who had had these cases before them. (this was written before "Obamacare"—a perfect example of the slippery slope).

Armed with these "health reports," "they," using tax payer money, instigated civil law suits upon civil law suits to force an out-of-court settlement. The tobacco companies, as large and rich as they are, soon realized they were no-match for the endless funding of the government. The result was exactly what the government (and the lucky {read, greedy} lawyers who handled the cases) wanted: money—lots and lots of money. The certainty that there is no constitutional basis for this rape of a legitimate industry is totally ignored by "they."

Already, the federally funded Center for Disease Control has come out with position papers saying that guns are a health risk. As this is being written, some cities, using the same tobacco- style logic of having the expense of medically treating gunshot victims with public money, have begun filing suits against gun makers. Only this time, in addition to money, money, money, "they" seek an outright ban on guns. Because we have slid so far down the slippery slope "they" just might be able to get away with it.

Incompetent and cowardly lawyers AND JUDGES, afraid to go against the political correctness of the day have failed to overturn the National Firearms Act, the 1968 Gun Control Act—and most other unconstitutional laws since passed. The die has been cast, the precedent established, and the ride down the slippery slope has begun. Since the ratification of the 21st Amendment (repealing prohibition) there have been only nine new amendments to the constitution. All of these new amendments apply to either voting rights or political functions. None deal with protecting former or future individual rights. Since 1933 all personal rights, privileges, guarantees or immunities spelled out in the Constitution have been dealt with exclusively by enacting laws regardless of their constitutional legality. The attitude of the politically correct has been and still is; let's pass the law because it feels good and is good for getting votes. We have slid so far down the slope the tobacco makers knew, same as the gun manufactures know, there isn't a judge in the country that will declare the government's tactics against politically incorrect, albeit legitimate, industries to be unconstitutional.

WHOSE DEFINITION OF ETHICS?

This brings us to JUDGES and the judicial branch in general. Used to be the wearers of white robes were the most feared gangs. Now it's those who wear the black robes. These pompous fate adjusters are so powerful they don't even have to abide by their own rules. After all, what do they have to fear? Appointed for life (on the federal level) by like-thinkers they can ignore constitutional demands and controls with impunity.

Case in point: Recently, I sent a question, via letter, to Thomas J. Moyer, Chief Justice of the Ohio Supreme Court. Four months later, a "Staff Counsel" responded, "Pursuant to the Code of Judicial Conduct, the Justices and employees of the Supreme Court are not permitted to give legal advice or to answer questions concerning legal issues." A copy of the Ohio Code of Judicial Conduct was enclosed. A careful study of this short, official set of Canons of Ethics found no statement saying "[justices] are not permitted to give legal advice or to answer questions concerning legal issues." In fact, Canon 2 contradicts: "(A)(1) A judge may speak, write, lecture, teach and participate in other activities concerning the law, the legal system and the administration of justice." The commentary to this section goes on to say: "...a judge is in a unique position to contribute *to the improvement of the law, the legal system and the administration of justice... [and] is encouraged to do so....*" In other words, the Canons recommend that judges "answer questions concerning legal issues."

In Ohio, like many other states, the state Supreme Court has jurisdiction over complaints filed against members of the bar, of which most attorneys and state court judges are members. The judges not only pass judgment on lawyers, but measure the judicial conduct of their fellow judges as well. They are in the position of acting as their own judge, jury and executioner when it comes to misconduct on the bench. This system is tantamount to the old proverb of the foxes guarding the hen house—and with the same predictable results.

Inasmuch as the aforementioned Ohio Canons lays out a code of judicial conduct it has the audacity to build into the code excuses for not disciplining fellow members. The Preamble to the Code of Ethics states: "It [the code] is not intended, however, that every transgression will result in disciplinary action." What they are saying: if one of the PC commits a crime or violates any of the Codes, we don't have to yank his license. While at the same time, if an attorney who is not PC, we have the power and right to disbar him for any transgression. Ohio should change its Code's name to Ethics by Arbitrariness and Capriciousness.

This is no surprise. Ohio is only emulating our federal system that, for example, used its power to adjudicate that the FBI agent did not commit murder—or any other crime—when he shot and killed Randy Weaver's wife during the Ruby Ridge incident. Legalities aside, where's the ethics in this?

A few years ago, an Ohio licensed attorney (Doris Houser Allen) was indicted for perjury, tampering with evidence and tampering with records. This was not just "code" infractions, but criminal felony violations. Ms. Allen's criminal acts caused the physical arrest and incarceration of an innocent person. The Ohio Bar's Board of Commissioners on Grievances and Discipline recommended Ms. Allen be suspended from the practice of law for six months for professional misconduct. The Supreme Court of Ohio voted 5−2, sans comment, to dismiss the complaint. In other words, some guy went to jail and the person who put him there—by her illegal conduct—walked. In Ohio, like most states and all federal jurisdictions, there is no appeal and no citizen panel to police lawyers.

Appointed for life, federal judges who commit misdeeds are subject to impeachment. The Bill Clinton impeachment process clearly showed what a long and drawn-out procedure it is. This is the primary reason there are such a low number of judges that are actually impeached, much less removed from office.

DUH:

It is a well-known truth the American Bar Association is anti-gun. The ABA does not deny or hide this fact. The over whelming majority of lawyers in this country are members of this trade association. Of the approximately 385K members most judges do or did belong at one time or another. Since the ABA is noted for its position against guns, per se, it stands to reason that any such member is presumed to be, at worst, anti-gun. At best, an ABA member (or in some cases, a former member) is tainted by association. If membership exposes readers of the association's publications, which are most certainly bias against firearms use or ownership, then a negative bent would not be unreasonable to assume.

Ethically, any judge who has a conflict of interest with any case before him must excuse himself from the case—even if the conflict is not brought to his attention by either side. This happens all the time. In civil cases involving some publicly traded company in which the judge owns stock, he will bow out, usually of his own accord. In criminal matters where he is known to harbor prejudice against the defendant or the defendant's position he will yield to another judge. When was the last time you heard of a judge in a firearm related case excuse himself—even at the request of the defendant—because he belonged to a known anti-gun association?

JUDICIAL ACCOUNTABILITY LAW:
SECTION I

In Any Criminal Or Civil Jury Trial The Defense Shall Have The Right To Argue The Law, As Well As The Facts, Before The Jury. No Judge Shall Issue Instructions Or Opinions To The Jury After The Start Of The Trial.

SECTION I—INTENTIONS OF THE FRAMER:

> *It is most important for all Americans, especially gun owners, that we reinforce this established concept of Jury Nullification. This is necessary because most judges, in violation of their sworn duties, have ignored this right and power and because there are many unconstitutional laws. This section is needed to enlighten juries of their rights and powers. Without this well established right and power, we gun owners will continue to be subject to constitutionally ignorant and anti-gun biased judges.*

SECTION 2.

No Judge Shall Issue Any Verdicts Other Than Affirmed, Denied, Guilty Or Not Guilty; Nor Shall A Judge Issue Any Orders, Edicts, Commands Or Decrees; Contempt Of Court Citations Excepted

SECTION 2 – INTENTIONS OF THE FRAMER:

Judges tend to propagate power, i.e., self- appointed power. Many "laws" are the result of court cases where a sitting judge ignored a petitioner's request for a yes or no decision and instead delivered his opinion – a bias that carries the weight of law. These unrequested edicts, commands, orders and decrees are in excess of his constitutional powers. Most of these "case laws," such as school busing, affirmative action or refusals to uphold the 2nd Amendment, are in violation of The Constitution.

SECTION 3.

Whosoever Violates Sections I Or 2 Of This Statute Shall Be Fined Not Less Than Twenty Thousand Dollars ($20,000).

SECTION 3 – INTENTIONS OF THE FRAMER:

If Representative Henry Hyde really means what he says about the third leg of the stool, then he and his fellow republicans should not have a problem supporting this "enforceable oath." For any law to have meaning it must have a definite and suitable penalty. Twenty thousand dollars, even to a judge, is not peanuts.

SECTION 4

Charges Of Violations Of Any Section Of This Law Shall Be Adjudicated By A Judicial Review Board Comprised Of Twelve Citizens, Randomly Selected From Voter Registrations. Each Judicial Review Board Member Shall Serve Not Less Than 12 Months Nor More Than 24 Months. Compensation Shall Be At The Same Level As Federal Appellant Court Judges.

SECTION 4—INTENTIONS OF THE FRAMER:

To judge the judges a review board, completely independent of any of the branches of government, is necessary for open and disinterested decisions. Since the constitution was written by lay men, average men and women are certainly competent to read, understand and apply its meanings.

Bringing America Together

We live in an extremely complex and dangerous society where there might not be solutions to some of our problems. Adding to our personal dilemma is the huge divide between the political parties. Our elected leaders must return to protecting our priority issues and refrain from getting bogged down with divisive matters. To help bridge this gap, I propose each candidate declare:

For the offices of President and Vice President:

1) I will not issue any Executive Orders, edicts or decrees, etc., expanding or reducing any abortion, religious or firearm issue;

2) I will neither sign nor veto any bill, statute, regulation, act or Executive Order, expanding or increasing any taxes, levies or fees;

3) I will support a constitutional amendment that requires all federal employees and elected officials to swear an oath that they renounce any group, person or political entity that the US government has determined supports or advocates violence against the USA or any of its citizens;

4) I pledge not to render any American funds or goods to any group, person or political entity that the U.S. government has determined supports or advocates violence against the USA or any of its citizens;

5) I will not criticize the proposals or acts of any member of another political party without tendering my own alternative;

6) I will support amending the Constitution to restrict the term for President and Vice President to one 6-year term.

For the offices of Senator, Congressperson or Governor:

1) I will not criticize the proposals or acts of any member of another political party without tendering my own alternative;

2) I will support a constitutional amendment that requires all federal employees and elected officials to swear an oath that they renounce any group, person or political entity that the US government has determined supports or advocates violence against the USA or any of its citizens;

3) I pledge not to support the distribution of American goods or funds to any group, person or political entity that the US government has determined supports or advocates violence against the USA or any of its citizens;

4) I will support amending the Constitution to restrict the term for President and Vice President to one (1) 6-year term.

Should these simple, basic, common-sense pledges be adopted, then, maybe we can all get back to the business of working together to keep America together.

Government Corruption with Solutions

It has been said that a government career is comprised of four distinct phases: Idealism, Pragmatism, Ambition and Corruption. For some the slide takes decades, others a significantly shorter period.

Recently, a mix of these types, in the name of safety (Idealism), but in the Pragmatism of reality (increasing government revenues), have invented the Stop-Light camera. This unmanned device photographs the license plate of a vehicle that runs a red light. The government then mails a ticket to the person to whom the plate is registered—regardless of who's actually driving. Up until now a police officer, to get a conviction, had to "place you behind the wheel" at the time of this criminal offense. To get around this sticky issue, the government has classified stop-light-camera violations as a civil **infraction** and thus no jail time or "points" are attached to your driving record should your vehicle be caught by the camera. Therefore, the only penalty is monetary.

A civil crime requires a significantly lower standard of proof, i.e., only a preponderance of the evidence and not beyond-the-reasonable-doubt requirement of a criminal matter. In other words, they don't have to prove—beyond- a-reasonable-doubt—that you were driving the car, just the preponderance of the evidence that you were most likely the driver of the vehicle. Think the O.J. case, where he was found not guilty in criminal court, but found responsible in the civil suit filed by the victim's family and had to pay big money. In the stop-light-camera matter, for all intents and purposes, the burden of proof will be on you to prove that you were NOT driving the vehicle, i.e., to beat the rap you'll have to produce the actual driver or evidence that you couldn't have been the driver.

PART 1

CIVIL CRIME OF CORRUPTION LAW:

Perhaps, we can apply this same analogy to those who make the laws. Local, state and federal statutes against corruption, such as lying, cheating and stealing, should be amended to create a Civil

Crime of Corruption Law. Therefore, instead of expending huge resources to prove a criminal corruption case against a government official to the beyond-a-reasonable-doubt standard, we create the Civil Crime of Corruption Law. This new crime would, as in the stop-light-camera, require a much lower level of proof. Of course, those found guilty of the *Civil Crime of Corruption Law* can't be jailed, but we can fine them and prevent them from ever receiving government funds (employment, grants, etc.) again.

To facilitate catching these violators we, the people, need a "stop-light-camera," to wit:

1) All elected and politically appointed officials shall be required to post on the Web their tax return and that of their spouses, if filing separately, while they are in office and for three years thereafter;

2) All elected and politically appointed officials shall be required to post on the Web a daily account of where they were and who they were with;

3) Those charged under the *Civil Crime of Corruption Law* shall be required to submit to a polygraph test (lie detector tests have not generally been allowed in criminal proceedings, but are acceptable in civil cases);

4) Establish the Investigative Reporter.

PART 2.

THE INVESTIGATIVE REPORTER:

Today, in order to detect government misdeeds and activities; a watchdog organization, the *Board of Licensed Investigative Reporters* (BLIR), is hereby tendered.

Much has been written about allowing reporters to enjoy the privilege of shielding their confidential sources. However, unlike police, clergy and doctors, reporters are not licensed and thus have no one to answer to should they abuse this privilege. Therefore, the BLIR shall license and monitor these special reporters, who must comply with the below privileges, immunities and rules. Of course, there will always be the temptation to abuse this power for political and/or monetary gains, thus the BLIR shall be made up of the most honored and trustworthy American citizens: Retired Police Officers.

The following criteria for members of the Board of Licensed Investigative Reporters shall apply:

1) Officers must be retired with 15 or more years as a full-time certified police officer and not less than five years at a supervisory level or the rank of detective;

2) Their pay shall come exclusively from membership dues of the BLIR;

3) They shall be term limited to eight years;

4) The officers, in addition to their investigative duties, shall also issue periodic public reports on each licensed investigative reporter.

These special **LICENSED INVESTIGATIVE REPORTERS** shall comply with the following rules and regulations:

1) In addition to other investigations, each licensee is obligated to investigate corruption of elected and appointed officials at all levels of government;

2) All reporters licensed under BLIR shall have the unrestricted right to withhold confidential sources from anyone—except information relating to a future event that will cause death or great bodily harm to others;

3) Licensed reporters, or their employers, shall pay a set yearly fee for these privileges;

4) All licensed investigative reporters and their employers shall be immune from liable and slander judgments when acting within the scope of their duties.

Yeah, I know this might seem extreme, but hey, we have to do something. My guess is, after a few years of this, the amount of corruption will be significantly reduced and the problem of downsizing the BLIR bureaucracy will become the problem.

> *The longevity of any republic or democracy is dependent upon:*
>
> *The 4th Estate's ability to identify and expose the 5th Column(s) in a manner framed by the 4th Dimension.*

Plans From Outside The Box!

ALTERNATE PARTY RULE: Suppose both houses of Congress agree to allow for Alternate Party Rule (APR) for four year periods. In other words, starting in, say, 2014, the Democrats are the only ones who can vote. Then in 2018, only Republicans have the power of the vote. In 2022 the common voters decide if they want to continue the APR or return to the old compromise/gridlock system. Note: Such a "rule" is not prohibited under the Constitution. Article I, Section 5 reads: "Each House shall be the judge of the elections, returns and qualifications of its own members ...."

SALES TAX WITH A TWIST: Create a National Sales Tax on everything except necessities (food, shelter, clothing). The Tax Rate and exemptions shall be established — and adjusted yearly — by the voters. This way, the poor pay no tax at all, while the rich decide what luxuries they believe are worth the tax. Allow the IRS to implement and collect the NST.

KEEP AMERICA STRONG: Institute a hiring freeze for all federal agencies, bureaus and staffs — plus legislation that for every reduction in military or sworn law enforcement personnel, an equal number of bureaucrats must be terminated.

VOTER QUALIFICATION: A Constitutional Amendment saying all those wishing to vote must prove they are at least 18 years of age, are American citizens, not convicted felons and they or any of their dependents are NOT receiving any government gratuities such as welfare, aid for families with dependent children, rent subsidies, etc..

Civilian Coup

If I was going to write a new fiction book this could be the outline:

PART I:

A compelling incident spurs a "leader" to emerge. The trip-wire could be rumors (truth is immaterial) that the government will begin confiscating firearms. Without rifles, pistols and shotguns the opportunity of a civilian coup is all but lost. This "leader" might not be a single person, but could be a group of persons. The person[s] who started/spread the rumor and the reason why will be divulged at the end of the book, or not.

The "leader/group" quickly develops and publishes — via Internet, Facebook, Texting and other electronic media — a platform spelling out its goals. This would include, but is not limited to: upholding The Constitution as the framers intended, swift and sure punishment of criminals (no more coddling), significantly reducing government size and scope, a strong military, a national sales tax to replace all income taxes — the rate of which is controlled by the voters (exemptions such as food, clothing, shelter will also be decided by referendum).

PART II

Coordinating their efforts via electronic communications, the "leader/group" gathers and bonds with followers. Organization and drafting of competent staff ready to assume vital government offices, i.e. Department of Defense, Public Relations, President, et al., begins.

A significant goal/tactic would be using contacts to secure oaths from the military commanders NOT to fire on revolutionaries, aka fellow Americans/neighbors.

Preparations are made for 10s of thousands of followers to gather — with arms — in D.C. (There are 315M people in this country, but less than 100K could take control, virtually without bloodshed).

PART III

The Capitol, White House and other select government buildings are surrounded. Once these designated locations have been sealed off, a demand is made: Within three hours all elected federal officials must surrender and present formal resignations. Entry is made into these buildings—any who have failed to resign are taken prisoners.

The new government:

a) Seals all borders and rounds up and expels illegals and/or anyone belonging to a group/sect/country that does not hold to our ideals;

b) Declares war on Islam and begins a campaign of nuking countries that are threats to the USA;

c) Terminates pensions of all politicians, requires all persons upon reaching the age of 18 to serve in the military for a minimum of two years and dismantles "entitlement" programs (to be replaced with "work for food" systems similar to the WPA of the 1930s).

d) All of the above or any combination thereof—or ?????????

EPILOGUE:

America emerges, again, as a strong, constitution-driven world power. The rumor starter/spreader is (is not) discovered and is (is not) killed or made a hero or imprisoned to formulate the next plan— haven't decided the ending. How would you treat it?

> *Leaders harbor visions of forthcoming years;*
> *visionaries envision decades hence.*

Proposed 28th Amendment

SECTION I.

Everyone Has The Inherent Right To Keep And Bear Arms Anywhere This Instrument Has Jurisdiction When All Of The Following Apply: The Person Is A Citizen Of The United States, Is Over The Age Of 18, Has Not Been Dishonorably Discharged From Any Branch Of U.S. Military Service, Is Not Under Indictment For, Convicted Of, Or While In The Act Of, Committing Any Felony Crime Of Violence; Or Felony Distribution, Or Trafficking In, Any Illegal Drug Of Abuse; Or Has Not Been Adjudicated As A Chronic Alcoholic, Drug Dependent Or Mental Incompetent; Or Is Not Under The Influence Of Alcohol Or Any Federally Controlled Narcotic Substance.

SECTION 1 – INTENTIONS OF THE FRAMER:

> *Any person who is a citizen of the United States (an inducement for those living here as foreign aliens) and does not fall under one or more of the disabilities has the right to own and carry guns. The section does not grant the right, it only recognizes this inherent and intrinsic right to keep and bear arms (a la the 2nd). The right extends to any physical location under the control of the U.S. Constitution. The Framer is not contending that carrying a concealed or unconcealed firearm is an absolute right anymore than free speech allows one to yell fire in a crowded building when there is no fire. However, the restrictions on bearing and keeping arms shall be limited to those enumerated in this amendment.*

SECTION 2:

The Bearing Of Arms Is Prohibited, When All Of The Following Apply: Within An Enclosure, Where Notification Is Made Restricting The Bearing Of Arms, Search Provisions Are Operational And Safe And Convenient Provision Is Made To Secure And Retrieve Arms Carried To The Ingress/Egress Point Of Enclosure.

SECTION 2 – INTENTIONS OF THE FRAMER:

310

Any public or private entity has the option of forbidding the carrying of arms into or onto its enclosure (building, fenced-in area) as long as said entity posts a notice, operates a metal detector or other means of detection and provides for the arms carrier to safely and conveniently store/retrieve his arms. This way, military bases, court houses, police stations and department stores, etc., that do not want persons to be armed within their enclosures, must establish a 'coat check' for guns and have metal detectors in operation.

SECTION 3:

Arms Means Any Rifled Barreled, Breech Loading Device Weighing Less Than Fifteen Pounds, Unloaded, And Capable Of Discharging By The Action Of An Explosive Or Combustible Propellant, A Non-Exploding Projectile Or Projectiles Of Which The Projectile[S] Is [Are] Not Greater Than .525 Inch In Diameter; Or Any Non-Rifled Barreled, Breech Loading Device With A Bore Diameter Not Greater Than .780 Inches; Bearing Of Arms Means To Carry, Either Openly Or Concealed; Keeping Arms Means Ownership And Having Control Of Arms.

SECTION 3—INTENTIONS OF THE FRAMER:

Most non-gun and many gun owners would feel uncomfortable with their neighbor hauling around a bazooka or other mega-destructive device. Barrel and stock lengths, rifle/handgun calibers (up to .50), shotguns up to 10 ga. and fully automatic arms are not restricted as long as the arm doesn't weigh more than 15 pounds—empty. This section does not preclude local governments from enacting and enforcing 'activity laws' such as pointing firearms (assault) or inducing panic by shooting in crowded public arenas. Keeping arms is not only protected, but it carries with it an obligation to be sure these weapons don't fall into the wrong hands, i.e., persons prohibited under SECTION I.

SECTION 4:

Each Territory Or State Of The United States May License/Test Persons Who Wish To Bear Arms In Public Or Purchase Arms; Fees And Complexity Of Testing For Such Licensing Shall Not Exceed That Which The Licensing State Or Territory Establishes For A Motor Vehicle Operator's License.

SECTION 4—INTENTIONS OF THE FRAMER:

Some may object to allowing states to license something one has a constitutional right to do. The state, however, also has rights, such as its need to know who is a citizen—a person entitled to own and carry deadly weapons. Requiring a license to purchase or carry arms, either openly or concealed, greatly enhances the likelihood for ratification. States might be more inclined to ratify the 28th AMENDMENT if they won't lose the income now generated from CCF or hunting fees. More importantly, and especially since the terrorist attack of September 11, 2001, anyone wanting to purchase or carry instruments of lethal force should be required to prove they are decent, law-abiding, American citizens. Qualifying for and possessing a "permit" card is a mark of citizenship—it is only available to those who are not drunks, mental patients or criminals. Establishing just who is and who is not a citizen when it comes to those who are part of America's First Line of Defense is paramount to a secure country.

Since **SECTION I** recognizes the right to keep and bear arms, all permits must be on a 'shall issue' basis. The tests and the procedure for securing the license cannot be any more complex than what a state requires for its motor vehicle operator's license, i.e., prove who you are, study a pamphlet and take tests (can't have those who can't comprehend use of lethal force laws packing heat).

SECTION 5:

No State, Local Or Federal Government Employee Or Agency Shall Maintain A Registry Of Arms.

SECTION 5—INTENTIONS OF THE FRAMER:

Registration of firearms is forbidden by any government person or government agency. This would not preclude manufacturers and gun dealers from keeping records of the original purchaser in case notification is needed for reasons such as recall or safety notices—as is already the law.

SECTION 6:

This Amendment Voids All Previous Federal, State And Local Statutes, Laws, Court Decrees, Executive Orders And Legislative Acts That Pertain To The Keeping And Bearing Of Arms, Except As

312

Applied To Arms Manufacturers And Licensed Arms Dealers In Force At The Time This Amendment Is Enacted; And No Future Restrictions On The Keeping And Bearing Of Arms Shall Be Permitted Except By Amendment To This Constitution.

SECTION 6 — INTENTIONS OF THE FRAMER:

This section is to make it clear that this new amendment has superseded all other current or future laws, statutes and executive orders and court rulings — federal, state or local! Arms laws pertaining to gun manufacturers and dealers, on the books at the ratification of this amendment, remain in force. There is no need for other controls on firearms as any such would be in violation of this amendment.

Football Scoring

Endlessly watching endless football it was clear there is a huge disparity in the scoring system: Touchdowns count for 6, 7 or even 8 points, while field goals count for only three. This doesn't seem sportsmanlike inasmuch as a team down by four or five points must score a touchdown as a 3-point field goal would not even tie the game. Perhaps, if after a team scores a field goal, they should get a "point-after try" just like after a touchdown. So that it's not a slam-dunk, this point-after-field-goal must be made from the 10 yard line. And, since we're trying to even things up, the point-after-field-goal — could be for two points if the team options to run or pass the ball (also from the 10 yard line) into the end zone.

This scoring realignment would make the game far more interesting and challenging to both team and coaching staffs. Because the actual scoring values wouldn't change, the game is still virtually the same. Throughout the history of the sport many changes have been made including equipment, penalties, instant-replay, location of the kick-off ... and even the 2-point conversion after touchdown. Like the 3-point basketball shot, this is a concept whose time has come.

Economic Solution: Daily Lottery

PART I

The Federal Government shall select ten (10) Social Security Numbers (SSN) per day and give to each winner (providing this person is an American citizen and is not incarcerated for a felony) $100K—tax free. The only stipulation is the recipient must spend this $100K during the next year on goods or services within the United States.

Each state will select ten (10) SSN per day and give to each winner (providing this person is a citizen of that state and is not incarcerated for a felony) $10K—tax free. The only stipulation is the recipient must spend this $10K during the next year within that state.

PART II

The Federal Government and all state governments shall not create any new or additional forms of income and must place a freeze on income from all sources—any form of income payable to that government entity (taxes, fees, tariffs, etc.). If the Federal Government or any state government needs cash for the short term to finance their lottery, they must reduce their size—but for every reduction in military or sworn law enforcement personnel, an equal number of bureaucrats must be terminated.

With this huge cash infusion being spent each year, it won't be long before the entire country is returned to economic recovery from the taxes collected on the sale of the items purchased by the winners and the number of people hired to make, transport and sell these goods.

PART III

This program will be phased out as the economy recovers and, in turn, reinstated as the economy demands.

~~~

315

America's Got Volunteer Talent

During every summer recess when elected members of Congress take a month or so off, let's appoint volunteers to fill those positions. To accomplish this, American citizens of all walks of life—except those who hold a political office—will be encouraged to submit their name, address and contact information to their representative district. Each Senator and each Congressperson shall, via public lottery drawing, select from this constituency pool a person to fill their seat for this vacation period. These Volunteer Members of Congress shall have the same powers as those whom they temporarily replace including the use of the elected person's staff. Any volunteer hopeful who submits his or her name more than once/year shall be disqualified and those who are selected shall not receive anything of monetary value for their services.

The elected officials who are being temporarily replaced may remain as advisers to their volunteer replacement—but only the volunteer may vote on issues brought before their respective Houses.

Hey, American's really do have talent and these volunteers just might come up with some significant concepts, ideas or solutions. They sure can't do any worse than the gridlock mess we've been locked into for so long.

Note: Article I, Section 5 of the Constitution says: "Each House shall be the judge of the elections, returns and *qualifications* of its own members...." (emphasis added). Thus, if each House decides to "qualify" of-age citizens for temporary status as a Senator or Congressperson, it is not prohibited by the law.

Red Lights

Recently, on a rainy day trip to the "big city," I noticed the difficulty of picking out the Red Traffic Control Lights from all the other signs, lights and distractions. It seems to me Red Traffic Control Lights should be made to pulse or flash. With the exception of these unblinking Traffic Lights, a flashing red light universally means stop:

- Railroad warning lights;
- 4-way stop intersections;
- Emergency vehicles.

all display "flashing" Red Lights—why shouldn't the common Traffic Control Light?

I'm sure we've all witnessed (or experienced) a vehicle drive right through a Red Traffic Control Light without even slowing down. When I was a police officer, many times I heard the excuse, "I didn't see the [Red] light." How many accidents occur each year because of this non-attention getting steady red light?

The technology exists to economically retrofit Traffic Control Lights so that when the Red Light is displayed, it either flashes or pulses (strobe). It might be an inexpensive and life-saving change.

Selected Klein's Laws

THEORY OF TIME:

When it comes to discovering the origins of the universe, all the earth/orbit telescopes, X-ray/radio scopes and infrared/laser gizmos are inconsequential should man conquer the 4th dimension.

COROLLARY TO KLEIN'S THEORY OF TIME:

God may not have provided mere mortals with the ability to conquer the 4th dimension, as thus empowered, man might be tempted to alter His plans and designs.

COROLLARY TO EINSTEIN'S THEORY OF RELATIVITY:

All matters that are not matters of matter, are matters of perspective.

LAW OF THE UNIVERSE(S):

The Commonality between scientist, creationist and evolutionist is the question: What lies beyond The Beyond?

LAW OF GRATITUDE:

If the question is: Is the glass half full or half empty? The answer is: Thank you for the half glass.

LAW OF PLANET EARTH:

The infiniteness of world population is inversely proportional to the finiteness of natural resources.

VII—SHORT TAKES

City Love

My first glimpse of her,
through rising river steam,
and teasing sculptured curves,
was everyman's dream.

My eyes swept her ample mounds
Surrounding central crests
And ancient, old world amenities;
There are others, but she's the best.

From that first moment, I was in love
Her friendly warmth and inviting way
Has kept me coming back for more
To fill an insatiable need to play.

The heart and soul of this beauty,
Like a theater in the round,
Is most sophisticated and vibrant
With an excitement so profound.

Statuesque and pillared, yet modern
Fed by flowing ribbons of diversity;
Ethnic, religious and political,
Like a free and good University.

Powerful leaders Taft, Harrison and Stewart;
And Sabin, Crosley and Stowe of fame;
Plus the old money of Kroger, Corbett and Gamble;
Can only mean...Cincinnati is her name.

~~~

Black History Month

A Short Refresher Course

Some of us have forgotten details to three very prominent Black American/symbols.

UNCLE TOM:

A pious and subservient slave character in Harriet Beecher Stowe's, Uncle Tom's Cabin (1851). The term has come to mean anyone who is overeager to win the approval of Whites. Though, it is a very derogatory term, it is also a symbol of truth of how some Black's had to behave in order to survive — and that's what we tend to forget. This behavior is similar to how other minority groups have been forced to behave when under the thumb of a vindictive, controlling majority.

DRED SCOTT:

This is more of a case about "the man" than the man himself. Dred Scott was a slave who was taken by his master, in 1834, from Missouri (a slave state) to Illinois and then to Ft. Snelling in the Minnesota Territory. In 1846, Mr. Scott sued to establish that he, and his family, were free because they had lived in a free state and free territory. The U.S. Supreme Court, embarrassingly, ruled:

1) Negroes were not citizens and therefore could not sue in federal courts;

2) A slave's residence in a free state did not make him a free man;

3) The Missouri Comprise of 1820 (forbidding slavery in that part of the Louisiana Purchase — except Missouri) was an unconstitutional exercise of congressional power.

The case had a polarizing effect on the slavery issue and was a factor in the conflict between the North and the South. After the Civil War, the case influenced the passage of the 13th and 14th Amendments — which gave freedom and citizenship to slaves.

JIM CROW:

There never was a real person named Jim Crow. However, there was a song-and-dance, minstrel routine—preformed by a White man (Thomas "Daddy" Rice), who blackened his face with charcoal paste or burnt cork and danced a ridiculous and degrading jig that depicted Blacks as inferior (c.1830). The term, post bellum, along with other White popular culture "code words," such as Sambo or Coon, were used to define any "person of colour." Jim Crow soon became synonymous with segregation and thus any law segregating Blacks from Whites became knows as "Jim Crow Laws." Some rail cars carried the sign "Jim Crow" to designate cars for Blacks only. In 1954 the U.S. Supreme Court finally got it right by declaring segregation in public schools to be unconstitutional. This led to similar decisions that outlawed any form of "Jim Crow" legislation.

My Psalm 23

The Lord is my shepherd and the guardian of our soldiers who make it possible for us to lie down in the green pastures and take of the still waters.

Thou anointest my soul with courage, my body with strength and the capacity to stand tall. Thou preparest me to face those who violate intrinsic rights Thou have bestowed upon us all. My cup runneth over with gratitude.

The Lord restoreth my soul and showest me the path of righteousness. For His name's sake I will strive to set the example for others to follow.

Should Thou command me into the valley of the shadow of death, I am prepared to fend off evil for Thou art with me; and my belief comforts me.

I am confident that my prayers to measure up to Thy commandments will be answered and I will be permitted to serve Thee in the hereafter forever and ever. Amen.

Articulate

Sam spent the better part of an hour describing, in extensive detail, the locomotive. However eloquent his narrative, it couldn't equate to personal presence when this articulated 4-8-8-4 engine, akin to a distant earthquake, rumbled, shook and bulled its way into the station.

Webster's New World Dictionary defines Articulated: Having parts connected by joints; expressing oneself easily and clearly.

The question is: Is the locomotive in the first paragraph "connected by joints" or is it merely the locomotive described by Sam? I wrote this with the intention of creating confusion as to the meaning of the subject word—to illustrate that, even today, the meaning of a single word can be in question. Thus, if one can be confused by a common word, how can anyone be sure of the meaning of words written (much less translated) hundreds or even thousands of years ago—before dictionaries or even the written word?

Case in point: Some versions of the Bible (Torah) quote one of The Commandments "Thou shalt not kill" while others cite, "Thou shalt not murder." By today's standards of literary correctness there is a significant difference between kill and murder. Obviously something was lost in translation of one (or both) renditions. Therefore, if this most important of Commandments is ambiguous, what else in the holy text is misleading, subjective or incorrect?

Note: *Most 4-8-8-4 railroad locomotives are connected by joints (hinged) between the first set of eight driving wheels and the second set of eight* (http://www.steamlocomotive.com/bigboy/).

Escalation

Trust not Gates
Gates before Fences
Fences before Barriers
Barriers before Threats
Threats before Guns
Guns before War
War before Death
Death before Dishonor
Dishonor before Annihilation?

Functions Of Government:

Our Constitution is unique inasmuch as it keeps the playing field level for the four players in all of the games of life. The four players are: the governed (citizens), those who make the laws (legislative branch), those who enforce the law (executive branch) and those who mediate (judicial branch). Each group is independent and at the same time dependent upon all of the others. This interdependence creates checks and balances so that one entity is never in a disadvantaged position. At least that's the way it's supposed to work.

There are four functions of our Constitution:

1) To establish a national government (Articles I, II, III, VI, and Amendments 12,16,17,20,22,23, and 25);

2) To control the relationship between the national government and the governments of the states (Article I [sections 8 & 10], Article III [section 2], Article IV, and Amendments 10, 11, 18, and 21);

3) To allow for adjustments in the Constitution to correct inadequacies or changing times (Article V);

4) To protect and preserve fundamental personal rights and liberties (Article I [section 9] and Amendments 1-10, 13, 14,15, 19, 24 and 26).

The Power To Ignore

One of the rights protected under the First Amendment is: *"Congress shall make no law...prohibiting the free exercise...to petition the Government for a redress of grievances."*

This says the Federal Government (state governments are included under the 14th Amendment) cannot pass a law to keep you from complaining about your government to your government. However, nowhere in the Constitution or in any statute is there any requirement for the "government" to answer, react to or otherwise acknowledge your petition — your complaint.

This was recently pointed out in a U.S. District Court for the District of Columbia decision (We the People, et. al., Plaintiffs vs. United States, et. al., Defendants, Civil action No. 04-1211). Here the court ruled that just because the government failed to respond to the plaintiff's complaint it was no reason for the plaintiff to be granted a favorable judgment against the government. Even a DEFAULT judgment is not possible when the government fails to respond to a suit filed in compliance with all laws.

In other words, though one has a right to complain to the government — that right doesn't mean the government has any statutory, constitutional, or even judicial obligation to respond to your "redress of grievance."

The hard evidence of this elitist attitude is further propagated in the functioning of the Supreme Court. Though they are empowered as the highest court in the land, there is no legal obligation to hear any cases — and they do refuse to hear far more cases than they accept. The justices, being appointed for life, are immune to retribution (yeah, I know they can be impeached, but in reality it just doesn't happen). Whereas, elected officials are, at the least, subject to the ballot box.

In addition, and to add insult to injury, this highest court, being the SUPREME court for which there is no appeal other than legislative, have no obligation to rule upon ALL issues of a case. In other words, they can select to review only minor portions of a case and ignore the main argument.

This power to ignore is not limited to the courts. If you ever need to contact government officials about something they don't want to be contacted about, keep in mind that while they might have to permit you to "redress your grievances," they aren't required to reply, much less take any action.

America Is Beautiful

Published in The United Stated Congressional Record,
Vol. 138, No. 104, 22 July 1992

Oh Beautiful For Spacious Skies: This canopy, so immense, it expands as high as the heavens and as broad as needed, not unlike a blanket of freedom, to cover Americans wherever they might be.

For Amber Waves Of Grain: Gold nuggets of life sustaining sustenance on whose shoulders all of those who seek the protection of the spacious skies depend.

For Purple Mountain Majesties: Forging straight up from the great plains of gilded grain, like a church spire paying homage to the heavens, these rugged resplendent pinnacles symbolize the strength and tenacity of the spacious sky people.

Above The Fruited Plain: Scattered among the violet mountains and meadows of wheat are the bounteous production yards of the fruits of American ingenuity and manufacturing. In the history of the world these plains and majestic plateaus have yielded the highest standards of excellence and an excellent people.

America — America: Saying it once isn't enough. To be an American is to be strong and fair, and honest and wise, and humanistic and realistic, and all the other virtuous attributes of those under the protection of the spacious skies.

God Shed His Grace On Thee: The Lord truly has blessed us with his benevolence, a covenant with all Americans, to do right by thee and thou and you and me.

And Crown Thy Good With Brotherhood: As we keep the compact with God so shall he continue to bestow the munificence that comes from loving and understanding, and helping our brothers and sisters.

From Sea To Shining Sea: Not just from Maine to Hawaii or Alaska to Florida, but to wherever those whose roots stem from the fruited plains, the fields of grain or the majestic mountains. For it is the duty of all Americans, an obligation that evolves from a pact with God, to stay the course and expand the spacious skies of brotherhood and freedom.

Pet Peeves, Things That Jerk My Trigger

LEFT TURNS:

When you wish to turn left, pull into the intersection and wait for a break in the traffic or the change of the light. That way, if the light turns red while you're in the intersection you won't be violating the law. It is only against the law to ENTER an intersection against a red light. Some bozos wait at the white/crosswalk line for traffic to clear — then when it doesn't they either run the light (very dangerous) or wait for another cycle (very dumb).

MJ:

A decade or so ago most jurisdictions decriminalized possession of small amounts of marijuana, i.e., get caught with a joint and the cops could only issue you a citation. Now the trend is to make possession of any amount of MJ a crime, again. The reason is NOT to harass pot heads or fill the already over crowded jails. The between the lines explanation is to allow the cops the right to search/pat-down the suspects for weapons and, of course, other contraband. It's a police safety issue because many junkies caught with a joint also are carrying saleable amounts of drugs AND guns. Heretofore, if an officer discovered evidence of MJ use, he was at a disadvantage — safety wise — when he approached the offender without the right to frisk him or her. If you're so immature or dumb enough to smoke grass — you've been warned.

IRAQ/IRAN/AFGHANISTAN:

One more time for all those who keep harping on how President Bush lied, twisted, usurped, and/or made up the WMD excuse for invading Iraq. We are at war — AS GW HAS TOLD US FROM THE BEGINNING — because we can either fight them over there or we can fight them over here. In other words, we have duped the enemy into expending all their munitions and suicidal warriors in THEIR cities and towns and on THEIR civilians rather than on our turf. In still other words: The Islamic fundamentalist have declared war on us in both word and deed and Mr. Bush was smart enough to redirect the fighting (which started on 9-11-01) from our shores to the place of his choosing — Iraq and Afghanistan. Finally, and whether his detractors accept this reasoning or not, if we suddenly bring the troops home these criminals will NOT just say, "thanks" and things will return to pre 9-11. Noooo, they will re-attack us over here. Duh!

Pop Quiz

Which of the following is the correct answer to the question:

Where, under our Constitution, is the mandate for the Federal Government to feed, clothe, evacuate, repair and/or provide money to victims of natural or other disasters?

a) Article I, Section 8 (Powers of Congress);

b) Article II, Section 2 (Presidential Powers);

c) Amendment XIV, Section 4 (Public Debt);

d) None of the above.

If you selected (d), go to the head of the class. It is NOT a function of the federal government to respond to natural or other disasters with food, water, shelter, evacuation, etc. Nowhere in the Constitution is it allowed, much less required, that federal money (taxes) or employees (military troops, et al) be used to "help" victims of disasters such as witnessed in the recent Gulf States calamity. Other than providing troops to maintain law and order, under martial law, there is no justification or expectation that our federal tax money be utilized for offering $2000 debit cards, transportation, direct payments to victims of 9-11 or any other misfortune.

I'm outraged, not shocked or surprised, just angry that the media—and our President—has shown such ignorance during a time of catastrophe. The lessons learned by the younger set (to expect the government to "take care of them") will not be lost and this is the real American tragedy.

The Preamble to the Constitution mentions "General Welfare" as a goal of forming a more perfect union. The Constitution then spells out exactly what powers, duties and controls this "more perfect union" has in attaining these goals. There is no empowerment, obligation or requirement mentioned in this, our rule of law, to feed, clothe, evacuate and/or conduct any other "general" much less specific welfare.

If the good people of America wish for its funds to be spent in such a way perhaps it is time to consider a constitutional amendment to cover these acts. But, until then, it is the sole responsibility of the individual states (see 10th Amendment) to decide if and how they wish to protect and care for their citizens. If you live in a state, or one of its political subdivisions, that is so incompetent as to leave you stranded during a catastrophic event, perhaps it's time to move or replace your elected officials—but your hardship is not the fault or obligation of the government.

Saying Good-Bye

Recently, I attended a eulogy for a lost friend. Somehow, the older I get the more of these there seem to be.

There are nice guys and gals; and then there are "nice" guys and gals. Some think of themselves as being kind in an attempt to fit that image. Those who try hardest usually fail. They're the ones, for example, who believe abruptly slowing up on the freeway to allow an entering vehicle to merge is being a decent person. It never seems to occur to them that somewhere behind, other cars and trucks might have to violently brake or swerve to avoid a collision.

Sometimes a person is eulogized because of their tangible accomplishments such as rising to high positions, earning peer recognition, or accumulating money. This brings up the question: Is it better to be a good person or a person that does good things? Maybe it's all in the words of the eulogizer... or the definition of good?

Daily TV news reports highlighting the misfortunes of fellow humans—for whom no eulogy is tendered—is disheartening. Most of us are by no means perfect now or in the past, but the common Judeo-Christian goal of "good" people is to be the best person we can be and to thank God everyday for the blessings of our extraordinary life. Extraordinary inasmuch as our sufferings are trivial when compared to some of those we see exposed by the harshness of these news programs.

Many who die in catastrophic events do not receive the honor of a eulogy as oft-times the survivors themselves usually don't have the occasion and energy for wakes. Or ... all that knew them also died in the same calamity. Maybe, for these good-who-die-to-soon, their tribute will come after a future generation has had the time and ability to reflect—or on the other side.

So, who or what is a nice guy or gal? Maybe the description or meaning is akin to U.S. Supreme Court Justice Potter Stewart's definition of obscenity. In deciding the Jacobellis v. Ohio (1964) case, the judge indicated he couldn't define it, but, he said, "I know it when I see it." That's the way it is with a truly pleasant and heartwarming soul. Words can't describe them, but you know it when they have touched your life.

As I scanned the room of long-time friends, I couldn't help thinking what would I say about any of them—or they about me?

God Has Blessed America

Lyrics by Irving Berlin
Annotation by Chuck Klein

God Bless America

And our troops, law officers and all of Her guardians.

Land That I Love

Those who know this love are truly the Blessed People.

Stand Beside Her, And Guide Her,

As God stands to safeguard us, we align ourselves shoulder to shoulder while bowing our heads in thanks for His protection and guidance.

Thru The Night With A Light From Above.

Dusk to dawn and sunrise to sunset, we are humbled by Your radiant supremacy and power.

From The Mountains, To The Prairies,

Forging straight up from the great prairies of gilded grain, like a church spire paying homage to the heavens, these rugged resplendent pinnacles symbolize our faith in You.

To The Oceans, White With Foam,

Seas of Blessed People of all colors, each seeking the purity only You can bestow.

God Bless America, My Home Sweet Home

May God continue to bless the Blessed People as this is their homeland forevermore.

Stress Test City

I just got back from a visit to the Southwest Regional/Marginal Medical/Hospital (used to be known as Brown County General Hospital). I don't know why they had to change the name; I mean BCGH says all you need to know. It would be like calling Apple computers pears or cucumbers. Anyway, I was scheduled for a stress test at 7:15 in the morning—the only time they say the test can be originated. But some caring person called me a few days before to say if I got there at 8 a.m. that would be just fine. In and of itself, that lowered my stress level. Living in a rural community has its advantages.

Though the doctor's main practice is in Cincinnati, I choose BCGH because I want to keep my business local. Registration was quick and easy and after a short wait of maybe 10 minutes I was readied for some kind of scan. They put me on a flat bed with crispy-clean sheets and allowed a huge box-machine to revolve inches above my chest— stress level up. The nurse/technician, Tammy, told me I would be under this thing for 20 minutes and I should breathe normally, but could not move. Ever try to breathe normally when you're thinking about it? What's normal? Tammy told me she would be in the room the entire time which reduced my stress—until I thought maybe she's staying to make sure I breathe normally. I fixated on a spot in the ceiling and built (in my head) the walnut cabinet I've been meaning to make someday. Time flies when you're having fun—at least that's what a jailer once told me.

Next, I was taken to the actual test room to be prepped for the walk-a-thon. Here, Charlie attached wires to patches stuck to my chest while another person inserted an IV in my arm to inject stuff to allow the stress machine to monitor my heart. I've got wires pasted to me, a needle in my arm, had nothing to eat or drink since last night and I'm freezing cold—stress city.

In due time Dr. Hattemer arrived and onto the treadmill I went. At first the stride was like a nice stroll in a park, but without the trees and grass. Just as soon as I began to relax with the pace they sped up the machine while adding an incline. At least I wasn't chilled any longer, beads of sweat now forming on my forehead. However, in all too long a time, the treadmill speed not only increased a second time, but so was the angle. I was now in double-overdrive—walking as fast as I could—up hill and wishing the room was cooler. At 14 hours, seven minutes and nine seconds into the test, I finally heard the doctor say, "stops in 10 seconds." Did he mean the machine or my heart? Fortunately, before I was totally stressed out, they lowered the ramp and slowed the tread way down. Whew! Wait… I lied about the 14 hour part—I was only on the treadmill a total of eight minutes, but it seemed a mite longer.

Pledge Of Allegiance

Annotations by Chuck Klein,

The Pledge Of Allegiance "…should be rendered by standing at attention facing the flag with the right hand over the heart. When not in uniform men should remove their headdress with their right hand and hold it at the left shoulder, the hand being over the heart. Persons in uniform should remain silent, face the flag and render the military salute." (36 USCS #172)

I Pledge Allegiance

Me, personally, do promise as an oath – a vow of loyalty, duty, devotion;

To The Flag Of The United States Of America,

The symbol, the representation of the United States of America; 50 states joined together as one people;

And To The Republic

A nation that lives by the rule of law;

For Which It Stands,

Not only do we pledge our allegiance to the flag and the Republic, but we promise our loyalty and devotion to the principals on which this Republic is founded;

One Nation Under God,

A unified nation, united as a single people, under God, the supreme being;

Indivisible,

We will not be divided against ourselves. Facing all enemies we stand together – back to back, shoulder to shoulder, rich to poor, liberal to conservative;

With Liberty And Justice For All

With freedom, sovereignty, emancipation, equality, fairness, truth, adherence to the rule of law for every one who is within our power to protect.

340

Getting It Straight

Let's Get A Few Things Straight — Once And For All.

1) Attention newspapers, cable companies, TV guides: There is no such time as 12:00 a.m. or 12:00 p.m. — it is a physical impossibility. The correct terms are 12:00 NOON and 12:00 MIDNIGHT, just plain Noon — Midnight or military time: 1200 hours-2400 hours.

2) If it wasn't for American know-how — the Arabs wouldn't know how to extract the oil under their land, much less that it was there in the first place.

3) Hybrid/electric cars are not the answer to reducing oil consumption for the following reasons — all of which the press, proponents and government seems to ignore:

- When the batteries begin to wear out, where are we going to dispose of this toxic waste?

- Our electric power grid is now at capacity (with black/brown-outs during peak times); just where is the extra power coming from to charge all these battery powered cars?

- The proponents of the hybrid/electric claim these cars can go 50-100 miles between charges. What they don't tell you is this is under ideal conditions with a relatively new battery. How many miles do you think you can go if most of your commute is spent in bumper-to-bumper, rush hour traffic with the headlights, windshield wipers and heater/AC fan on?

4) For the long term it is NOT Iran, Korea, China... our greatest worries are:

- Depletion of the ocean's fishes;

- Pollution from the residue of wars, pesticides, herbicides, human waste and consumption of fossil fuels;

- Viruses and diseases that exceed scientific control;

- Pollution generated by devastating hurricanes, blizzards and tsunamis;

- OVER-POPULATION: Continent wide droughts and famine just might be: God's message to us to Get-it-Straight.

5) If all the guns in the world could somehow be magically removed; the weak, frail and vulnerable would have no way of protecting themselves from the thugs with bats, clubs and knives.

6) Muslims who don't, won't or can't renounce their fellow Muslims for committing and/or preaching violence are wolves in sheep's clothing.

7) All Americans have the inherent and constitutional right to be free of fear from armed citizens. However, this right does not extend to usurping or disparaging other American's inalienable, 2nd and 9th Amendment rights to be free of fear from thugs intend on doing them harm.

Tribute To Those Who Serve

Memorial, Veterans and Independence
Are American tear producing days;
When we honor our soldiers;
Past and present.

We are so blessed
To have such patriotic citizens
Who have unselfishly "served" this country;
So many times.

But right here on our soil,
And in highly visible positions
Are others of every affiliation;
Who "serve" this great nation.

Everyday our first line of defense;
Our police officers and firefighters;
Unflinchingly "serve" at risks
That cost some their livelihood, and lives.

There are, of course, far more
Who "serve" America and Americans;
Monetarily and via countless philanthropic groups;
That contribute to our common good.

Complementing these benevolent associations
Is a multitude of unorganized volunteers;
Who quietly "serve" at hospitals, libraries;
And the vast number of eclectic, charitable fund-raisers.

America is unique;
Inasmuch as this cadre of unpaid citizens
Take such good care of each other;
That the impersonal socialization
Found in other countries;
Is not needed here.

Many decent, law-abiding citizens;
The over-whelming majority of Americans;
Also "serve" their country:
By challenging unjust rules, standing up to wrong-doers;
Or facing down bullies.

If warfare ever threatens our front door
There should be no doubt that our neighbors;
The ones who keep and bear arms;
Will stand back-to-back and shoulder-to-shoulder;
To tender their "service."

May God bless America and every American;
Where ever they may be;
And in whatever capacity they may "serve."

Bullies

During my year in the 5th grade, a 6th grader bullied me almost daily on the home bound bus. I made up my mind that I would be tough and take it — and not cry-baby to the authorities. I also, resolved that when I became part of the oldest class in the school, I not only would not bully the little kids, but would confront (fight if necessary) any of my classmates if they were doing the bullying. In high school, after a kick, punch, roll-on-the-ground fight with a fellow classmate that took a teacher to pull us apart, I gained a reputation of being tough and that had the effect of keeping bullies at bay.

Perhaps it would be beneficial if schools taught a class in extrapolation. Obviously, many current administrators and politicians fail to consider the consequences of some of their laws, edicts and rules. For instance: Today's zero tolerance bullying mantra quite possibly will produce a generation of future police officers who will have no clue of how to deal with bullies and violent criminals thus subjecting the populace to these uncontrolled jerks. Regardless of how many restrictions are placed on kids or adults, there will always be predators. Another example of society's failure to extrapolate is establishing of gun-free-zones. They are not. To the law abiding citizens (victims of the bullies and violent jerks) — they are self-defense free zones. Some people seem to have more dollars than sense.

I'm not saying schools should condone fisticuffs or serious bullying, but a little more "let 'em work it out among themselves" might go a long way in developing character — and future protectors of society.

Asthma: It Is Life-Threatening

With two children so afflicted, I did my share of rushing the inhaler to school or other places when they experienced an attack and had forgotten to take it with them.

Once, when the county road was flooded and the youngest was staying at a neighbors, so he could go to school, I walked a half mile through the night woods in the snow and at 15 degrees to meet the neighbor with my son's inhaler.

However, the scariest was the time he awakened me in the middle of the night. He could only shake his head to the question of "can your breath?" I instantly realized I had two options:

a) call the life squad, or,

b) drive him myself to the hospital. This was 1980 and our farm was in sparsely populated Switzerland County, Indiana.

I knew the all-volunteer squad would take at least 20 minutes to arrive and then 30 minutes or more to transport him two county lines east to Lawrenceburg General in Dearborn County. I chose plan "B." I threw on a pair of pants and helped him into the car, setting out as fast as I dared over two-lane state and county roads.

The only town, Rising Sun with its single stop sign, was 15 miles and then 15 miles to the hospital. Coming through the little village in the dead of night, I slowed to maybe 60, changing down to third for the stop sign. Speeding out of town it soon became apparent the local police were in pursuit. I pulled over, got out and ran back to the scout car where I quickly told him my name, address, and that I was in route to the hospital with my ailing son and his life-threatening condition. I also told the officer, and before he had said a word, he could write all the tickets he wanted and I'd pick them up on the way back or he could follow me to the hospital and arrest me there—but I wasn't going to wait even a minute.

He jumped out of the cruiser, following me back to my car where he shined his flashlight on my obviously ill child. The officer only said, "Be careful," as I accelerated away. I'm sure he radioed ahead as a Dearborn County Sheriff's Deputy merely watched as we flew past at the county line. Lawrenceburg General did what they do best and we were home by noon

Today's Slavery

Perhaps a solution to the illegal immigrant issue could be found in the 13th Amendment.

Ratified in 1865, the 13th says: "*Neither slavery nor involuntary servitude, except as a punishment for crime ... shall exist within the United States ...*" Thus, to punish illegitimate aliens for their crime of unlawfully entering our country they could be:

Forced (involuntary servitude) to work on state/local road gangs,

and/or

Sold, as slaves, by the government to "big AG" for picking crops.

Whoa, before you hop on a PC, liberal, bleeding-heart horse, please consider what they've been doing to us. I call it involuntary servitude when American tax-payers are forced to pay the health care, welfare, education, etc., for illegal immigrants and others criminally in this country. You can call it charity, humanitarian or compassionate aid—with your money, but when you punish me—without my ever committing any crime—that's slavery.

My Nightly Prayer

Thank You, God, For A Great Day (The day's events flash through my mind, and even though several might not have been pleasant, I am still thankful).

Thank You, God, For A Wonderful Life (Various occasions are brought to mind, and though some are not happy, I am still thankful).

Thank You, God, For A Loving Wife (Her presence is comforting, cherished and loved).

Thank You, God, For A Noble Family (Names and faces flash through my mind).

Thank You, God, For All My Friends, Past And Present (Names and faces flash through my mind).

Thank You, God, For My Guardian Angel (The identity and image of the person I believe to be my Guardian Angel is revered each night).

Thank You, God, For The Privilege Of Deciding My Own Paths (Only in a free country am I able to choose my own direction).

Thank You, God, For The Grit To Accept The Challenges And Consequences Of Exercising That Privilege (From the strength of and the faith in the almighty, I am able to meet each day).

I Remain Ready, Willing And Able To Serve You, God, And/Or Your Agent. Amen (Amen).

Chuck Klein:
Author,
Firearms Expert,
Hot Rodder,
Adventurer

To come up with the selections for **The Best of Chuck Klein** the author had to wade through a collection of writing samples greater by far than that produced by the most proficient of writers. That's because Chuck Klein has lived a fuller life than most authors and those life experiences have produced volumes of adventures, opinions, reminiscences and astute observations that cry out to be compiled in a "best of" edition.

Now a fulltime author, Klein is a retired licensed private investigator, a former certified police officer and firefighter, a firearms editor, street rod columnist, former staff instructor for the Tactical Defense Institute, Bill of Rights columnist, and security columnist.

Klein built his own car at the age of 15 and can set-up and operate milling machines, metal working lathes and other machine tools. He earned a Bachelor of Laws in 1972 and has been listed in Who's Who in America for 13 years. He is a member and past president of Kiwanis Club of Cincinnati, an active member of the International Association of Law Enforcement Firearms Instructors.

Author of The Best of Chuck Klein, his books include: **The Badge**, stories and tales from both sides of the law; **Laws and Ideas**; truths and observations; **Guns in the Workplace**, a manual for private sector employers and employees; **The Power of God**, a novel exposing a de facto hole in America's civil defense; **Klein's CCW Handbook**, a requisite for those carrying concealed handguns; **The Way It Was**, nostalgic tales of hot rods and romance; **Klein's Uniform Firearms Policy**, a manual for private detectives and security guards; **Circa 1957**, the coming of age in '57—girls, cars, and rock and roll; **Instinct Combat Shooting**, defensive hand gunning for police; and **Lines of Defense,** police ideology and the constitution.

Klein and wife Annette have five children and 10 grandchildren and live on a 125-acre farm in Brown County, Ohio.